£7.15.

THE ARABIC BOOK

MODERN CLASSICS IN NEAR EASTERN STUDIES

SERIES EDITORS

Charles Issawi • Bernard Lewis

THE ARABIC BOOK

JOHANNES PEDERSEN

TRANSLATED BY
GEOFFREY FRENCH

EDITED
WITH AN INTRODUCTION BY
ROBERT
HILLENBRAND

PRINCETON UNIVERSITY PRESS
PRINCETON, NEW JERSEY

Published by Princeton University Press, 41 William Street,
Princeton, New Jersey 08540
In the United Kingdom: Princeton University Press, Guildford, Surrey

This book has been composed in Linotron Bembo

Clothbound editions of Princeton University Press books
are printed on acid-free paper, and binding materials are
chosen for strength and durability. Paperbacks, although satisfactory
for personal collections, are not usually suitable for library rebinding.

Printed in the United States of America by
Princeton University Press
Princeton, New Jersey

Translated from the Danish, *Den Arabiske Bog* (Copenhagen, 1946)

The translation and preparation of this volume were made possible
through a grant from the translation program of the
National Endowment for the Humanities,
to which we would like to express
our deep appreciation.

Library of Congress Cataloging in Publication Data

Pedersen, Johannes, 1883-1977.
The Arabic book.

(Modern classics in Near Eastern studies)
Translation of: Den Arabiske bog.
Bibliography: p.
Includes index.
1. Book industries and trade—Islamic Empire.
2. Civilization, Islamic. I. Hillenbrand, Robert.
II. Title. III. Series.
Z464.I8P413 1984 070.5'0917671 82-61379
ISBN 0-691-06564-0
ISBN 0-691-10148-5 (pbk.)

CONTENTS

LIST OF ILLUSTRATIONS

(following page 175)

INTRODUCTION

THE LONG-OVERDUE publication of *The Arabic Book* in an English translation is matter for celebration. The work was written before its time and has yet to be superseded. It deals with a subject that of its very nature touches upon every branch of Islamic studies, though it cannot be said to belong principally to any single one of them. This wide-ranging relevance made such a work a natural task for one of the polymaths of Islamic studies. At the same time, it sufficiently explains why earlier scholars were so chary of attempting to cover the same ground. The author compresses into 150 pages an extraordinary quantity of material bearing on every aspect of book production in medieval Islamic society. He was the first European scholar to confront the numerous problems in this field as a group and not as separate objects of enquiry. How were books duplicated before the advent of printing? What were the safeguards against forgery or pirated editions? What governed the price of books? By what means were they made available to the general public? How did booksellers operate?

To deal with such subjects intelligently a scholar of unusual attainments and interests was required. Johannes Pedersen fell into this category. In an earlier publication, *Islams Kultur* (Copenhagen, 1928), he had already manifested a capacity to illuminate Islamic material culture by setting it within a detailed framework of social history. *The Arabic Book* is a triumphant synthesis of the same two interests, but this time accomplished within a much narrower compass. Pedersen was no narrow specialist. Born in 1883, he grew up in an age that had a more spacious view of scholarship than that which prevails nowadays. In his generation it was still standard practice for a prospective Islamicist to acquire a broad grounding in Semitic languages before embarking on research. In the case of Pedersen—who studied with Snouck Hurgronje and Ignaz Goldziher, themselves great masters in that very tradition—such a background was particularly apropos, for he maintained throughout his career a keen interest in comparative philology, principally in the Semitic field. This aspect of his scholarship is accurately reflected in the remarkably wide range of specialties represented in his two *Festschrifts*, one published in Stockholm in 1944, the other—entitled *Studia Orientalia Ioanni Pedersen . . . dicata*—in Copenhagen in 1953. They include, apart from the Biblical and Islamic subjects that one would expect, material on Ugaritic, ancient Egyptian, Akkadian, Avestan, modern Persian, and Turkish, as well as articles on ancient Egyptian and Islamic art. There is even a contribution by a world-renowned physicist.

Like many great European orientalists before him, Pedersen made his way into Islamic studies after an initial training in Hebrew. Indeed, his principal contribution was made in that field rather than in Islamic studies, though of course both areas of his scholarship were reciprocally enriched as a result, a process that is especially obvious in the second chapter of *The Arabic Book*. His magnum opus was devoted to Old Testament studies; entitled in its English translation *Israel: Its Life and Culture*, it was published in two massive volumes in 1926 and 1940. Its approach was marked by that ability to see a complex culture as a whole, and to analyze the subtle interaction of religious and social factors, which distinguished *The Arabic Book* and his shorter works on the mosque and the madrasa. All these works share too a steady emphasis on cultic practice, which is examined in minute detail and illumined by reference to a wide range of primary sources. Although it was *Israel* that marked the culmination of his scholarly career, Pedersen's niche in Islamic studies is assured. His output in that field may be limited, but it is of superlative quality. Finally, it might be added parenthetically here that although Pedersen did train younger scholars, his principal contribution to Near Eastern studies—apart from his scholarship—was as an administrator. He discharged a variety of offices, some of very specialized interest (such as the chairmanship of the Excavation Committee of the Danish expedition to Hama) and some of much wider scope, such as the Presidency of the Carlsberg Foundation, a most influential post of which he had a long and distinguished tenure.

Pedersen's impressive credentials in Islamic religious studies—studies that he consistently pursued within the broad framework dictated by his training as a historian of religions—are best demonstrated by his magisterial article *masdjid* in the first edition of the *Encyclopaedia of Islam*. That article testifies to an astonishing range of reading in difficult sources. So too does *The Arabic Book*. The lack of a single major medieval source devoted to this subject meant that relevant information would come from many disparate quarters—biographies, literary histories, *ḥadīths*, the Qur'ān, historical chronicles, poetry, and geographical literature among them. Pedersen's book is the kind of work that cannot be researched in a hurry; it needs to mature for years as the material gradually accumulates. Most of that material was drawn from primary sources, none of them extensively exploited for such purposes by earlier scholars. As a result, the wealth of anecdote and detailed evidence presented in the book cannot be found in any secondary source. For the art historian it provides the natural complement to Sir Thomas Arnold's *Painting in Islam*, while for specialists in Islamic history, theology, and literature it would long ago have been an indispensable vade mecum if it had not been published in a generally inaccessible language.

Pedersen was careful to include within the compass of his work all the subjects that had a significant bearing on it. He therefore found it necessary to evaluate the evidence for literacy and for the existence of books in the *jāhiliyya*, to deal with the role of the Qur'ān in Islamic book production, and to write a lengthy excursus on the various forms of Islamic script. His interests extended also to the physical details of preparing a book; hence the chapters on writing materials—including paper—and on bookbinding.

The core of his work, however, and the section that is at once most original and most valuable, consists of the third and fourth chapters. These give a careful step-by-step account of the stages between the conception of a book and the moment that the finished article was bought by some bibliophile. The complexity of the process thus lucidly summarized will come as a surprise to many students of Islamic culture. The rate at which books were composed, for example, must occasion wonder. One of the most celebrated authors of medieval Islam, the great historian al-Ṭabari, maintained—according to some reports—a steady pace of some forty pages per day for forty years. Many an author took employment as a copyist to supplement the slender income he derived from his writing. Others turned to bookselling. The picture that emerges is of a much more integrated publishing industry than might be suspected—an industry in which the same man might compose, copy, publish, and sell a single work, and thereafter earn a substantial income by authorizing and authenticating copies of that work. He would thus receive the equivalent of royalties in a society that made no direct provision for such matters.

In these key chapters of the book, therefore, Pedersen has been at pains to encompass the significant source material relevant to the physical production of Islamic books. Thus the reader learns exactly how books were composed, calligraphed, published, copied, illustrated, bound, sold, stored, and—though centuries later—printed. But the author's aim is wider than this; it is to outline the role of literature and scholarship in medieval Islamic society. It will be evident to anyone who uses the texts of the period, whether in manuscript, printed editions, or translations, that such information about the production and transmission of the source material in question is of central importance. So far as the authenticity of these texts is concerned, it is comforting to reflect that the precautions taken against plagiarism, forgery, and tampering with the text were more far-reaching and ingenious than any that seem to be recorded in western European society before the invention of printing. The world of books was very different in the two cultures. The high regard in which scholars were held in the Islamic world was reflected in the lavish scholarships and gifts that they so often received.

Pedersen is never at a loss for an illuminating anecdote, and his intimate knowledge of the sources is woven seamlessly into the texture of the book. Indeed, the material is presented throughout in a relaxed and readable way. Thus over and above the basic value of the work as the only comprehensive handbook in the field is the unexpected bonus that the first attempt at such a summary should also be so successful. Moreover, while its details intrigue and instruct the specialist, its lightness of tone ensures that the general reader too can derive profit and pleasure from it. The book is informed by a deep familiarity with medieval Islamic society, and it is for this reason that Pedersen's assessment of the place of books within that society carries conviction.

It is a measure of the difficulty of the task that Pedersen set himself that in the crucial area covered by the third and fourth chapters of his work no significant progress has been made since he published his book, and it seems that nobody has seriously challenged its principal findings. However, in areas that were somewhat incidental to the main focus of his research, Pedersen's investigations were superficial and largely confined to summarizing published material. In these areas considerable progress has been made since Pedersen published his book in 1946. These remarks apply especially to the chapter on painting, which is now entirely outdated. Pedersen seems to have had no special affinity for art history, and it has to be admitted that his attempt to indicate the major concerns and stylistic trends of Islamic painting miscarried. As a result it has proved necessary to annotate his text rather fully here and to amplify or modify his findings. Such editorial comments are given at the foot of the page in notes indicated by letters; Pedersen's own notes are numbered.

A brief outline of the progress in these fields since *The Arabic Book* was published may be useful at this stage. The unchallenged classic in the field of Arab painting is the work of that title by Richard Ettinghausen. Persian painting is well served by the four solid volumes of Ivan Stchoukine, and by the much more concise handbook of Basil Gray. For Turkish painting, the basic documents are those assembled by Stchoukine in two volumes. Research on Persian painting in particular has advanced at unprecedented speed in the last generation, with numerous doctoral theses and monographs already indicating the need for the serious revision of current handbooks.

In the more specialized field of bookbinding, where technical factors—which play a much more significant role than in studies of painting—had already been adequately treated in earlier works, Pedersen's summary of existing knowledge has not been seriously invalidated in the interim. However, the major study of the craft by Weisweiler has replaced Sarre, the source most used by Pedersen, as the standard textbook. Several detailed studies by Ettinghausen have revealed the existence of some rare techniques in this craft and have pinpointed the interdependence of designers in bookbinding, manuscript illumination, and the textile arts.

In calligraphy, too, Pedersen's conclusions—a summary of current knowledge that lays no special claim to originality—can stand substantially unchallenged. Very little work has been done since his time on the oeuvre of individual calligraphers or on individual manuscripts, though the monograph by D. S. Rice on the Ibn al-Bawwāb manuscript in the Chester Beatty Library is an honorable exception. However, a variety of other publications has appeared. They include several exhaustive treatments of the development of Islamic epigraphy and calligraphy; two useful, concise, and reliable handbooks, by Annemarie Schimmel and Yusuf Safadi, respectively; and many lavish picture books that have helped to make the subject accessible to a far larger public than hitherto. Several major exhibitions devoted either entirely or in part to Islamic calligraphy have also given a major impetus to studies in this field. Chief among them have been the exhibitions entitled "The Qur'an" and "The Arts of Islam" in London in 1976 and "Calligraphy in the Arts of the Muslim World" in New

York in 1979. All have been accompanied by major exhibition catalogues. The section that Pedersen devotes to writing materials can now profitably be supplemented by the work of Adolf Grohmann, who has also summarized the results of a lifetime of study on Arabic papyri in a concise handbook. On the other hand, the material assembled by Pedersen on libraries and on the development of the printed book in Islam draws on rich and varied sources and holds its own admirably.

ROBERT HILLENBRAND

THE ARABIC BOOK

ONE

Writing and Books in Arabia before Islam

THE ARABIC BOOK owes its origin to Islam, and this has given it a character that it has retained. This does not mean, however, that written records were unknown in the Arabian peninsula before the coming of the Prophet around the year 600 (his emigration from Mecca to Medina, the starting point of the Muslim calendar, took place in A.D. 622). From information brought back by Niebuhr's expedition from Yemen, where it had sojourned in 1762-1763, it was known in Europe that there were inscriptions with a distinctive script in southern Arabia. During the course of the 19th and 20th centuries, a large number of these became known in Europe, partly through squeezes. The south Arabian characters,[a] which are monumental and symmetrical in shape, are derived from an adaptation of the oldest Semitic alphabet writing, which originated with the Canaanitic people. This south Arabian script was called in the Arabic tradition *musnad*—"supported"—probably because of its stiff, pillar-like form.

The language is a branch of the Arabic family of languages, differentiated into various dialects but quite distinct from the north Arabic language, which later became classical Arabic. The inscriptions, most of which are incised in stone, are largely dedications and building inscriptions, but they also include laws, documents, and expressions of religious feeling; they give an impression of the rich culture that flowered in these regions that conducted trade both with India and with the Mediterranean lands. Most of the inscriptions are from the

[a] Now usually called Himyaritic.

first millennium B.C., but there are some from later centuries; a couple of long inscriptions, dealing with the collapse of dams, date from 449–450 and 542–543.

In the later Arabic tradition, southern Arabia plays a large role as a starting point for popular movements in Arabia, and it would not be remarkable if the impulse for the writing activities of the Arabs had come from here, the more so since commercial intercourse brought the southern Arabs into continuous contact with their northern kinsmen. We do have evidence, in fact, that the south Arabian script spread beyond its own boundaries. This was of greatest significance in a country beyond Arabia, namely, Abyssinia, the leading language of which is close to Arabic, probably because the ruling people had migrated thither from southern Arabia. A script derived from the south Arabian one is still used there today, but with the important improvement that it can depict vowels. The oldest inscriptions extant in this script date from the fourth century A.D.

But offshoots of the south Arabian script have also been found in northern Arabia. At the oasis of al-ʿUlā, which lay on the caravan route leading from southern Arabia via Mecca and Medina to the countries of the Mediterranean, purely south Arabian (Minæan) inscriptions, originating from a south Arabian colony, have been discovered. Other inscriptions have been found at the same place, but with a more cursive adaptation of the south Arabian script called Lihyanic, after the people among whom it originated. A number of inscriptions, often scratched graffiti, have been encountered, in a script also derived from the south Arabian one, but showing a greater degree of modification. These are all comprehended under the description "Thamudic." A third group, closely related to these with regard to both script and language, composes the Safaitic, which are found as far north as Ṣafā, a place situated in the Ḥaurān mountains southeast of Damascus. Most of these inscriptions are incised in rock walls and on the remains of ancient buildings. They are not very informative, but they do constitute evidence of the expansion of the south Arabian script in the period between the second century B.C. and the third century A.D.

Nevertheless, it was not the southern Arabs whose script came to furnish the basis for the Islamic book. The south Arabian alphabet and its offshoots did not achieve any widespread dissemination in northern Arabia beyond peoples of the southern Arabian type. The script that became of historical world importance throughout Islamic literature came into existence as an offshoot of Aramaic.

The Aramaic script came into existence in close association with the north Semitic type, which was used in the Canaanitic region and has strong affinities with the later Hebrew script. It was in use during the centuries before and after the start of our era over virtually the whole of the Near East, where Aramaic had become both the universal popular idiom and an international second language. It goes without saying that over such a vast region local variations would occur in both language and script. Thus, one characteristic subgroup consists of inscriptions from the busy trading settlement at the oasis of Palmyra; the Nabataean inscriptions form a second. The latter are of particular interest in this context, for they stem from Arabs who in the Hellenistic age had pushed into the region of the dominant culture and had adopted the language and script of the host population. Therefore they wrote Aramaic, but their Arabic mother-tongue shines through clearly, especially in the names. From about 100 B.C. to about the third century A.D., the Nabataeans controlled the northern section of Arabia's western caravan and trade routes, from the oasis of Madā'in Ṣāliḥ via Petra and southeast of the Dead Sea northward to Damascus. Their inscriptions have been found in this region, and others not very different from them are met with in the Sinai peninsula.

Once the Arabs had gone this far, it was but a short additional step for them to use the same alphabet for writing their own language. This step is taken in an epitaph to the Arab King Mar' al-Qais found at al-Namāra, southeast of Damascus, dated 328 in our chronology. This is the oldest inscription in the north Arabic language so far known. The inscription proclaims the deceased to have been king of all the Arabs enumerates various northern Arabian tribes subdued by him, and includes even Najrān in southern Arabia; it says also that he set his sons over the tribes and sent them on missions to the Persians and the Byzantines.

This inscription shows Mar' al-Qais to have been a powerful Bedouin chieftain, who gathered the northernmost tribes of Arabia around him and made contact, like so many later great Arab chieftains, with the imperial civilizations of East and West. Thus, the first genuine Arabic inscription comes from the Bedouins. Such use of the Nabataean-Aramaic script led to the development of a distinctive Arabic script. We find this in three inscriptions from the pre-Islamic era, all of them from Syria. The oldest is from Zabad, in northern Syria, and is dated A.D. 512; it contains a Syriac, a Greek, and a short Arabic text, the latter consisting mainly of proper names. The second, at Harrān in the province of al-Lajā, southeast of Damascus, is to be found together with a Greek translation, dated A.D. 568, on the lintel over the portal of a now-ruined church. The third is from Umm al-Jamāl, and likewise dates from the sixth century. The new script differs from the Nabataean in its more rounded shapes, in its predilection for giving the last letter of the word a distinctive form, and in general in its simplification of the more monumental lines of the Nabataean characters. It may be presumed to have sprung up in the period between the Namāra inscription and the Zabad inscription, namely, in the fourth or fifth century A.D., somewhere in northern Arabia or neighboring Syria. It is worth noting, perhaps, that it resembles the Sinai inscriptions more than the other inscriptions of Nabataean origin. In the same way as it spread northward to the outermost margin of the Arabic-language region, as the Zabad inscription shows, so also it moved southward, reaching at least as far as Mecca, where it attained its historic significance with the emergence of Islam. That it was this and not the south Arabian type that prevailed results from the fact that the inhabitants of al-Ḥijāz, the territory in which Mecca and Medina are situated, had close linguistic affinities with the northern Arabian tribes.[1]

No Arabic script other than those just noted has survived from the pre-Islamic era. Before Islam, the Arabs had innumerable stories of the lives and exploits of the tribes, and they also had a highly developed poetry bound by fixed rules of rhythm and construction, but both the stories and the poems were handed down orally. The tribes had their special reciters and narrators. A narrator, or *khaṭīb*, needed to command every shade of meaning of which his language was capable in order to uphold the honor of his tribe when recounting its heroic deeds, and he had to have a large fund of knowledge that others could inherit from him. Poets did recite their poetry themselves, but a prominent poet would have his transmitter, a *rāwī* or *rāwiya*, who knew all his poems by heart and who was master of the fine art of recitation. Such a *rāwī* was a living edition of the great poetry collections, and naturally he had pupils, who represented new editions of the poems. Such a mode of transmission could ensure the survival of the poems for no more than a few generations, as a rule; the oldest poems to have come down to us date back no further than the first century before Islam.

These same poets, however, do furnish evidence of the use of writing in the late pre-Islamic age. A major poem usually begins with descriptions of a deserted campground where the loved one had tarried with her tribe; the black markings etched into the white sand by the refuse of the camp evoke in the poet's imagination the shapes of letters twisting and turning across the white pages of a book.[2] One of these older poets,

[1] On older Semitic writing, see J. Pedersen, "Schrift. E. Semiten," in *Reallexikon der Vorgeschichte*, edited by M. Ebert, 11 (Berlin, 1927-1928), 347-57; and H. Jensen, *Die Schrift* (Glückstadt and Hamburg, 1935), and the works cited therein.

[2] Examples of these comparisons of campground traces to writing have often been collected; see for example T. Nöldeke, "Fünf Moʿallaqāt, übersetzt und erklärt," in *Sitzungsberichte der Kaiserlichen Akademie der Wissenschaften in Wien. Philosophisch-Historische Klasse*, Bd. 142 (1900), 65; F. Schulthess, *Der Dīwān des Ḥātim Ṭej* (Leipzig, 1897), p. 40, note 4; F. Krenkow,

Imru' al-Qais, begins one of his poems thus: "From whom stem the campground's traces, so painful to mine eye, resembling the writing in a book of Yamanī palm-bark?" In another poem he likens the campground's traces to "the lettering in the books of monks."[3] Other poets speak in the same way of "lettering on parchment."[4] And Labīd, who lived to see the coming of Muḥammad, is reminded by the remains of the loved one's camp both of weathered inscriptions on stone tablets and of "books whose pages are filled afresh by the reed pens." He mentions also a gold-striped table on which missives are placed, both sealed and open (that is, when they are to be delivered to a prince). Thus, Labīd is acquainted with rock inscriptions, parchment books, and missives, and it seems as if he has in mind parchments used for a second time, i.e. palimpsests. When he speaks of "characters like those written by a Yamanī slave,"[5] and we compare this with the mention by Imru' al-Qais of "a book of Yamanī palm-bark," this suggests that the southern Arabs did produce other written works than the inscriptions—quite monotonous for the most part—that they incised in stone.

In fact, the frequent stress laid in the northern Arabic poems upon Yamanī writing surely constitutes evidence that their authors saw something alien in it, and this is borne out by their special mention of Jewish and Christian books. We have seen that Labīd's thinking on the subject of writing and books is bound up with the ideas of southern Arabia and of monks. Al-Shammākh, a Bedouin poet of the time of Muḥammad, says of the campground traces that they are "like unto the

"The Use of Writing for the Preservation of Ancient Arabic Poetry," in *A Volume of Oriental Studies Presented to Professor Edward G. Browne*, edited by T. W. Arnold and R. A. Nicholson (Cambridge, 1922), pp. 261-68.

[3] Imru' al-Qais, pp. 63 verse 1; 65 verse 2 in *The Divans of Six Ancient Arab Poets*, edited by W. Ahlwardt (London, 1870).

[4] Ṭarafah in the above-cited edition by Ahlwardt, p. 19 verse 2; Ḥātim al-Ṭā'i: see Schulthess, *Dīwān*, p. 42, verse 1.

[5] The verses by Labīd are in his *Muʿallaqah* (C. J. Lyall, *Commentary on Ten Ancient Arabic Poems* [Calcutta, 1894]), vv. 2 and 8, and in al-Khālidī's edition (Vienna, 1880), p. 91 verse 3 and p. 61 verse 4.

lines dashed off by a Jewish scholar in Taimā writing Hebrew with his right hand."[6] There is no doubt that Jews and Christians coming in from the north helped make the use of books and writing known in Arabia.

The Arab tribes in the pre-Islamic period penetrated farther and farther northward into Syria and Mesopotamia, as indeed the finding of the inscriptions noted above also testifies. The Byzantines and Persians saw how important it was for them to obtain friends among these tribes in order to secure tranquillity on the frontiers, and in place of some great Arab prince such as Mar' al-Qais, whose tomb is found in al-Namāra and who held the balance between the two great powers, they each created in the sixth century their own Arab buffer states. In the western part of the Syrian desert the Byzantines had the Ghassānid dynasty as their—somewhat troublesome—vassals, while the Persians had the Lakhmid dynasty in Ḥīra a little to the west of the lower course of the Euphrates. Christendom little by little extended its sway over these peoples, and a number of religious houses were established. In Syria east of Damascus in the sixth century there were 137 monasteries for monks for the Monophysite confession, whereas their Christian opponents, the Nestorians, who stressed the distinction between the divine and the human natures of Christ, had a bishop in Ḥīra. Monks and anchorites of both groups spread southward into Arabia. In Najrān, a province northeast of Yemen, there was a Christian community having close links with Ḥīra. A fearful persecution launched against the community by a Jewish king in Yemen named Dhū Nuwās in the year 523 is described in accounts in the Syriac tongue, including a letter from bishop Simeon of Ḥīra written the year after the events in question.

All this leads us to understand that the Christians must have been important in introducing the use of writing into Arabia; and if we can believe a report that Khusrau, the Persian king,

[6] Al-Shammākh's poems (Cairo, 1327/1909), p. 26.

appointed the Christian poet Adī ibn Zayd[7] to his chancellery at al-Madā'in with the duty of drafting letters in Arabic, then it would seem that Arabic was already being employed in administrative correspondence in Iraq as early as the sixth century. It would be remarkable if the Meccans, whose soil is quite barren and who therefore have to depend upon what they can earn from outside through trade, had been able to dispense with the aid afforded to business life by writing. Tradition has it that writing was used in the entourage of the Prophet. In the tenth century, Ibn al-Nadīm states in his book *al-Fihrist* ("Index" [of Books]), written in Iraq, that the caliph al-Ma'mūn (813-833) had in his library an I.O.U. in the sum of 1,000 silver *dirhams*, inscribed on leather, owed by a certain Himyarite living in Ṣanā' to the Prophet's grandfather ʿAbd al-Muṭṭalib, and that it was written in the latter's hand.[8]

The veracity of this story may be doubted, but that agreements were committed to writing in the Mecca region is shown by a poem of al-Ḥārith ibn Ḥilliza composed in the time of King ʿAmr, in Ḥīra (554-568 or 569). Al-Ḥārith, lamenting a breach of the peace between his own and another tribe, says: "Remember the oath sworn at Dhu'l-Majāz, the obligations entered into and the hostages exchanged so as to avert broken words and violations; unbridled fancy surely cannot revoke what stands in the parchments."[9] This is an allusion to a reconciliation between the Bakr and Taghlib tribes brought about through the mediation of the king of Ḥīra. It is of interest that a pact between these northern Arabian tribes was concluded at a holy place close to Mecca,

[7] Al-Iṣfahānī, *Kitāb al-aghānī* II, 3rd ed. (Cairo, 1346/1928), pp. 100, 102 line 4. His father Zayd "was skilled in writing and in Arabic."

[8] Ibn al-Nadīm, *al-Fihrist*, edited by G. Flügel (Leipzig, 1871), p. 5, lines 18-20.

[9] *Muʿallaqah* verses 41f. Mutalammis also mentions a written promise in a poem to King ʿAmr in Ḥīra in the middle of the sixth century; see K. Vollers, *Die Gedichte des Mutalammis* (Leipzig, 1903), II, 2; III, 1. ʿAmr sent him and his nephew, the celebrated poet Ṭarafah, to the governor of Bahrain with a letter ordering him to put the bearers to death.

whose central significance was acknowledged even before Islam, and that the agreement was inscribed on parchment. Nuʿmān ibn al-Mundhir, a king of Ḥīra who reigned about 580-602—that is, immediately prior to the coming of the Prophet—is said to have had a collection of poems that had been composed in his praise by various poets.[10] On the face of it there is nothing improbable in this, but we have no traces of this kind of pre-Islamic writing. All we have are the few rock inscriptions mentioned above.

[10] See Krenkow, "The Use of Writing," p. 266.

TWO

The Qur'ān and Arabic Literature

ARABS USE the same term, *kitāb*, to denote both a book and any other piece of writing, short or long, whether a letter, inscription, document, or anything else. If they speak of "the book," *al-kitāb*, that is, the book in its truest sense, they mean the Qur'ān. In no other religion does the book play such a role as it does in Islam. Every word found "between the two covers" is literally the word of God: therefore it is eternal and uncreated, and therefore a miracle of linguistic perfection.

Muḥammad had no very profound acquaintance with the Jewish and Christian books, but he marveled over them no less than did the poets. He doubted not that they were the revelation of God; it must have been that much more distressing to him that they were not revealed to his people in their own tongue. The Jewish books were written in Hebrew, of course, and those Christian books that he may have seen were probably in Aramaic. When he himself received revelations and became sure that they came from God, therefore, it was a special joy to him to perceive that God was now also revealing Himself in Arabic. God says in the Qur'ān: "This is the miracle manifested in the book's revelation, that we have sent it down as an Arabic Qur'ān" (Sūra 12, 1-2). The word Qur'ān really means "recitation," and so also, by extension, that which is recited as holy writ. God says to unbelievers: "Had We made it a Qur'ān in a foreign tongue, they would have said: Why is the miracle of its revelation not performed in plain view? Why a foreign speech and an Arab listener?" (Sūra 41, 44).

In speaking of revelation, vouchsafed first to the Jews, then to the Christians, and now to Muḥammad, the Qur'ān manifests a mystical view of the book. For all the revelations granted to men are regarded as messages culled from something we can call the first writing, a Celestial Book existing with God and brought to man's knowledge piecemeal through prophetic revelations. The Celestial Book is the materialized expression, as it were, of God's knowledge and will. Everything in heaven and on earth, and everything that happens, is recorded in the Book: the deeds of men whereby they shall be judged are written in the Book, and so are their fates. On the Day of Judgment every man will receive his own book, his private transcript from the account, on which his fate depends. It was written in the Book on the day of the Creation that the number of months should be twelve, and all the duties that God has seen fit to impose upon man are to be found there: "We bind no soul beyond its capacity, and We have a Book that sets forth the Truth: they shall suffer no injustice" (Sūra 23, 62).

This idea of a Celestial Book was not invented by Muḥammad, of course. Its origin is to be found with the Babylonians, at whose New Year festival the gods assemble for their deliberations and the tables of destiny are inscribed. These divine tables are filled with all that happens in heaven and on earth, the fates of men and their good and evil works. We encounter this conception again in the Old Testament, where it is said that Jehovah has a Book in which is written down that which he wishes to do, and a Book of Life with the names of those who act rightly; at the Judgment, when the case will be heard, the books will be opened. The later Jewish literature, especially the Book of Enoch and the Book of Jubilees, is even more explicit on the subject of the celestial tables or books in which are inscribed all that happens and is to happen as the world runs its course, and in the New Testament, too, we find traces of the same idea.[1]

[1] On the Celestial Book see J. Pedersen, review of E. Meyer, *Ursprung und Geschichte der Mormonen* in *Der Islam* 5 (1914), 110-15.

These ancient conceptions, which raise the book into the sphere of the divine and invest it with cosmic signficance as the source of all knowledge and wisdom, were adopted by the Prophet to form the basis of the Islamic view of the book. "The Mother of Books," *Umm al-kitāb*, or "the well-preserved table," as it was called (Sūra 43, 4; 85, 22), is written by noble scribes, namely, angels (68, 1; 80, 15-16), on pure and venerable sheets with the celestial reed pen. "It is sent down" by the angel Gabriel, and is recited to Muḥammad in Arabic, little by little as time and opportunity serve, in the ingenious form of rhymed prose. By being granted a share in the wisdom of the revelation, the Arabs are raised to an equal footing with Jews and Christians, "the People of the Book," *Ahl al-kitāb*, who had been admitted to "the Book's" secrets earlier on; but the Prophet goes still further and relegates the former People of the Book to a lower rank, since Muḥammad was the last recipient of the Word and the revelation attained its final and conclusive shape in Arabic. This meant that God need not abide forever by what he had revealed in the past to the earlier people of letters, and even revelations imparted to Muḥammad could be revoked or altered afterward, as indeed happened in a number of instances.

Muḥammad was in a trance-like state when he received his revelations, at any rate in the opening stages; immediately thereafter he recited to his believers what had been revealed to him. But how were these fragmentary messages turned into a book? Muḥammad himself did not write down his revelations, and curiously enough it is the general opinion of Muslim scholars that he would have been unable to do so because he was illiterate. They find this evidenced in the Qur'ān's description of him as a "layman," *ummī* (Sūra 7, 157, 158); but the context shows that the term denotes him as one who has no share in the revelations of the Jews and Christians, for which reason the word is also used of the Arabs in general (Sūra 62, 2). We are faced here with a dogmatic assertion shining clearly through the explanations of the interpreters, which are rooted in the notions that the Prophet's credibility as an instrument of revelation will be corroborated by his inability to read the revelations of others, and that the miraculousness of his own revelation is that much the greater.

It is highly improbable, however, that Muḥammad, who as a young man was engaged in trade, and whose revelations in the Qur'ān contain a wealth of reminiscences of business life, can have been ignorant of the art of writing. In actual fact, Muḥammad, in handing down his Divine Word, proceeded in the same manner as the poets, to whom in other respects he so emphatically refused to be compared. Just as the poet recited his production to his *rāwī* until the latter knew it by heart, so also did the Prophet recite his revelation to one or more believers until they were able to repeat it. The fragments thus recited began at a very early stage to be written down on whatever material lay to hand—the bones of camels or asses, flat stones, or palm leaves; the same probably began to happen to poetry at that time.

The revelations were not collected together until after the Prophet's death; four compilers in particular are mentioned. One of these, Zayd ibn Thābit, is said to have been commissioned by the caliph Abū Bakr (632-634), to make an authentic compilation. In executing the task he made use of both written records and the oral reports of persons who knew the texts by heart, the "bearers of the Qur'ān." Later on, under the caliph ʿUthmān (644-656), a definitive text was arrived at by a commission, thus giving the Qur'ān its final form.

So the Arabs now had a book, a work of an extraordinary character, emanating not from men but from God Himself. When the new religion spread over the former Christian lands, and Hellenistic philosophy penetrated Islam, the followers of the latter became familiar with the concept of the eternal Logos, issuing from God and ruling the world; and just as this concept had been applied in the past to Christ, the Son of God, so now it was almost a matter of course to apply it to the holy book of the new religion. Naturally the Celestial Book was divine and eternal: of that there could be no doubt.

As to the book that was manifested in the speech of men, written in characters formed by men, its eternity was discussed as the Christians had discussed Christ's eternity and consubstantiality with God. The result was the establishment of the doctrine that the Arabic Qur'ān, as it was recited and known, was eternal and uncreated. For it was God who spoke therein in an incomparable tongue, and its coming into existence in earthly form was a miracle, the greatest that had ever happened.

Thus Arabic literature started off with an unattainable exemplar, and this was of paramount importance to the Islamic book. It was established at once that the Arabic language was a perfect instrument for dealing with the very highest topics, and the form of the language represented by the Qur'ān, namely, the one prevailing in the Hijāz around the year 600, stood above the rest; all other Arabic dialects were thereby relegated to the background.

The vast energies expended later in producing sumptuously worked editions of the Qur'ān reflect the reverence nourished for the Holy Book. A handsome copy of the Qur'ān was a joy to behold, but more than that, it drew forth blessings upon its owner—and still does so—by virtue of his possession of it. It is used but little for reading. The written Qur'ān was necessary in order to fix the correct text and thus establish a check on deviations. But otherwise the Qur'ān has continued to be transmitted from generation to generation by rote learning, just as in its early days, and just as poems formerly were. Every Muslim of a certain level of education knows at least large parts of the Qur'ān by heart, and for a learned man it is a matter of course that he knows it all. For example, the candidate's ability to recite the whole of the Qur'ān without faltering is a condition of acceptance as a pupil in the Azhar Mosque, and these are lads of about ten years of age. An adult recites the holy text, and the boy repeats it after him until he has mastered it.

Thus, throughout the history of Islam, oral transmission of "the Book" proceeds alongside the written. Muslims say that even if every copy of the Qur'ān were to be burnt, the Qur'ān would still live, for it dwells in the hearts—that is, memories—of the faithful. Indeed, it is a peculiarity of Islam that despite the great respect paid to the Book, written exposition is not regarded as an independent mode of expression, valuable in its own right, but as a representation of oral communication. To an Arab, therefore, reading always means reading aloud. He recites what the letters tell him, swaying his upper body from side to side in rhythmic movements. If one enters the Azhar mosque during the afternoon, for example, when the students are sitting reading their lessons, the sound of their voices is like the polyphonic roaring of the ocean. The conception of the written word here described is clearly observable in the scholarly tradition of Islam, and in legal actions a written document does not carry the same inherent evidential weight as with us but merely furnishes corroboration of the memory. It has proved impossible, however, to maintain this position with total consistency.

The spread of Islam over the neighboring lands is one of the marvels of world history. By about twenty years after the death of the Prophet in 632, not only Arabia but also Syria, Iraq, and the Persian Empire had come under the dominion of the caliph, and in another twenty years after that Egypt and North Africa had been won. Shortly after 700, Spain was conquered in the west and further territories secured in the east, so that the caliph's empire now extended from the Atlantic to the frontiers of China. Although political unity could not be sustained, nevertheless a common culture, whose kernel was Islam, was created over this vast region, and with Islam came the Arabic tongue. The Aramaic, Greek, Coptic, Persian, Turkish, and Berber languages were all forced to yield before it, and even in those lands where the national dialects survived beneath the surface and became powerful again later on—as in the three last-mentioned cases—Arabic continued to be the language of religion, scholarship, and higher culture until the most recent times. The Persian language alone, from about A.D. 1000, achieved some measure of importance as a literary language alongside Arabic, notably in the domain of poetry, and gradually also of historical writing; but it was now full of loan words from Arabic. The Arabic alphabet was and still is used, and many of the most important Arabic authors were Persians.

Arabic, which had hitherto led a very quiet existence, was now a world language, and in a short time an immense body of Arabic literature was born. Copious use was made of the Arabic script in the public service, where much work was done on its form, and this too was of importance to the development of books. There emerged an Islamic branch of scholarship whose first task—immediately after the determination of the Qur'ānic text—was to collect and arrange the traditions of the Prophet's deeds and words, setting norms for every action of a Muslim; this led to the creation of great systems encompassing at once doctrine, law, ethics, and standards of behavior—the whole being termed *fiqh*. The struggle with Christendom and the other forms of religion, especially Gnosticism, led to the development of an Islamic theology, with an entire literature of its own, showing strong indications of having evolved in a milieu frequented by Christian thinkers. Hellenistic learning lived on and now became embodied in the new Arabic-stamped culture. Systems of thought were derived from Platonic and Aristotelian philosophy. Hellenistic natural science, especially medicine, found its continuation among scholars who wrote Arabic.

The bulk of the ancient Arabic scientific literature consisted of translations from Greek, which were promoted at academies such as the one established by the caliph al-Ma'mūn at the beginning of the ninth century. Many books were translated from Persian as well; a single author, Ibn Marzubān (d. 921) is said to have been responsible for over fifty,[2] but little of this translated literature has survived. Ibn al-Nadīm, who lived in the heyday of this activity, compiled a survey of the

[2] Yāqūt, *Irshād al-arīb ilā maʿrifat al-adīb*, edited by D. S. Margoliouth (London, 1907-1926), VII, 105.

translations and original works then current in his *Fihrist* (Index [of Books]), completed in 987.

The Arabic language became an object of study, and a new science of language developed, embracing grammar, rhetoric, prosody, and so on. The closely associated science of philology, concerned with editions and interpretations of the ancient works, also emerged, as did a body of commentaries on the Qur'ān, on the collected traditions, and on the ancient poems. Poetry had now become literature. A historical literature of colossal scope was produced, comprising general world and Islamic history and the histories of individual countries and cities, with an incessant stream of biographies forming by no means the least important element. The lands of Islam were described, partly by public functionaries and directors of posts, who were acquainted through their official duties with the various regions and their roads, and also by private travelers, who recounted their personal observations and experiences. In addition, there was a wide range of light literature, poems, stories, and so on.

Only a small portion of the vast body of literature that evolved in this fashion was written by Arabs, but its language was Arabic, and Islam must have the credit for it, since Islam was indissolubly bound up with the Arabic language through the Qur'ān.

THREE

Composition and Transmission of Books

THE STARTING point and center of the prodigious literary activity that developed in Islamic lands was the mosque. People did not merely foregather for religious services: the government's public announcements were made in the mosque; judicial proceedings were held there; and, most notably, every aspect of the intellectual life of Islam was cultivated in the mosque. Education took place in the mosque, where the teacher sat surrounded by a circle (*ḥalqa*) of young people, drilling them in the knowledge required of a Muslim; but it was not mere instruction alone that went on. In the mosque scholars of distinguished reputation recounted the results of their studies, their audiences consisting not only of young pupils but also of other scholars and educated lay people. The cultural basis was common to the entire Islamic world. Scholars formed a kind of fraternity, and though each might have his special field of learning, there were no hard and fast boundaries.

Every scholar was knowledgeable in all branches; the philologist was also a Qur'ānic interpreter, a theologian, philosopher, historian, and so forth, and every man of education had his portion of this universal knowledge. The functionaries seated in their offices, including the *wazīrs* and other powerful men, were often scholars who did not merely listen to lectures in the mosques but might themselves attract a circle around them now and then as they discoursed. Scholars might also, of course, address gatherings of people in their own homes. Al-Aḥmar (d. 810), who succeeded al-Kisā'ī as tutor to the children of al-Rashīd, delivered his lectures in his own palatial residence, where his audience was supplied with all necessary writing materials and he himself arrived with his clothes smelling of musk and incense. The audience preferred al-Farrā', who sat at the door while they squatted in the dust in front of him.[1]

The rooting of intellectual life in religion, the basis of Muslim society, created a respect for it such that rulers and rich men opened their doors to the representatives of the intellectual life and frequently lavished large sums of money on them. Notables would often assemble at the mosque as a group to deliberate upon scholarly and literary questions, and scholars themselves commonly came together in concourse (*majlis*) for discussions (*munāẓara*); sometimes these might take place in the mosque as a supplement to the discourses. One renowned grammarian, Thaʿlab (d. 904), says of a colleague: "I have not missed Ibrāhīm al-Ḥarbī at a concourse on language in fifty years."[2] Muslims love company and conversation, and from the very beginning communication of the products of the intellect has had a personal character.

This is the reason why people of intellectual pursuits traveled so widely: they wanted to hear eminent personages discoursing about their own works. The many books written about learned men leave a strong impression of this intense life of study, which leads young and old from one end of the far-flung world of Islam to the other. We may cite as a random example the account by Yāqūt (d. 1229), in his seven-volume work on "Learned Literary Men," of the wanderings of a certain Muḥammad ibn ʿAbdallāh, who was born in Murcia, Spain, in 1174. He journeyed to Cairo in 1210, proceeding thence to Mecca and Medina and on to Baghdad, where he remained for some time at the Niẓāmīya College; next he went to Wāsiṭ, another town in Iraq, then to Hamadhān in western Persia and Nīshāpūr in eastern Persia; again he traveled further eastward to Marv and to Harāt in Afghanistan, returning thence to Baghdad; in subsequent years he so-

[1] Yāqūt, *Irshād al-arīb ilā maʿrifat al-adīb*, edited by D. S. Margoliouth (London, 1907-1926), V, 110.

[2] Ibid. I, 40 lines 14f.

journed in Aleppo, Damascus, and Mosul, where Yāqūt met him; then he spent more time in Mecca, Medina, and Damascus; finally he went to Cairo, where Yāqūt encountered him again in 1227. Thus he was traveling for seventeen years, and of course he made notes everywhere he went. Yāqūt was able to enumerate a long list of books written by him.[3]

Yāqūt relates of another individual that he traveled for twenty-seven years and that the scholars whom he heard numbered three thousand. This itinerant life developed most fully in Egypt and the eastern lands, the region within which Yāqūt's own journeyings took place. When a man had heard a sufficient number of scholars and compiled his notes, he could set himself up as an author. Authorship is colored by the above-described intercourse between cultured people, and books reflect the oral nature of communication. The author has "heard from"[4] or "taken from"[5] this or that authority, and now "he is handing it down from him" (*rawā ʿanhu*),[6] that is, he is transmitting the oral communication further, and the book is speaking to an invisible circle of listeners.

Every book begins with the formula "In the name of God the Merciful, the Compassionate," for any enterprise not beginning in this way must inevitably fail; thus has the Prophet spoken, it is said. Then follow praises to God and His Prophet and the latter's family and associates, in which the poet displays all his stylistic capabilities. The transition to the subject is signaled by an ancient pre-Islamic formula, *ammā baʿdu*, "as regards the following," but discussion of the subject proper still does not begin. As a rule there first come certain general remarks, interwoven with citations from the Qur'ān, selected with great skill so as to approach the subject imperceptibly while drawing attention to its inherent interest. The author will probably next relate why—not infrequently under heavy

[3] Ibid. VII, 17.

[4] *Samiʿa min*, e.g. ibid. VII, 40 line 10; 43 line 16.

[5] *Akhadha ʿan*, e.g. ibid. VII, 43 line 4; 47 line 3; 173 line 19.

[6] *Rawā ʿan*, e.g. ibid. VII, 43 line 4 from bottom; 47 line 4; 50 line 3; 174 line 8.

pressure from friends—he has brought out this book, and he begs God to grant him the grace and strength to carry through the enterprise. At this point the structure of the book is often explained. It very quickly became customary to give books grandiose titles, such as "The Vast Ocean of Qur'ānic Interpretation," "The Priceless Pearl for Defining the Doctrine of Unity," and so forth. To us there often seems a glaring contrast between the poetic title and the dry contents.

The author of the Islamic book seldom reveals himself as a person. The purpose of a book is not to express personal feelings or originality; even the erotic poems move in fixed phrases determined by custom. A very large proportion of the contents of Islamic books are presented as traditions handed on from others. The author picks from his notes and sets down an item that he finds useful, stating the authority from whom he has heard it, and the informant from whom this authority received it, and so on back to the original source. This painstaking recording of the chain of informants (*isnād*) reflects the fact that the book represents a continuing and unbroken oral tradition. The great importance attached to it certainly stems from the fact that the oldest Muslim literary activity centered upon the compilation of the sayings of the Prophet, the genuineness of which had to be attested, and that the form of transmission thus developed had percolated into other fields.

Thus, for example, in his great work, "The Book of Songs" (*Kitāb al-aghānī*), ʿAlī al-Iṣfahānī begins his exposition with these words:

> "We were told by Abū Aḥmad Yaḥyā ibn ʿAlī ibn Yaḥyā the Astronomer, who said: I heard it from my father, who said: I heard it from Isḥāq ibn Ibrāhīm al-Mauṣilī that his father told him that al-Rashīd—may God's mercy rest upon him!—commanded the bards, and they were many at that time, to choose for him three melodies from all the songs, and they agreed upon three melodies, to which I shall refer later, if God wills.

The item of information continues to its conclusion, and then comes a new *isnād*. The author of the work in question lived from 887 to 967, and the oldest person in the chain, Ibrāhīm al-Mauṣilī, Isḥāq's father, from 743 to 804. He was a highly esteemed bard, who gained widespread popularity for his art by training young slave girls in his methods and placing them in wealthy houses. The character of the particular subject determines the chain of informants, but the one who is named first has certainly been heard by the author. The chain is often considerably longer and consists of a series of scholars who, one after the other, have handed on the particular item of information. One author acts as transmitter, *rāwī*, to the next.

This form of narrative gives the exposition a heavy and disjointed character, and it contributes to the further effacement of the author's personality; he does not shape his material independently. If he wishes to put forward a personal opinion or an item of information of his own, it is often written in the third person like the others: "Abū Jaʿfar says" is a stock phrase in Abū Jaʿfar al-Ṭabarī's great historical work. Another phrase frequently employed is "the author says." This is connected with the fact that the published book was as a rule a transcript of the author's discourse.

The word employed in Arabic to denote publication means "let (it) go out" (*kharraja* or *akhraja*), and "go out" (*kharaja*) can also mean "come out, be published." The procedure was rather more complex than with us, resulting from the fact that, until the most recent times, the Islamic book was a handwritten production.

The oral path was followed in publishing. A work was published by being recited and written down to dictation, *imlāʾ*, usually in a mosque. This was the only method by which the Muslims of former days could conceive of a work being made public and brought before a wider circle. Even poets, who in fact still had their *rāwīs* in the period of the Umayyads (661-750), published their works in the mosque. One of the minor poets from the beginning of the tenth century describes a situation in which he sat and dictated one of his works in the principal mosque of Kūfa, "and people wrote it down after me."[7]

Even when the writing of a book was commissioned privately, publication would still be effected in this way. One of the prominent early philologists, al-Farrā' (d. 822), was asked by a friend to compose a book capable of guiding him in the understanding of the Qur'ān, so that he need not be ashamed if the amīr to whom he was attached should question him about any passages from it. Al-Farrā', who resided in Baghdad, then made it known that he would recite a work of this character in the mosque, and so the work was produced.[8]

During the vigorous political struggles that took place in the eighth to eleventh centuries, the very era in which culture and literature were flowering, it could be a risky business for an author to recite his work in a mosque where the general mood was adverse to his school of thought. A contemporary of al-Farrā', who had also written a Qur'ānic commentary, wished to recite it in the principal mosque but lacked the courage to do so because he was an adherent of the Muʿtazilite theology.[9] This theology did not find favor with the multitude, since it made use of concepts that the ordinary man did not comprehend, and transformed the old Islam by its interpretations. A contrary instance is that of the orthodox author al-Ṭabarī, who had to break off a discourse he was holding during a sojourn in Ṭabaristān because he offended the ruling Shīʿī sect by his account of the early history of Islam; he had to leave the country hastily.[10]

It could happen that dictation of a work might not be completed because the author broke off for one reason or another. When Ibn ʿAsākir had dictated seven discourses on the early history of Islam, he broke off to give lectures on the repre-

[7] Ibid. V, 239.
[8] *Fihrist*, p. 66.
[9] Yāqūt, *Irshād* VII, 105.
[10] Ibid. VI, 456.

hensible qualities of the Jews.[11] We have reports of a couple of occasions when Ṭabarī began dictating works that he did not finish. He had composed a work in four parts on "The Formation of the Noble Soul and Fine Character," but suddenly stopped dictating "and did not give it out to the public by dictation." Those who had taken down the five hundred pages that he did dictate thus had to be satisfied with a truncated work. On another occasion, there was a polemical tract that he ceased dictating when his adversary died. It is said that what was published came into the hands only of a few people, and that it was not passed on any further.[12]

The lecturer would sit crosslegged, as is still done in the mosques, with his listeners seated in a circle (*ḥalqa*) before him in the same position. If the teacher was a regular one, he might well have a famulus (*mustamlī*), who would sit close by him; this was his most intimate pupil, who acted as an intermediary between him and the audience. A famulus was of course a particularly faithful transcriber of all his teacher's works. The numerous "circles,"each centered around its dictating lecturer, filled the mosques with a humming life not very different from that of today, although actual dictation seldom takes place nowadays.

The dictation was often delivered from memory: this is stated again and again in the biographies of scholars and literary men. Al-Nīsābūrī (d. 1066) dictated his great Qur'ānic commentaries from memory, and at his death only four volumes of them were found in his library.[13] It was thus a real feat of memory, of the sort that Muslims are masters of. The philologist al-Bāwardī (d. 957) dictated from memory 30,000 pages on linguistic topics,[14] and it is said of the Spaniard Ibn al-Qūṭīya that he dictated the history of Spain "from his heart," that is, from memory,[15] but in fact he was censured for in-

[11] Ibid. V, 144.
[12] Ibid. VI, 450f.
[13] Ibid. V, 232.
[14] Ibid. VII, 26.
[15] Ibid. VII, 53.

accuracy of transmission, since he was content to give the sense instead of the exact expression. Fantastic stories are often told of the memories of dictating authors: for instance, Abū Bakr ibn al-Anbārī (d. 939) is said to have dictated from memory 45,000 pages of traditions concerning the Prophet and to have been able, according to his own account, to recite thirteen chests of books by heart.[16] To us this hardly seems credible; we must remember, however, that Orientals are accustomed to train their memories in a manner inconceivable to us. "You have your knowledge in books," they say to Europeans, "but we have it in our hearts."

The rule of course was that the author himself wrote out his work and followed the manuscript in his dictation. This original manuscript (*aṣl*) was called the "draft" (*muswadda*, meaning actually "made black," as opposed to *mubayyaḍa*, "made white," that is, copied fair). Such a draft naturally had its value and became of interest to bibliophiles later on. Yāqūt recounts that he came into possession of some sheets of the drafts of Kamāl al-Dīn, the Aleppan historian.[17] A factor for a son of the Mosul prince Nāṣir al-Daula, who was searching for a copy of al-Iṣfahānī's *Kitāb al-aghānī*, experienced the mortification of seeing the author's draft sold under his nose at a very low price.[18]

Nevertheless, a draft is not the same thing as an authorized book. The latter might come into existence as a result of being copied fair in final form by the author himself, or, as usually happened, through the authorization of transcripts produced via public dictation. The prerequisite of such authorization, naturally, was that the author should have checked the transcript. The normal method of doing this was for the copyist to read out his manuscript to the author (*qara'a ʿalayhi*). This aspect of scholarly life was just as important as the author's actual discourse. Biographies of scholars constantly declare not only that "he heard it from so-and-so" but also "he read

[16] Ibid. VII, 73f., 76.
[17] Ibid. VI, 21.
[18] Ibid. V, 164.

it to so-and-so." The genesis of this laborious procedure is probably to be found in the way the Qur'ān was transmitted. When a young man had crammed the whole of the Qur'ān, he would very likely want to recite it before a Qur'ānic scholar of high standing to be assured that he had learned the text correctly. The caliph al-Rashīd made his son al-Ma'mūn recite the Qur'ān for (*qara'a ʿalā*) the great Qur'ānic scholar al-Kisā'ī. During the lesson al-Kisā'ī sat with head bowed; when al-Ma'mūn made a mistake, he raised his head, and the young man corrected himself.[19] The same sort of method was carried over to other books.

There was plenty for a scholar to do with his books, both in dictating them and in listening to their recitation. The copyist had to execute the recitation in order to obtain authorization. A man by the name of al-Ziyādī was reading Sībawayh's grammatical work to the author, but did not complete it and so had to transmit (*rawā ʿan*) on the authority of others.[20] Authorization was the prerequisite before transmission could be undertaken. It is related of the fanatical Spanish theologian Ibn Ḥazm that one of his pupils, who was born in Majorca, "read most of his works to him."[21] It was not a matter of indifference who received authorization for one's works. Al-Mubarrad (d. 898) received little satisfaction from his principal work, because it was transmitted by the heretic Ibn al-Rāwandī, who was influenced by Manichaeism, and the animosity aroused by the copyist spilled over upon the author of the book as well.[22]

An author could not, of course, give unlimited time to the hearing of check-reading for authorization, and so he would assemble his audience for check-reading in the same way as for his own dictation. It is said of al-Ṭabarī that he refused to allow Abū Bakr ibn Mujāhid to read for him alone because

[19] R. E. Brünnow, *R. Brünnows Arabische Chrestomathie aus Prosaschriftstellern*, 4th ed., edited by A. Fischer (Berlin, 1928), pp. 5f.

[20] Yāqūt, *Irshād* I, 62 line 15.

[21] Ibid. VII, 59 line 3.

[22] Ibid. VII, 143ff.

he wanted the knowledge contained in the work in question to be proclaimed publicly. Al-Ṭabarī's great historical work "appeared before the public through the medium of authorization, including the year 294 (907)." Only a little more was needed for the whole work to become authorized, since the narrative stops at 302 (915).[23] We do not know for certain what those of the audience who did not recite got out of the proceedings. But it may be presumed, perhaps, that they followed the reading in their own transcripts and that they too received authorization even though their copies cannot really be said to have been checked.

If the author had not completed his manuscript before the check-reading, the latter could form a stage in the composition of the book. This is illustrated by what Ibn al-Nadīm tells us about the production of a work of philology by Abū ʿUmar al-Muṭarriz (d. 956). He repeats an account by Abū'l-Fatḥ:[24]

> He began dictation of this book, *Kitāb al-yāqūt* [The Book of the Gem] on Thursday, 29 Muḥarram in the year 326 [December 6, 937] in the principal mosque of Abū Jaʿfar's city [Baghdad], from memory, without any books or notes, and he continued with the dictation at regular hours until he reached the end. And I wrote what he dictated, hour after hour. Then he began to make additions, and he added twice as much as he had dictated, and extemporized other gems. Abū Muḥammad al-Ṣaffār was especially busy with this addition, because he was closely attached to him, and also with the reading of this book for Abū ʿUmar [the author]. I had the addition from him. After that he assembled the public for Abū Isḥāq al-Ṭabarī's reading of the book; this reading was called "the statement";[25] he read it out to the author, and the public heard him. Next the author made further additions to it, and I collected all the additions in my book. And

[23] Ibid. VI, 443 (middle), 445.

[24] *Fihrist*, p. 76.

[25] This word, *fadhlaka*, is taken from bookkeeping.

I began the reading of the book for him on Thursday, 27 Dhu'l-Qaʿda in the year 329 [August 23, 941] and continued until I finished it in the month of Rabīʿ II in the year 331 [December 13, 942 until January 10, 943]. And I had all the transcripts at hand during my reading: Abū Isḥāq al-Ṭabarī's and Abū Muḥammad al-Ṣaffār's and Abū Muḥammad ibn Saʿd al-Qurṭubī's and Abū Muḥammad al-Ḥijāzī's copies. He [Abū ʿUmar al-Muṭarriz] gave me some additions during my reading for him, and we were in accord concerning the entire book from first to last. Then he again extemporized further gems and twice as many additions as the length of the book. The man particularly concerned with these additions was Abū Muḥammad Wahb, for he was now attached to him. So he assembled the listeners and promised them that Abū Isḥāq (al-Ṭabarī) should recite this book for him, and that this would be the last reading,[26] so that by it the book would be finished, and that there would be no further additions thereafter. This reading was called "the curative."[27] The public now assembled on Thursday, 14 Jumādā I in the year 331 [January 25, 943] in his [Abū ʿUmar's] dwelling in the presence of . . .[28] Abu 'l-ʿAnbar, and he dictated to the people verbatim: Abū ʿUmar Muḥammad ibn ʿAbd al-Wāḥid [that is, I myself] says: "This version is the one that Abū Isḥāq al-Ṭabarī alone recited as the last version I allow to be read out now that he has written it down. If anyone transmits the present version of this book from me with a single word (added), then it is not my word, and by it he imputes lies to me. This version accords with Abū Isḥāq's reading for the public at large, hour by hour, for I conducted this reading word for word."

[26] *ʿUrḍa*, actually "submission," the same word as is used later of the thing submitted, namely, "edition" or "version."

[27] The meaning of this word is uncertain. The vowels have not survived; I read it as *al-buḥrānīya* and take it to be an adjective from *buḥrān*, which signifies the crisis of an illness, with recovery about to set in.

[28] The word that has come down to us bears no meaning.

We see from this how laborious the proceedings were. The book is recited first to the public by the author himself, then it is read publicly three more times in different versions by a copyist in the presence of the author. In the meantime the changes and addenda are produced by being dictated to a famulus, who then reads the dictated version back to the author. The work only attains its final shape by being read aloud to the author in the presence of the public, and the author gives his authorization to this version.

The authorization of the book is called *ijāza* which means "to make lawful." The author placed his *ijāza* [license] on the copies that he approved. It signified that he granted permission "to transmit the work from him" in the form as approved, an expression which occurs very frequently. It was important to have an *ijāza* directly from the author, "with hearing by him," *samāʿan lahu*,[29] that is, after the author had heard it read. Sometimes one might have a transcript of a work and then have the good fortune to meet the author and get him to authorize it. Yāqūt relates that he had used a book about his own family written by the Aleppan historian Kamāl al-Dīn, "and I read it to him, and he verified it" (*aqarra bihi*).[30] Yāqūt recounts another episode in which Yaʿqūb ibn Aḥmad, who had produced an anthology of poetry by himself and others, met one of the other poets, Abū ʿĀmir, and asked him to inscribe the book. Yāqūt saw the copy with Abū ʿĀmir's endorsement, "about which I entertain no doubt." It consists of a series of compliments, and so forth, partly in verse, and finally a statement to the effect that Yaʿqūb had read back to him, in the presence of two other persons, such of his manuscript as he had used and that he besought God to grant him benefit and satisfaction therefrom.[31] This is a tactful way of expressing authorization, since of course he is thereby saying at the same time that he regards the inclusion of his poem in the anthology as an honor.

Direct transcription of the author's dictation, followed by

[29] For example, Yāqūt, *Irshād* VI, 429 line 13.

[30] Ibid. VI, 18 line 1 from bottom.

[31] Ibid. VI, 128ff.

authorization, was and remained the best form of publication. But of course the number of people who could obtain books from a particular author in this way was limited, and this opportunity came to an end in any case on the author's death.

Muslims have never abandoned their skepticism toward the written word: it might be falsified, they feel. This general skepticism is what underlies such a remark as that of Yāqūt cited above, to the effect that he entertained no doubt as to the genuineness of Abū ʿĀmir's endorsement. But when the person who wanted a book could not go to the author himself and get his authorization, he would have to make do with authorization of a secondary nature.

When the author had given his authorization, this meant, as we have seen, not only that the copyist had an assurance that he possessed the book in the form determined by the author, but also that he in turn was empowered to transmit the book in the same form. Anyone so empowered could similarly empower others, provided he first assured himself that their transcripts agreed with his own. This was done in exactly the same way as when the author conferred his *ijāza*: the new copy was read over to the holder of *ijāza*, who then granted his own *ijāza* to this copy. The guarantee of the copy's genuineness rested upon there being an unbroken chain of *ijāzas* going back to the author himself. Yāqūt relates that in Cairo in 1215 (or 1216) he saw a copy of al-Iṣfahānī's *Kitāb al-aghānī*, "Book of Songs," with consecutive authorization (*ijāza muttaṣila*) going back to al-Dihakī, who had read it to the author and received his authorization. But others claimed to have a better *ijāza* for this work.[32]

[32] Ibid. V, 78. The formula *akhbaranī ijāzatan*, "he informed me with authority," frequently occurs; for example, al-Khaṭīb al-Baghdādī, *Ta'rīkh Baghdād* (Cairo 1349/1931), VI, 260 line 6 and often in *Kitāb al-aghānī*. The boundary between the history of a book's production and of its transmission is somewhat blurred. There is an instructive example of this in Yaḥyā ibn Ādam's *Kitāb al-kharāj* (On Taxation), which was published in Leiden in 1896 and whose textual history is fairly clear. The editor, T. W. Juynboll, states that in the manuscript used (the only one extant), there is an endorsement

The difference between the value of the various "warranties" might arise from the author's having himself dictated the work several times, so that there would be numerous published versions, as we saw in the example of al-Muṭarriz. But most commonly it depended upon whether the intermediate copyists had transmitted the book conscientiously without making any alterations. The value of a version hinged upon whether it was transmitted by way of a series of trust-

---

after each of the book's four chapters, in the same hand as the text itself, to the effect that four men mentioned by name heard the entire work, while a fifth heard half of it, all according to Abū ʿAbdallāh al-Ḥusayn ibn ʿAlī ibn Aḥmad ibn al-Buṣrī, and read out by Muḥammad ibn ʿUbaydallāh ibn Muḥammad; the check-reading was completed on May 22, 1096. This is to be understood as meaning that the check-reading was based on a manuscript by al-Buṣrī, authenticated by *ijāza* whether or not he himself attended the check-reading, and that it was transcribed by the four persons in question or at least by one of them. However, Ibn al-Buṣrī is himself mentioned in the text of which he is the transmitter, for several of the passages begin thus (pp. 3, 26, 52, 88): "Abū ʿAbdallāh al-Ḥusayn ibn ʿAlī ibn Aḥmad ibn al-Buṣrī has told us." "Us" must mean the group of listeners referred to above and the individual among them who was acting as scribe writes in the manner of an author citing a work as transmitted by Ibn al-Buṣrī. The text continues with Ibn al-Buṣrī having said: "Abū Muḥammad ʿAbdallāh ibn Yaḥyā ibn ʿAbd al-Jabbār al-Sukkarī has informed us in the year 415/1025" (52 cf. 26 with the addendum "with reading for him"). Ibn al-Buṣrī's *ijāza*, with which his initial copy was endorsed, is cited in a marginal note (fol. 22 v.); it says that he heard the work in company with his father and two other persons during the check-reading by Muḥammad ibn ʿAlī ibn Mujallad in the year 1025, namely, the year mentioned in the text above. Al-Sukkarī's name is not mentioned here, but the information in the text suggests that it was his manuscript that was read and that this took place in his presence. It goes on to say that al-Sukkarī said: "Abū ʿAlī Ismāʿīl ibn Muḥammad ibn Ismāʿīl al-Ṣaffār has told us, with reading for him in the year 340/952. He said: We have been told by al-Ḥasan ibn ʿAlī ibn ʿAffān al-ʿĀmirī al-Kūfī in Kūfa, who said: We have been told by Yaḥyā ibn Ādam." The last-mentioned died in 818 or 819. That he was the actual author is confirmed by the fact that he cites various authorities for his individual statements while the chain Ibn al-Buṣrī, al-Sukkarī, al-Ṣaffār, al-ʿĀmirī is unaltered. Thus, these four quite simply transmitted Ibn Ādam's book to one another by the process of transcription and check-reading, each being the authority for his own transcript, but the text reads as though they were transmitters who had been involved in its composition.

worthy authorities. It was hardly universal, however, for every one of the preceding *ijāzas* to be specified in a manuscript.

It was possible for one of these early authors to be transmitted by some scholar's dictating his work, in the same manner as the scholar dictated his own. Thus, the great al-Ṭabarī dictated from memory in the ʿAmr mosque in Cairo the works of Tirimmāḥ, a poet of the Umayyad era.[33] But when one of the early classics was involved, the normal procedure was certainly to borrow a copy and make a transcript of it. Yāqūt relates that al-Balūṭī, a Spaniard, asked a teacher whose discourses he attended for the loan of the latter's copy of Khalīl's *Kitāb al-ʿayn*, one of the basic works of philology from the eighth century, so as to make a transcript of it, but his request was refused because he had irritated the scholar with his questions, so he got a transcript made of another copy "as transmitted by Abu'l-ʿAbbās ibn Wallād."[34] Those who were to tread the path of learning became accustomed from their early youth to copying. Al-Khaṭībī, who lived about 1200, as a boy copied daily five pages of a philological work by Ibn Fāris, and afterwards he read it over to a distinguished teacher.[35]

The reading over to a teacher of repute, who then gave the book his *imprimatur*, was what imparted authority to the transcript of an early work. Therefore we hear of such a scholar that he was much in demand "for reading to him."[36] Each had his own speciality. One of the basic works of Arabic grammar is Sībawayh's book, which indeed was entitled simply "The Book." An authority on its text who was much sought after in the century after the author's death (in the 790s) was al-Mubarrad (d. 898). It is explicitly stated that he did not have a copy of Sībawayh's book direct from the author, but he had read it over to two scholars. He was himself reluctant to lend out his copy for transcription; however, one

[33] Yāqūt, *Irshād* VI, 432.

[34] Ibid. VII, 178, 184.

[35] Ibid. V, 424.

[36] Ibid. I, 45 line 3.

of his pupils, Muḥammad ibn Wallād, did get possession of it in return for a clear promise, apparently to do with payment, but after having transcribed it he refused to pay until al-Mubarrad had let it be read over to him. The learned philologist sought the support of the authorities against his pupil, but the latter also had his connections, and al-Mubarrad was compelled to let him read the book to him.[37] This example shows that the reading over to an authority, and of course the latter's approval, were crucial.

In the next generation we find further evidence to the same effect. A Persian named Abū ʿAlī al-Fārisī came to Muḥammad ibn al-Sarī (d. 929), who had check-read Sībawayh's book to al-Mubarrad, to read over the same work to him. By the time he reached the middle of the book he was strongly tempted to give up; but he told himself that when he got home to Persia and was asked if he had gone through the whole book, he would be lying if he said yes, and if he said no, then his transmission (that is, his authority as transmitter) would be worthless.[38] The picture is always of transmission being maintained by way of personal authorization from man to man. About a hundred years later al-Daqīqī (d. 1024) was the authority for Sībawayh's book, which he had read over to ʿAlī ibn ʿĪsā al-Rummānī, who had given it his attestation.[39] Al-Rummānī himself (d. 994) is referred to in connection with the al-Fārisī mentioned above, from whom he may have received his version. About another hundred years later Muḥammad ibn Masʿūd al-Andalusī (d. 1149) is spoken of as a man to whom people traveled in order to read Sībawayh's book to him.[40]

The transmission by prominent scholars of a book in very considerable use could result in the emergence of distinct versions of the work, in the same way as there developed a number of schools of Qur'ānic textual tradition displaying

[37] Ibid. VII, 133f.
[38] Ibid. VII, 9, 11.
[39] Ibid. V, 271.
[40] Ibid. VII, 106.

minor deviations from one another. Al-Wāḥidī (d. 1075 or 1076) reports that Saʿīd al-Ḥīrī "transmitted to us Abū ʿAlī al-Fasawī's writings directly from him, and I read over to him with my words al-Zajjāj's book according to his transmission from Ibn Muqsim, who transmitted it from the author, and many persons listened to my reading."[41] The importance of specific transmission is more strongly highlighted by another example. ʿAlī ibn Jaʿfar al-Saʿdī (d. 1120) "read over to al-Ṣiqillī; one of the works he transmitted from him was al-Jauharī's *Ṣiḥāḥ* (a well-known dictionary), and through his reading (*ṭarīqah*, mode or method) the tradition of this book became known in every clime."[42]

The *ijāza* conferred upon such an early written work transmitted by a scholar may take different forms. The same Abū Isḥāq al-Ṭabarī mentioned above, who was a pupil of al-Muṭarriz, transcribed a poem by al-Ḍabʿī and read it over to al-Muṭarriz. On the manuscript could be read: "I entrust my book to you with my writing from my hand to yours: I give you authorization for the poem, and you may transmit it from me. It has been produced after having been heard and read."[43] It seems to have been the copyist himself who wrote this to the person to whom he gave the book. Yāqūt found on one copy of al-Ṭabarī's great Qur'ānic commentary an *ijāza* in the following form, written in al-Farghānī's handwriting: "I give to you, ʿAlī ibn ʿImrān and Ibrāhīm ibn Muḥammad, authorization for the Qur'ānic commentary that I have heard read by Abū Jaʿfar al-Ṭabarī—may God have mercy upon him!" The two copyists had presumably transcribed the work and read it over to al-Farghānī, who then endorsed it with his authorization. At the same time he granted authorization for other books by al-Ṭabarī, which he had not received directly from the author but through the authorization of others.[44]

[41] Ibid. V, 101.
[42] Ibid. V, 107.
[43] Ibid. I, 36.
[44] Ibid. VI, 426.

FOUR

Scribes and Booksellers

In scarcely any other culture has the literary life played such a role as in Islam. Learning (*ʿilm*), by which is meant the whole world of the intellect, engaged the interest of Muslims more than anything else during the golden age of Islam and for a good while thereafter. The life that evolved in the mosques spread outward to put its mark upon influential circles everywhere. Princes and rich men gathered people of learning and letters around them, and it was quite common for a prince, one or more times a week, to hold a concourse (*majlis*), at which representatives of the intellectual life would assemble and, with their princely host participating, discuss those topics that concerned them, just as they were accustomed to do when meeting in their own milieu.

The industry of these scholars was prodigious, often inconceivable. Al-Marzubānī, who died shortly before the year 1000, wrote over 37,580 pages, according to Ibn al-Nadīm;[1] Yāqūt managed altogether 33,180 pages, of which only one minor work survived even in his own day.[2] He was wont to write with the wine goblet next to the inkstand—a gross breach of Islamic law and by no means a general custom, in fact. The Spaniard Ibn Ḥazm, who lived at about the same time, is reputed to have written about four hundred volumes, totaling about eighty thousand pages,[3] and according to Yāqūt was surpassed only by al-Ṭabarī, the oft-cited historian and commentator on the Qur'ān; al-Ṭabarī's commentaries on the

[1] *Fihrist*, pp. 132-134.

[2] *Irshād* VII, 50-52. However, C. Brockelmann cites four works by him still extant in manuscript (*Geschichte der arabischen Literatur, Supplementband* I [Leiden, 1937], 191).

[3] *Irshād* V, 88 lines 1ff.

Qur'ān are said to have filled thirty thousand pages originally, but to have been abridged to three thousand. When he died in 937 at the age of eighty-six, his disciples counted the days of his life from the time he attained adulthood and divided them into the number of his written pages, a calculation that showed him to have written an average of fourteen pages every day. It was claimed by some, indeed, that he wrote forty pages every day for forty years.[4] All records seem to have been broken, however, by the Egyptian Jalāl al-Dīn al-Suyūṭī, who died in 1505 at the age of sixty, that is, two or three centuries after Yāqūt. His books numbered 600, according to the Egyptian historian Ibn Iyās.[5]

When it is borne in mind that the literary man as a rule spent long periods on study tours, took part in pilgrimages to Mecca, and devoted a fitting amount of time to his religious duties, it is hard to grasp that such prolific writers also had time for conversing with friends as host or guest, and that as well as all this they had their family lives, often with several wives and many children. It shows how literary work could utterly enthral Muslims and dominate their lives. But, of course, a substantial share of this vast productivity is accounted for by the fact that the literature consisted in large measure of reports of traditions, which make less demand upon the creative, constructive powers. Even with an author like al-Ghazālī (d. 1111), who as theologian and thinker was fighting for an idea, this aspect played some part; all the same it is a proof of the considerable spiritual force developed in Islam that this man was able to leave behind him over seventy works encompassing all branches of knowledge apart from the natural sciences ("the ancient sciences") and linguistics, of which he believed more was made than was justified.

At an early stage, books based upon other books began to

[4] Ibid. VI, 424, 426.

[5] *Die Chronik des Ibn Ijās*, edited by P. Kahle and M. Muṣṭafā (Leipzig, 1932), V, 93 lines 19ff. Brockelmann cites the titles of 330 works by him still extant in MS (*GAL* II [Weimar, 1902], 144ff. and 295; and *Supplementband* II, 405).

be written. As time went on and writings with the authorization of the author became available, it became possible to copy from them without referring to one's own teachers as intermediaries. As early a writer as al-Iṣfahānī often uses in his "Book of Songs" the formula: "I have copied (*nasakhtu*) the following from such-and-such a book." The more indeterminate *naqaltu*, "I transmit" from X, is also used.[6] Yāqūt says of the above-mentioned Marzubānī, "Most of his traditions are cited from *ijāza* [authorized manuscripts]; nevertheless he says when he cites them 'X has told me.' "[7] This formula is interesting, for it shows that Yāqūt found it natural to make this explicit statement even when his only source was written tradition, but there is little doubt that al-Marzubānī's mode of procedure was the general one, so that the formula originating from the oral tradition was carried over to the purely written. In later times, however, it became the general practice to cite a book by stating simply, "X says." Scholarly literature adhered closely to the traditions of the past, both in form and content, often to the point where the ancient classical works were transcribed and embellished with commentaries that in the next generation were amplified by super-commentaries, to which super-super-commentaries might be added later on.

How were the representatives of the literary life in a position to perform the vast labors that took up all their time and abilities? First, most of them lived a life of great contentment. "Learning," that is, the life of the intellect, was intimately bound up with religion, and to devote oneself to it both afforded an inner satisfaction and was a service to God that on the Day of Reckoning would count to the credit of the one who performed it. It not only made men of letters willing to

[6] As, for example, in *Kitāb al-Aghānī* I, 40f.

[7] *Irshād* VII, 50, 3f. According to ʿAbd al-Razzāq, *Dictionary of Technical Terms*, edited by A. Sprenger, I, 282, the expression *ḥaddathanā* "he told us" ought to be used only of direct oral statements, whereas *akhbaranā*, "he related to us," is used for statements lacking such a direct character. Terminological usage does tend somewhat in that direction but cannot really be said to be applied consistently.

accept deprivation; even more, it prompted others to lend them aid. A wide variety of institutions endowed innumerable scholarships in the mosques to provide stipends for teachers, whose means of subsistence were thereby assured, often in liberal measure. This source was frequently supplemented by rulers and other notables who made cash donations earmarked for individual scholars who had aroused their interest.

Generally speaking, it was regarded as unseemly to take a wage in return for learning, and many pronouncements to that effect are on record. On the other hand, gifts could always be accepted. The mosque scholarships were regarded in this light. It was also a general practice for the well-to-do to make donations from their own abundance to some scholar in want. Ibrāhīm al-Ḥarbī (d. 898) was an indigent man of letters who spent his time in a small room in his house, "meditating and copying." One evening a man brought him a costly kerchief in which were wrapped food and 500 dirhams.[8] The anonymity of the gift increased the merit it conferred upon the donor. When he who possessed worldly goods was unable to create knowledge himself, he repaid by his gift some small part of the debt that he, as a Muslim, owed to those who devoted themselves to intellectual labor.

An author would very often dedicate his work to someone of princely rank. The dedication consisted of the prince's being presented with the first fair copy of the work, either by the author himself or through some intermediary. The prince then had to show his recognition of the honor thus paid to him by giving the author a sum of money, that is, a kind of author's honorarium. It was a point of honor for a prince not to be parsimonious in affairs of this sort. In the "Book of Songs" we continually hear of large sums being lavished by the caliph or some other potentate upon poets who come to court and recite poems for him. ʿAlī al-Iṣfahānī, the author of this work, himself dedicated it to the Ḥamdānid Sayf al-Daula, who in the middle years of the tenth century estab-

[8] *Irshād* I, 39.

lished a powerful hegemony in northern Syria and held a court of some splendor, at which men of letters foregathered, in Aleppo.

Al-Iṣfahānī toiled over his work for many years, then he himself produced one fair copy to present to Sayf al-Daula, who then gave him a thousand dīnārs.[9] Another devotee of literature in that era, Ismāʿīl ibn ʿAbbād, *wazīr* to the Būyid prince of Baghdad, who was the real ruler at the caliph's side, declared that Sayf al-Daula had been niggardly and that the author had merited a donation many times larger.[10] Al-Iṣfahānī wrote other works that he sent to the Umayyad rulers in Spain, and they gave him generous honoraria. Al-Ḥakam II of Córdoba is said, in fact, to have given him a thousand dīnārs for the "Book of Songs."[11] Later on again we hear of the liberal aid furnished by the western princes to the devotees of learning. For example, a not particularly prominent scholar living in Seville around 1200 received a thousand dīnārs from the "Ruler of the West," to whom he had given a commentary on Sībawayh.[12]

The boundary between a gift and a wage was not absolute, of course, and the principle that wages were not to be accepted for learning could not be observed to the letter. Cases could occur, for instance, where a young student might be working as a craftsman on the side and handing over half his earnings to his teacher.[13] Many teachers entertained no scruples about accepting some reward for their labors. This was particularly so when it was a matter of furnishing a pupil with guidance regarding older works.

Reports of such instances are especially frequent when a

[9] One denarius was equivalent in value to about thirteen gold francs.

[10] *Irshād* V, 150ff. Ibn ʿAbbād's biography is to be found in II, 273ff.; see also *Encyclopaedia of Islam*, 1st ed., II, 374. To the references to the literature given in the latter we may add Niẓāmī-yi ʿArūḍī al-Samarqandī, *Chahār Maqāla*, revised translation by E. G. Browne (London, 1921), pp. 19, 107.

[11] Al-Maqqarī, *Nafḥ al-ṭīb* (Cairo, 1302/1885), I, 180.

[12] *Irshād* V, 421 in middle.

[13] Ibid.

work such as Sībawayh's grammar is involved. We have already noted the episode of al-Mubarrad's quarrel with a pupil over payment for scrutiny of Sībawayh's work. This particular scholar was indeed somewhat on the acquisitive side. One pupil, a glass polisher earning 1½ dirhams a day, offered to pay him one dirham daily as long as he lived in return for instruction from him. Al-Mubarrad accepted, and the indigent pupil fulfilled his promise, even after his path had taken him far away from al-Mubarrad.[14] A hundred dīnārs seems to have been the price for a check-reading of Sībawayh's book, for it is reported of one of al-Mubarrad's teachers, al-Māzinī, that he refused a request by a Jew for such a check-reading at that price, not wanting to allow a non-Muslim to recite his work's many Qur'ānic passages.[15] Al-ʿAskarī, a younger contemporary of al-Mubarrad, charged the same honorarium and was very close-fisted about it. Yāqūt reports, not without malice, how a student—who, in fact, subsequently became a celebrated theologian—played a trick on him by first giving him a casket supposedly containing valuables as a pledge for cash, then going off and leaving him with the casket, which was filled with stones.[16] It has to be admitted in defense of the student—al-Jubbāʾi—that a hundred dīnārs, about 1,300 gold francs, was a substantial sum for checking a copy of Sībawayh's book.

Even though it might be doubtful whether it was quite in order for scholars to accept honoraria in return for checking and authorizing a transcript, there is another branch of book production in which it was certainly permissible to make a charge, namely, transcription on behalf of others. It was inevitable in the course of time that only a limited number of books came into existence by being transcribed or dictated in the mosque. Under the necessity of obtaining books, scholars would borrow copies—authorized if possible, of course—and transcribe them for their own use; in such instances the ques-

[14] Ibid. I, 47f.

[15] Ibid. II, 382.

[16] Ibid. VII, 42f.

tion of authorization of the transcript did not arise. When they died, their books might be sold. The indigent al-Ḥarbī, who passed his days in a little room engaged in transcribing, showed his wife that there were twelve thousand volumes on linguistics that he had written himself, and when he was dead she would be able to support herself by selling a volume a day for one dirham each. But of course a man of letters who lacked independent means could also transcribe books exclusively for sale. In this way, indeed, an entire professional caste emerged that was of very great importance in the dissemination of books.

A man who made a profession of transcribing was called *warrāq* (from *waraq*, *waraqa*, "a sheet"); as a scribe he was also called *nassākh*, "a copyist." As anyone occupied with study had to undertake a large amount of transcribing, the position of *warrāq* emerged naturally from the scholarly life, and many important scholars and literary figures have the description *al-warrāq*, "the copyist," appended to their names. Through this status a way of life was created that was of the utmost importance to the perpetuation of the literary class. It embraced people of all levels of education, including prominent authors. A well-known Christian Arab philosopher, Yaḥyā ibn ʿAdī (d. 974) made his living as a copyist; inter alia, he twice transcribed al-Ṭabarī's Qur'ānic commentaries, which in their present printed edition fill thirteen thick volumes. Ibn al-Nadīm, who wrote the *Fihrist* frequently cited above—a survey of the Arabic and other literature known to its author—was a *warrāq*, and the same is true, according to Yāqūt, of a number of the literary personages of whom he writes. At all events it was a calling on which a man of letters could always fall back. Yāqūt reports the case of one Muḥammad ibn Sulaymān (d. 1223), a well-to-do man who squandered his inheritance and was forced to become a scribe for wages until the day should come when he might find a post.[17] Yāqūt himself was originally a slave, and after being freed in 1200

[17] Ibid. VII, 14.

he lived by transcribing (*naskh*) for payment.[18] We can often read complaints by copyists over the disproportion between their labor and their remuneration. But there were differences between one *warrāq* and another, as well.

Copyists worked both for authors and for princes and rich men who wanted to build up a library. We hear of them in the early period of the ʿAbbāsid dynasty, around 800, when the literary movement was beginning to gather momentum and the work of translating from the older literature was starting in earnest, notably at al-Maʾmūn's new academy, *bayt al-ḥikma*, "The House of Wisdom," in Baghdad. It is plain that there would have been employment here for large numbers of copyists. The story of the great philologist Abū ʿUbayda tells us how one influential man obtained books. He was brought to Baghdad from Basra by Ismāʿīl ibn Sabīḥ, a powerful official who had played an important role in the fall of the Barmakids under Hārūn al-Rashīd. Ismāʿīl got hold of Abū ʿUbayda's books, whereupon he sent for a skilful *warrāq*, al-Athram, whom he installed in one of his houses, bidding him remain there and transcribe the books. Al-Athram, however, gave the requisite paper to some younger people who came to him, and got them to carry out the transcription within an agreed short time limit. It is said that Abū ʿUbayda was very ungenerous with his books, and had he known what al-Athram was doing, he would have stopped it.[19]

The caliph al-Maʾmūn (813-833), whose promotion of translating activities has just been noted, also procured original works by contemporary scholars. Thus he attached to himself the philologist al-Farrāʾ (d. ca. 820) and asked him to write a work on language. The scholar was accommodated in an apartment of the palace with good servants, and the caliph provided him with scribes. It took some years to complete the work, and al-Maʾmūn then commanded that it should be transcribed in the libraries. Next, al-Farrāʾ dictated pub-

[18] Ibn Khallikān, *Wafayāt al-aʿyān* (Cairo, 1310/1893), II, 210.

[19] *Irshād* V, 421f.

licly a book of Qur'ānic interpretation. There were so many listeners that their number could not be determined, and among them were eighty *qāḍīs*. Al-Farrā' had with him his two copyists, Salāma ibn ʿĀṣim and Abū Naṣr ibn al-Jahm. It is said that when the dictation was completed, the copyists withheld the book from the public so as to make a profit on it; they would only release it on being paid one dirham for every five pages. People went to al-Farrā' to complain, and he attempted persuasion on the *warrāqs*, but in vain. They said bluntly that they had only followed his discourse to make money on it; this was their daily bread. Al-Farrā''s efforts to bring the parties together came to nothing. But then he announced that he would hold a new discourse on the same subject in a considerably expanded form. Just the opening words of the first *sūra, al-ḥamdu*, "The Encomium," filled a hundred pages. At that point the copyists yielded and agreed to supply what was being demanded—ten pages for one dirham.[20]

Evidently the *warrāqs* were available to make copies for people who did not themselves take down dictation, either because they were not present or because they listened to the discourse but could afford to spare themselves the trouble of transcribing it. By having copyists present, the author assured his book of wide dissemination. But the story recounted above shows that the copyists were an independent class and that there were no economic commitments between them and the author. The pressure put upon them by al-Farrā' depended upon the threat that his more detailed discourse would make the original one valueless.

Numerous examples show that it was not uncommon in the time of the early ʿAbbāsids for an author to have his special *warrāq*. Of course this can sometimes mean merely a private secretary, to whom the author dictated his work instead of writing it himself, in the same way as al-Farrā' dictated the work commissioned by al-Ma'mūn. Thus the phi-

[20] Ibid. VII, 276f.; al-Baghdādī, *Ta'rīkh Baghdād* (Cairo 1349/1931), XIV, 150.

lologist Ibn Durayd (d. 934) is said to have dictated one of his great works to his *ghulām*,[21] which may denote either a pupil who served him or a slave. Mention is made elsewhere of his *warrāq*, who was called al-Duraydī, obviously after himself, and to whom his books passed on his death.[22] Whether the latter is the same as the former is not stated. It is impossible to say precisely what the relationship was in individual cases, but the general pattern was apparently that the *warrāq* was an independent businessman. It may be taken for granted that the *warrāq* and others used slaves as scribes, and a slave who could write fetched a high price. An example of fraudulent trading cited in legal tracts is that of splashing a slave's clothes with ink to give the impression that he could write.

Ibn al-Nadīm records the names of a couple of al-Mubarrad's *warrāqs*.[23] The much-read man of letters al-Jāḥiẓ (b. 767), who wrote one dissertation on the virtues of the *warrāq* and another on his shortcomings, also had his copyist, Zakarīyā' ibn Yaḥyā, who was dubbed "Abū Yaḥyā, al-Jāḥiẓ's *warrāq*."[24] Isḥāq ibn Ibrāhīm al-Mauṣilī (b. 767), who was particularly skilled in discoursing on songs and on whose writings al-Iṣfahānī's "Book of Songs" was based, had a *warrāq* of whom Isḥāq's son declares that in collusion with a colleague he falsified a written work, a "Book of Songs" that appeared under Isḥāq's name after his death although he had written only the first part. Al-Iṣfahānī states the name of the *warrāq* in question and the place where his booth was situated.[25] What was probably involved was a publication not put into its final form by Isḥāq to which the two *warrāqs* therefore gave the finishing touches when transcribing it.

This shows that the certification of copies made by these scribes as authorized was not carried out consistently. It may not have been feasible when the business in hand was on a

[21] *Fihrist*, p. 61, line 25.

[22] *Irshād* V, 81.

[23] *Fihrist*, p. 60.

[24] *Irshād* VI, 75, 78.

[25] *Fihrist*, p. 140; *Kitāb al-aghānī* I, 5f.

large scale. But of course one of the copyist's duties was to check that what he wrote down agreed with the original. The comparing of the manuscripts, *muqābala*, "the collation," was a necessary stage in the book's production. Abū Ḥayyān al-Tauḥīdī, who became sick and tired of books and transcribing in his old age, actually burned his books, said: "Why should my eye strain itself any more with ink and paper and parchment and reading and collation and correction and draft and fair copy?"[26] Sometimes special correctors (*muḥarrir*) are mentioned. Collation would probably be effected as a rule by reading aloud, as was also the case, of course, with the author's check for authorization. It was always of value to a copyist if he could read his transcript to a scholar of high repute. Al-Bāḥḥāthī, who lived in the eleventh century, was a copyist who is said to have made a copy of a book of traditions of the Prophet. He read it over to two men as a "hearing-reading" (*qirāʾat samāʿ*) and later to a third as a "proof and correction reading" (*qirāʾat taṣḥīḥ wa itqān.*)[27] The latter check was concerned with orthography and matters of that sort. Just as an author authorized a book with his *ijāza*, so a recognized scholar could certify that he had verified a manuscript by appending his *samāʿ*, "hearing," that is, an attestation that he had checked it by hearing it read over.[28] An older manuscript might sometimes be subjected to a proofreading by being read over to a scholar of standing. A manuscript in Leyden, written 252/868, bears an inscription saying "that its proofreading and correction for the high Imām Ibrāhīm ibn Muḥammad was completed . . . on Monday, 24 Jumādā II, in the year 378 [October 8, 988]."[29] There are also manuscripts that a later reader has collated with another manuscript and in the margins of which he has made corrections.

[26] *Irshād* V, 390.

[27] Ibid. VI, 410.

[28] Ibid. VI, 359.

[29] M. J. de Goeje, "Beschreibung einer alten Handschrift von Abû ʿObaid's Ġarîb al-ḥadîṯ," in *Zeitschrift der deutschen morgenländischen Gesellschaft* 18 (1864), 786.

As a rule, at least, the manuscripts handed down to us contain at the end of the book the copyist's name and the date of completion of the work, often accompanied by a sigh of relief that it has reached its conclusion, followed by prayers and benedictions. We may cite as an example the copyist's remarks on a manuscript by al-Sulamī, "The Classes of Ṣūfis," now to be found in the Berlin National Library. He writes,

> The end of the book "The Classes of Ṣūfis," may God have mercy on them! God be praised first and above all! The completion of its transcript was accomplished on Sunday evening, the 16th of the month of Dhu'l-Qaʿda in the year 785 [the evening before Sunday, January 11, 1385]. And the slave, who flies to God the Exalted, who hopes for the mercy of his Lord and pardon for his sins, and who hopes for the intercession of God's Prophet Muḥammad—blessing and peace be unto him!—wrote it with his corruptible hand, and he is Muḥammad ibn Muḥammad ibn Muḥammad ibn Aḥmad ibn ʿAffān ibn ʿAbd al-ʿAzīz ibn Manī, *sharīf* of the blood of Ḥasan, who dwells at Furn al-Ifrīt . . . may God forgive him and his parents and all Muslims, and them that read the book, and them that look in it, and them that crave pardon and forgiveness for him who copied it and for his parents and for all Muslims, and God is sufficient unto us and our best Guardian. God bless our Lord Muḥammad, Seal of the Prophets, and his family and campanions and grant unto them manifold peace and favor and mercy.

As a rule, a manuscript will also bear the names of those who have owned it, sometimes accompanied by a verse or a sentence.

The problem of the accuracy of the transcript was of course a persistent one despite all the checks, and authors were wont to complain from time to time about the unreliability of copyists. At the end of his great world history, al-Masʿūdī begs pardon for the errors that may be introduced by the copyist. The author's best guarantee, of course, was to transcribe his work himself, and for the scholar too it was probably best to transcribe personally those works of particular importance to him. Yāqūt tells us that he himself transcribed al-Iṣfahānī's "Book of Songs" in ten volumes, since he used it for a work on the poets. But naturally there were limits to how much the individual could do in this direction.

Copyists were the connecting link between men of letters and the general public. They themselves belonged more or less to the literary class, but their livelihood lay in multiplying the works of authors. They were not only copyists but booksellers as well. A *warrāq* had his stall or booth (*ḥānūt, dukkān*) where copying went on and business in books was conducted. An illustration of the activities of these places is furnished by what we are told of al-Shaʿūbī, who lived in Baghdad at the beginning of the ninth century under the caliphs Hārūn al-Rashīd and al-Ma'mūn. He was the author of various books, and for a time was a copyist in the recently established institute of science and letters (*Bayt al-ḥikma*). He had a booth in which he sold books and where he had people who transcribed for him. He was recommended to a rich man, who sent for him, and he then stayed in the rich man's house for a time engaged in transcribing. One day, however, there was a breach between them, al-Shaʿūbī having failed to meet the standards of politeness set by his employer. Al-Shaʿūbī declared that he was not to be taught good manners by others: rather the reverse, for he had not come to beg for anything but to execute a task for which he had been commissioned and for which he received his wages. But now he swore that he would never again write a single letter in the house of another.[30]

We see that the *warrāq* had his sense of importance both as a representative of the world of learning and as an independent entrepreneur, but although he obviously conducted a considerable business in his own booth, it was still normal for such a man to go out to work for others for payment.

The books written in the course of the *warrāq*'s business

[30] *Irshād* V, 66f.

were produced either to order or with a view toward sale on the open market. To this end he also obtained books by purchase. We have seen that the original draft of the "Book of Songs" came onto the market on one occasion. A *warrāq* might hold quite a considerable stock of books. Al-Jāḥiẓ, who was a versatile author and a great bookworm, hit upon the idea of hiring booths from the *warrāqs* and spending the nights in them reading; it was cheaper than buying the books.[31] Anyone wanting a particular work approached a *warrāq* and got him to procure it. Thus one *warrāq*, al-Ḥusayn ibn Ḥubaysh, relates that al-Ṭabarī asked him to obtain whatever writings were to be had on analogy (*qiyās*), an important and disputed point of legal doctrine, and the bookseller gathered more than thirty works for him.[32]

An independent *warrāq* performed a function that in our day in the West is shared between the printer and the bookseller, and also, perhaps we may add, the publishing house. An author's *warrāq*, having the first copies of the work, was the obvious person to be approached by anyone wanting to obtain it. A *warrāq* of the mid-tenth century relates that one day he was passing the poet al-Nāshi'ī, who said to him, "I have composed a *qaṣīda* (a lengthy poem of fixed form) that is in demand, and I should like you to write it by your hand, so that I may have it published."[33] Books were produced and brought out on the book market through the *warrāq*.

We have seen one example of a *warrāq*'s ascribing to an author a work he himself and not the author had put into its final form. We also hear of instances in which a *warrāq* steals a manuscript from a known author, naturally with publication in mind. This happened to al-Ṭabarī on one occasion.[34] This did not signify much economic loss for the author, since in all probability he had no share in the income from sales. But it is not difficult to believe that a *warrāq* may sometimes have

[31] Ibid. VI, 56; *Fihrist*, p. 116, lines 26ff.

[32] *Irshād* VI, 453.

[33] Ibid. V, 241.

[34] Ibid. VI, 450 in middle.

bought a work from an author in order to transcribe it and sell the copies. However, he did not thus acquire any copyright in such a work, apart from the copies he himself bought or produced.

The selling of books was conducted like all trade: buyer and seller bargained over the article in question, then as now. In an age when every book was produced individually, fixed prices were unknown, and, indeed, price-haggling is still not uncommon in the Orient. A person of princely rank was looking for a copy of the "Book of Songs" and procured a fine one for 10,000 dirhams at a rate of eighteen dirham per dīnār, which is equivalent to a little over 7,000 gold francs. On receiving the magnificent work, he upbraided his agent who had purchased it for having treated the poor *warrāq* badly, for the book was worth over 10,000 dīnārs.[35] A person of princely rank might view a transaction thus; ordinary folk behaved otherwise. Sometimes book sales were conducted by auction (*nidā'*, "call"). People sat in a circle and the book was called out, bid following upon bid. Whereas in an ordinary selling transaction the purchaser tried to beat the vendor's price down little by little, at an auction the price moved gradually upward. Generally speaking, auctions were not unusual and did something to satisfy the gambling instinct condemned by the Qur'ān.[36]

The booksellers' booths came by degrees to take up a good deal of room in the towns and, as was customary in the Near East, they tended to cluster in a particular quarter, a tradition that has still not completely died out. Al-Maqrīzī mentions the "bookmen's quarter" in his description of Cairo in the

[35] Ibid. V, 164.

[36] Ibid. V, 164 line 2 from bottom; 417 line 5. According to a tradition going back to Anas ibn Mālik, the Prophet himself is supposed to have conducted sales at auction, thereby legalizing this method of selling; see al-Tirmidhī, *Kitāb al-buyū'*, *bāb* 10, *apud* his *Ṣaḥīḥ* (Cairo, 1292/1875); and Ibn Māja, *Kitāb al-tijārāt, bāb* 25, *apud* his *Sunan* (Delhi, 1282/1865 and 1289/1872). An amusing account of the auctioning of a slave, whose price increased as he appeared in successively finer clothes, is to be found in *Irshād* VII, 213f. and *Kitāb al-Aghānī* I, 330.

fifteenth century, and we often hear of the "quarter of books" or the "*warrāqs'* quarter" in Baghdad. It was situated a little outside the oldest part of the capital, the round city founded by al-Manṣūr, toward the southeast, by one of the canals. The corresponding quarter of Damascus, wrote Ibn Baṭṭūṭa in 1327, lay in the vicinity of the magnificent Umayyad mosque, with booths selling paper, pens, ink, and other articles associated with books.[37] Literary folk frequented these quarters, sitting in the booths and whiling away the hours with literary gossip and discussion of the issues of the day. This milieu forms the setting for a good many of the anecdotes that abound in scholarly biographies, affording us a glimpse of daily life.

Like other professions, the "bookmen" were organized in a guild headed by a shaykh, who occupied a position of standing. Among the important events of September 1516 recorded by the historian Ibn Iyās is the death of Shams al-Dīn, the shaykh of the Aleppo booksellers' quarter, who was said to belong to the sultan's social circle.[38]

Ibn Khaldūn (d. 1406) states in his celebrated "Prolegomena," an introduction to his historical work surveying the culture of his day, that the increases in literary pursuits brought "the emergence of the occupation of *warrāq*, which is concerned with transcribing, proofreading, binding, and everything else that has to do with books and office work."[39] This demonstrates the immense importance of the *warrāq* to the world of books. Everything connected with their production was in his hands, and as Ibn Khaldūn says, his activities were

[37] In Baghdad, the "bazaar of the warrāqs" (*sūq al-warrāqīn*) is mentioned, *Irshād* V, 164 line 4 from bottom, and p. 240 in middle; the "books' bazaar," *sūq al-kutub*, VII, 291, situated in the vicinity of the goldsmiths' quarter, V, 24. There were about a hundred stalls; see G. Le Strange, *Baghdad during the Abbasid Caliphate*, 2nd ed. (London, 1924), p. 92. For the "bookmen's bazaar" (*sūq al-kutubīyīn*), in Cairo, see al-Maqrīzī, *Al-mawāʿiẓ wa'l-iʿtibār fī dhikr al-khiṭaṭ wa'l-āthār* III (Cairo, 1325/1907), 165f. In Damascus the "warrāq's bazaar" and "bookmen's bazaar" are mentioned by Ibn Baṭṭūṭa, *Riḥla* (Cairo, 1323/1905), pp. 65f.

[38] Ibn Iyās V (see note 5 above), 65.

[39] Ibn Khaldūn, *Muqaddima* (Cairo, 1322/1904), p. 334.

particularly associated with the larger towns and their advanced culture.

In our own day, when most of the books sold are printed, "bookmen" do not of course exist in the same way as of old, and the function of the copyist has been taken over by the printer; but the book trade continues on essentially the same lines as before, and the bookseller is the successor of the *warrāq* of earlier times. If he wants a text to be duplicated he gives it to a printer, just as he formerly handed it to a scribe. Other booksellers and the ordinary purchaser can then obtain the book from him at a price agreed upon by the parties in each instance after the appropriate bargaining. Literary folk foregather in the booksellers' booths for mutual entertainment, as before.

Even now, however, the work of the copyist has not died out entirely. Scholars both from Europe and from the Orient often have a need for a copy of a manuscript in an Oriental library, and this has provided work for the copyist (*al-nassākh*) down to the most recent times. Fifty years or so ago in the large libraries of Cairo and Damascus, for example, there were copyists offering their services; in Cairo a special desk was reserved for them, where they sat with their pencil-cases and inkstands and transcribed manuscripts with reed pens, which they emphatically preferred to steel pens. Many of them wrote a fair and clear manuscript, but individuals could be found among them who felt it their duty to correct in their transcripts real or imagined errors in the manuscript they were copying, so that one could not always be certain of receiving an accurate representation of it. The old complaints over the copyist's poor remuneration were still to be heard, and were certainly not unjustified, even though books acquired in this way were expensive. Photography has now cut the ground from under this last remnant of an occupation that engaged the energies of a whole class of people for centuries and that has been of the greatest cultural significance. Only in out-of-the-way regions may one still expect to encounter the old-fashioned copyist.

FIVE

Writing Materials

IBN AL-NADĪM gives in his work a survey of the materials used by various peoples for writing on. Apart from stone and metal, which were used for inscriptions "for eternity," he mentions wood, bark, the leaves of trees (especially palm), silk, skin, parchment, papyrus, and finally paper.[1] In the days when the Qur'ān was coming into existence, Arabs used to avail themselves of the bones of camels, sheep, and asses, as well as thin white stones and potsherds, as we have already seen.

Most of these materials are of little interest for our present purpose. Wood was used for tablets, and according to al-Suyūṭī was used for the Qur'ān, and it was also employed for amulets, but is otherwise best known for its use in schools. Silk was used by the Byzantines and Indians, and was also employed for writing purposes in the early Islamic era. It was immersed in gum and had to be smoothed with a mussel shell or a special stone (*muhra* in Persian, from which the Arabic term *muhraq* is derived) before it could be used for writing on, and it was never widely employed. For the rest, linen (*kattān*) was also used in Egypt; so we find in Vienna a linen shawl with the whole of the Qur'ān written on it, and single documents on linen are also found.[2] These three materials—wood, silk, and linen—were also employed as writing materials in China.

Potsherds, which were sometimes pressed into service in the various societies of antiquity, were used very little. How-

[1] *Fihrist*, p. 21.

[2] On wood and linen, see A. Grohmann, *Allgemeine Einführung in die arabischen Papyri nebst Grundzügen der arabischen Diplomatik* (Vienna, 1924), pp. 59-62.

ever, we do hear of the poet Abu 'l-ʿAtāhiya (d. ca. 820), who was a dealer in jars, that young people came to him to hear him recite his poems and write them down on potsherds that they picked up in the workshop.[3] Inscribed bones are rare, but there is a solitary example in the Dār al-Kutub in Cairo.

The Qur'ān mentions only parchment (*riqq*, Sūra 52,3) and papyrus (*qirṭās*, Sūra 6, 7.91) as writing materials, always in connection with the Revealed Book, the Celestial Pages (*ṣuḥuf*). We may hazard the guess that the oldest complete Qur'ān was written on one of these two materials, probably parchment.

People generally used skin if they did not use parchment. Numerous writings on skin or leather have survived from ancient Egypt.[4] In Arabia, where the leather industry was long-established and generated a considerable export trade,[5] leather was employed as a writing material. This is attested by a number of the early poets, and we have already noted above that al-Ma'mūn of Baghdad is traditionally reputed to have owned a document, written on leather, that originated from the Prophet's grandfather. The Persians, as Ibn al-Nadīm relates, were accustomed to write on the skins of buffalo, oxen, and sheep. Several such pieces of writing on skin, in the Persian language (Pahlavi), are to be found in Archduke Rainer's collection in Vienna.[6]

It is said that the reports from the tax authorities to the

[3] *Kitāb al-aghānī* IV, 9.

[4] A. Erman, *Aegypten und aegyptisches Leben im Altertum* (Tübingen, 1885), p. 598; Grohmann, *Einführung*, p. 51.

[5] The leather industry was particularly prominent in south Arabia; see al-Maqdisī, *Aḥsan al-taqāsīm fī maʿrifat al-aqālīm*, edited by M. J. de Goeje (Leiden, 1873), pp. 87 lines 1-4; 97 line 14. It was also practiced in Ṭā'if in the vicinity of Mecca; see H. Lammens, *L'Arabie occidentale avant l'hégire* (Beirut, 1928), pp. 128ff.; *idem*, "La cité arabe de Tāif à la veille de l'hégire," in *Mélanges de l'Université Saint-Joseph* 8/4 (1922), 115.

[6] Grohmann, *Einführung*, pp. 51-53. The following story of King Khusrau Parviz according to al-Balādhurī, *Futūḥ al-buldān*, edited by M. J. de Goeje (Leiden, 1866), p. 464.

Persian king Khusrau Parviz were made on a roll of white skin, but the smell of the latter displeased the king, so it was colored with yellow saffron and sprinkled with rosewater. The use of yellow skin as a writing material was introduced, following the Persian example, into the public administration in Baghdad. Ibn al-Nadīm relates that the skins employed for writing on were generally cured with lime, but that made them too dry. Another method of curing was introduced using dates, which made the skins moist; this was termed the "Kufic" method after the town of Kūfa.

Special treatment of skin produces a thinner and stronger parchment, which was probably used by the Persians and certainly came into service in the West in the second century B.C. That it was known in Arabia before the time of Muḥammad is apparent from numerous references to it by the early poets, some of which are cited above. The Arabic term *raqq* or *riqq* refers to the thinness of the parchment, obviously in contrast to skin, which was thicker. Sometimes used parchments were wiped clean and written on again; such reused parchments (*ṭirs*) are mentioned now and then in literature.

Parchment was much employed for Qur'āns, as may be seen from the magnificent Qur'āns surviving from the seventh[a] to tenth centuries, and for other books as well. Arabic parchment manuscripts are somewhat rare, however. In the field of administration, the founder of the Umayyad caliphate in Damascus, Muʿāwiya (661-680), made use of parchment in his chancellery. The ʿAbbāsids (750-1258), whose capital was Baghdad, also used it, and references are still made to it in the twelfth century.[7] Ibn al-Nadīm tells us that for many years the Baghdad authorities had to make do with used parchments because the offices had been plundered. Parchment was employed in Spain, too; the geographer al-Maqdisī tells (in A.D. 985) of its being used there for Qur'āns and for

[a] It seems that no indisputably seventh-century Qur'āns have survived. For "seventh," therefore, read "eighth."

[7] Grohmann, *Einführung*, p. 57.

account books.[8] The most recent parchment in any European collection appears to be a document of 1059 or 1060 preserved at Heidelberg.[9]

The reason why parchment was used relatively little for Islamic books is that it was an expensive material, and so had to yield preference to a cheaper one. In the earlier era this meant papyrus. It is evident that papyrus sheets were known in Arabia in the time of the Prophet because of the statement in the Qur'ān that the Mosaic revelations were written on this material, and because Allah says to the Prophet that even if he sent down a book of papyrus for his adversaries to hold and feel, they would still reject the revelation (Sūra 6, 7.91). Admittedly there is an element of uncertainty in this, inasmuch as the word employed (*qirṭās*, from the Greek χάρτης), which generally denotes papyrus, is also applied now and then to parchment.

At all events, it was not until after the conquest of Egypt by Islam that papyrus became an article in everyday use by those writing Arabic.[10] For papyrus was, as it had always been, virtually an Egyptian monopoly, since it was along the banks of the Nile that the serviceable papyrus plant throve. It was used for plaited cordage and mats, even for clothing; its roots were eaten; and first and foremost, by the time of the Middle Kingdom (the beginning of the second millennium B.C.), the Egyptians had already discovered how to turn it to use as a writing material. Long strips were cut from the three-sided stems, dried, and placed in two layers at right angles to one another, then wetted and hammered together, pressed, and smoothed into sheets that were extended by being pasted end-to-end and then rolled up into thick rolls. The Muslim conquest of Egypt in 640 and subsequent years did not change any of this, but soon Arabic began to appear on the papyrus sheets side by side with Greek and Coptic. The sheets still extant include an Arabic one from as early as 642, and through

[8] Al-Maqdisī, p. 239 line 5.

[9] Grohmann, *Einführung*, p. 57.

[10] On Arabic papyri, see Grohmann's *Einführung*.

these discoveries we can trace the inroads made by the Arabic language until it became absolutely preeminent. Of the many thousands of Arabic papyri that have come to light and have been placed in museums and libraries, only a modest number have yet been published. The bulk of these consist of official correspondence, legal documents, ledgers, tax receipts, and so forth. There are some literary fragments to be found, as well, but there are fewer of these.

The Arabs call the papyrus plant *bardī*; the terms *fāfīr* and *babīr*, which are Arabizations of the Graeco-Egyptian *papyros*, are encountered, as well. The sheets were produced in a number of workshops and exported in large quantities. They were used at the principal seat of the caliphs under both the Umayyads in Damascus (658-750) and the ʿAbbāsids in Baghdad (from 750). Some caliphs, such as Muʿāwiya, preferred parchment and others papyrus; as a rule both were employed. Under the first ʿAbbāsid caliph, al-Saffāḥ, his *wazīr*, Khālid ibn Barmak, who founded the mighty Barmakid dynasty of officials, introduced the codex to replace the scroll in the taxation and army offices. There were caliphs who preferred papyrus to parchment for their correspondence because it was impossible to make erasures on papyrus and change the caliph's missives undetected. Hilāl al-Ṣābī records in his "Book of the *Wazīrs*" an example of this kind of falsification by an official.[11]

The interest of the ʿAbbāsids in papyrus manifested itself in an attempt to create a papyrus industry in Iraq. The person responsible for this was Caliph al-Muʿtaṣim, who founded a new royal residence at Sāmarrā, which then became the seat of government for a number of years (836-878). In this town, which like Baghdad was situated on the Tigris, though a little further north, al-Muʿtaṣim established a papyrus factory with Egyptian workers. The implicit precondition for this was that the papyrus plant grew in Iraq, whither it may have been introduced from Egypt. However, the experiment does not

[11] *The Historical Remains of Hilâl al-Sâbî, Kitâb al-wuzarâ*, edited by H. F. Amedroz (Beirut, 1904), p. 66.

appear to have attained any substantial success, for we hear no other reports of Iraqi papyrus. The only place, apart from Egypt, where we hear of the papyrus plant being grown is Sicily, at Syracuse and Palermo, where Ibn Ḥauqal found it in large quantities in 972-973.[12] The local potentate made use of it as a writing material, but otherwise it seems to have been used mostly for cordage and similar purposes, because even here papyrus rolls were imported from Egypt.

The attempt to introduce the manufacture of papyrus rolls in Iraq reflected a desire to make the chief province independent of imports. We hear on a number of occasions of the caliph's anxiety lest the civil service should find itself one day without writing materials, and officials were frequently exhorted to exercise economy. In point of fact, there was a major problem here, for offices were by no means the largest consumers of writing materials. The rapid growth of Arabic literature, which was gaining momentum from about 800 all over the far-flung world of Islam, generated a demand for writing materials in unprecedented quantities. But precisely as the problem was emerging into prominence it was, in fact, being solved by the introduction of paper manufacturing. It is true that paper was invented in China, not in Islam. But the Muslim peoples made use of new materials that facilitated manufacturing on a large scale, and they also devised new methods. In so doing they accomplished a feat of crucial significance not only to the history of the Islamic book but also to the whole world of books.

After large quantities of papyrus and paper documents had been brought out of Egypt and placed in European libraries and museums in the late seventies and eighties of the last century, the study of paper was set in motion both through microscopic analyses of plant physiology and by research into the information contained in Arabic literature; attention was thus drawn to an anonymous tract bearing the title "Writers' Aids and Intelligent People's Tools," which attained its final

[12] Edited by M. J. de Goeje, p. 86.

form around 1200 and contains a description of paper manufacturing. The work comprises three manuscripts, from which it is evident that there must have been an earlier version of the text. These researches have clarified the essential features of the history of paper and its method of manufacture in the Arabic-speaking world.[13]

The difference between papyrus and paper consists in the fact that whereas papyrus sheets are simply cut from the plant, sheets of paper are fabricated artificially from a liquid mass composed of the fibers of certain plants that have been subjected to special processing.

Paper was first made in China, its year of origin being 105 B.C., according to tradition. The raw materials for its production were the best fibers of the paper mulberry tree and young shoots of bamboo, to which were added rags, fishing line, and hemp fiber.[14] A fair amount of this Chinese paper was sold in the regions bordering on the west, notably in Samarqand. At the beginning of the eighth century, the Arabs conquered Transoxania and other eastern provinces, thus

[13] The credit for clarifying the history of Arab paper belongs to J. von Karabacek of Vienna, assisted by the plant physiologist J. Wiesner. An account of their researches, including publication of the anonymous tract cited, is given in *Mitteilungen aus der Sammlung der Papyrus Erzherzog Rainer* (hereafter cited as *MSPER*) 2-3 (1887), 87-178 (von Karabacek) and 179-260 (Wiesner); 4 (1888), 75-122 (von Karabacek); also in *Papyrus Erzherzog Rainer. Führer durch die Ausstellung* (Vienna, 1894), in which the introduction and the passage on Arab papyri are written by von Karabacek.

[14] The Chinese had earlier used wooden tablets, bamboo sheets, silk, and linen, and later silk remnants decomposed in water and hammered together. By this step the transition to paper manufacturing seems to have been taken. This is demonstrated by Henri Alibaux in an article in the *Gutenberg-Jahrbuch* of 1939 entitled "L'invention du papier," which was drawn to my attention by the late Svend Dahl, National Librarian of Denmark, and in which this much-debated issue is subjected to a critical scrutiny. The author reaches the conclusion that, in fact, the invention of paper, ascribed by tradition to Tsaï Lun in 105 A.D., took place gradually, and that Tsaï Lun put the finishing touches to the discovery in some manner or other in the year stated. The oldest known papers are found in Turkestan and date back to the second century A.D. A reproduction of a couple of examples is to be found in the article cited.

reaching the frontiers of China. During a struggle between two Turkish princes (of Farghāna and Shāsh, the present Tashkent), one of the parties obtained Chinese help, and as a result both came under Chinese domination. Thereupon the conquering Arabs intervened, and in July 751, the latter inflicted a crushing defeat on the two Turkish princes at a small town in the vicinity of Samarqand, where the Arabian deputy governor had his residence. Among the many prisoners of war carried off to Samarqand in the course of this affair there were not only Turks but Chinese, as well. Some of them were paper-makers, and they introduced the manufacturing of paper by the Chinese method into the domains of Islam.

The mulberry tree, however, whose bark was supposed to be used, did not grow in these regions, and so recourse was had to the fine fibers found in linen rags. "As to the Khurāsān paper, that is made of linen," says Ibn al-Nadīm.[15] Thus was rag paper invented. The Arabs called the paper *kāghid(h)*, a term they took over from the Persian-speaking people of Samarqand, who in turn had got it from the Chinese *kog-dz'*, "paper from the bark of the paper mulberry tree."[16] Under the name of "Samarqand paper" or "Khurāsān paper" (after the Far Eastern province of that name), the new writing material gradually spread over the whole Islamic world. During the time of Hārūn al-Rashīd, paper was introduced as an article of use in Iraq by Jaʿfar ibn Yaḥyā, grandson of the Khālid ibn Barmak mentioned above, who introduced the parchment codex. This is stated by al-Maqrīzī (d. 1442), and Ibn Khaldūn says that it took place at the prompting of Jaʿfar's brother al-Faḍl, who was governor of Khurāsān in 794-795.[17] This sounds very plausible, although it is doubtful whether he is right in saying that paper began to be produced in Iraq at the same time.

The oldest pieces of paper to have come down to us are contained among the finds made in Egypt, and can be dated

[15] *Fihrist*, p. 21 lines 15f.

[16] *Führer durch die Ausstellung*, p. xx, after Hirth.

[17] Al-Maqrīzī, *Khiṭaṭ* I, 147; Ibn Khaldūn, *Muqaddima*, p. 334.

around 800. Diverse references in literary works, however, show that papyrus still had the upper hand in the first half of the ninth century, and a remark by al-Jāḥiẓ, who died after the middle of the century, is based on a presumption that the papyrus rolls of Egypt performed the same function for the West as did Samarqand paper for the East.[18] The above-described efforts of al-Muʿtaṣim to develop a papyrus industry in Sāmarrā in 836 may be regarded as an attempt to strengthen the old product against the new. Success was impossible, for the new product was cheaper and in many respects better than the old. Around 900 parchment, papyrus, and paper were all in use. That this was also the case in the westernmost territories of Islam can be seen from the book. "The Costly Pearl," written about 900 by the Spaniard Ibn ʿAbd Rabbih, in which the author describes which kinds of reeds are best suited for skin, paper, and papyrus, respectively.[19] About 903, al-Hamadhānī says that Egypt is alone in producing papyrus, and al-Kindī says something of the sort a little later.[20] From this time onward, papyrus entered upon a drastic decline. The most recent dating established for a papyrus in a European collection is the year 334 after the Hijra, which began on August 13, 945 A.D. After this date papyrus manufacturing died out, and paper documents became more numerous; there

[18] *MSPER* 2-3 (1887), 99, after al-Thaʿālibī, *Laṭā'if al-maʿārif*, edited by P. de Jong (Leiden, 1867), p. 97. In his work on Egypt, *Ḥusn al-muḥāḍara fī akhbār Miṣr wa'l-Qāhira* II (Cairo, 1321/1903), 194, al-Suyūṭī (d. 1505) cites a statement by al-Kindī (d. 961): "In Egypt there is papyrus, and there is none else in the world but in Egypt." Al-Suyūṭī continues, "Another writer says: among the specialties of Egypt are papyri, that is, sheets (*ṭawāmīr*, pl. of *ṭūmār*, from the Greek τομάριον, a sheet ⅙ the length of a roll), and these are the best for writing on; they are made from a plant growing in the soil of Egypt. They are made in lengths of 30 ells and more, to a hand's width. It is said that Joseph—may God give him peace!—was the first to have used papyri and written on them."

[19] Ibn ʿAbd Rabbih, *Al-ʿiqd al-farīd* II (Cairo, 1322/1904), 183.

[20] Ibn al-Faqīh al-Hamadhānī, *Kitāb al-buldān*, edited by M. J. de Goeje (Leiden, 1885), p. 66. On al-Kindī see note 18 above. Von Karabacek in *MSPER* 2-3 (1887), 98 and 103; and Grohmann, *Einführung*, p. 44, oddly enough, state the year of al-Kindī's death as 246/860 instead of 350/961.

is still a reference to papyrus in Egypt by al-Masʿūdī in 956,[21] but al-Maqdisī, who wrote his account of the Islamic lands around 985, says nothing of papyrus as being among the products of Egypt, and a traveler of the year 1216 declares explicitly that papyrus manufacturing was quite forgotten.[22]

It is a remarkable fact that al-Iṣṭakhrī, writing in the middle of the tenth century, says that paper (like sal-ammoniac) is not produced in any of the Islamic lands save Transoxania.[23] This statement originates, admittedly, from Ibn al-Balkhī, who was writing at the beginning of the century and on whose work al-Iṣṭakhrī relied for his information; nevertheless, if it is correct, then the manufacturing of paper remained confined to its first Islamic home for more than a century and a half, although it had become a worldwide article and although the raw materials for it were easily obtainable everywhere. No answer to this riddle is to be found in the sources so far available, since the above-cited report by Ibn Khaldūn concerning the introduction of paper manufacture into Iraq is from a much later period and does not quote any authority.

We do, however, have reliable evidence from the latter half of the tenth century of the manufacture of paper in the West. Al-Maqdisī, writing about 985, mentions paper as an export commodity in Damascus and Tiberias,[24] and according to his account there seems to have been papermaking even in distant Ṣanʿāʾ in southern Arabia. If, indeed, there were paper industries in these places, then it is to be presumed that they also existed in principal provinces such as Iraq and Egypt. The latter especially, with its large linen weaving mills, was well suited for paper manufacturing, and about the year 1000,

[21] *Kitāb al-tanbīh wa'l-ishrāf*, edited by M. J. de Goeje (Leiden, 1894), p. 22 line 2.

[22] The traveler was the botanist Abuʾl-ʿAbbās al-Nabātī, mentioned by his contemporary, Ibn al-Bayṭār (d. 1248) in his work on curative and nutritive substances, especially plants; see von Karabacek in *MSPER* 2-3 (1887), 101.

[23] Edited by M. J. de Goeje, p. 288.

[24] *Ahsan al-taqāsīm* III 180 line 16; 181 line 1. On Ṣanʿāʾ, see ibid., p. 100; cf. von Karabacek in *MSPER* 2-3 (1887), 138 and 140.

in fact, there is a report of its paper being extra fine and smooth,[25] an assertion confirmed by the finds that have been made. A Baghdad doctor named ʿAbd al-Laṭīf, who visited Egypt about 1200, relates that Bedouin and fellaheen stole linen from the mummies and sold it to the papermakers.

In the eleventh and twelfth centuries we have evidence of the production of paper in numerous places, including not only Samarqand and Baghdad but also Egypt, where al-Maqrīzī mentions a book- and papermaking *khān* with a mill;[26] Syria, where Ḥamā and Tripoli are mentioned as well as Damascus and Palestinian Tiberias; North Africa, where around the year 1200 the town of Fās (Fez) had 472 millstones, some of them certainly in the service of paper manufacturing;[27] Spain, where in the twelfth century, according to al-Idrīsī, Shāṭiba (Xátiva), the present San Felipe in Valencia, produced finer paper than any other center and exported it to both East and West; Persia, where after the Mongol conquest in 1221 a new paper industry emerged under revived Chinese influence in Tabrīz and other towns. The industry was implanting itself in Europe at that time, and in the thirteenth century paper from the Franks was being used in Egypt—"Franks" serving as a label for Europeans generally at the time of the Crusades.

Complete paper manuscripts have survived from about 900; for example, one in Damascus from the year 266 after the

[25] Al-Thaʿālibī (see note 18 above) calls Egyptian paper "the best, finest and smoothest"; see J. von Hammer-Purgstall, "Auszüge aus Saalebi's Buch der Stützen des sich Beziehenden und dessen worauf es sich bezieht," in *Zeitschrift der deutschen morgenländischen Gesellschaft* 7 (1854), 526. The statement of ʿAbd al-Laṭīf al-Baghdādī is in *Relation de l'Égypte par Abd-Allatif, médecin arabe de Bagdad*, edited and translated by S. de Sacy (Paris, 1810), p. 198.

[26] *Khān al-wirāqah*: al-Maqrīzī, *Khiṭaṭ* III, 37. A *khān* is a large business establishment with booths, workshops, warehouses, offices, stables and living quarters.

[27] Ibn Abī Zarʿ, *Annales regum Mauritaniae*, edited by C. J. Tornberg (Uppsala, 1843), p. 46 lines 1f., cf. von Karabacek in *MSPER* 2-3 (1887), 125f. On Spain and Persia see ibid., pp. 126f.

Hijra, a year that began on August 23, 879,[28] and one in the Azhar mosque in Cairo from 923. There is an even older manuscript in Leiden, namely, Abū ʿUbayd's book on unusual terms in the traditions of the Prophet; it was written in the year 252 after the Hijra (A.D. 865-866), but two-fifths of the work is missing.[29]

Paper was made from flax or hemp fibers, not in the raw state but in the form of linen, cordage, and so on, so that they had already undergone processing. Cotton was never used for papermaking, as was formerly supposed.[30] The first thing done with the rags or cords, after sorting, was to unravel them; then they were softened by combing. Next they were steeped in lime water, and then the pulp was kneaded by hand and bleached in the sun. This process was repeated several times. Scissors were used to cut up the fibers of the pulp, which was then washed in clean water that was changed daily for a week. The lime having thus been removed, the hydrated pulp was then pounded in a mortar or ground between millstones until comminuted and even. The preparatory process was then complete and molding could begin.

The mold consisted of a frame with a screen stretched across it, as in a sieve. A quantity of pulp was placed on the screen and smoothed out to an even thickness. It was then put on a board, possibly felt-covered, and transferred to a smooth wall, to which it adhered until eventually it became dry and fell away. The sheets, being ribbed by the interlacing pattern of the mold, were now rubbed with a mixture of fine meal and wheaten starch, which had first been pulverized and softened in cold water and then stirred into boiling water. This rubbing process, which was followed by sprinkling, "filled out" the sheet and whitened it. The sheets of paper could now be piled and the stacks pressed prior to individual polishing of each

28 M. Kurd ʿAlī: *Khiṭaṭ al-shām* IV (Damascus, 1926), 243.

29 See p. 47 and note 29 to previous chapter.

30 The account given here and later is based upon von Karabacek's and Wiesner's studies cited above, especially the anonymous Arabic paper mentioned in *MSPER* 4.

sheet on a board, using agate or onyx, or sometimes glass, as a polishing stone. Cockleshells were originally employed for this process.

The last stage, for strengthening the paper and preventing the ink from running, was a "treatment," *ʿilāj*, or sizing, as it is known to us. It consisted of immersing the paper in, or rubbing it with, wheaten starch paste, as has been ascertained from the discoveries of paper made in Egypt. Rice water was also employed for sizing, this being a viscous decoction of rice that was strained through a piece of clean linen; less often, use was made of gum tragacanth produced from astragalus. The latter has not been proved from the samples tested, however. Sizing filled up the pores of the paper and made the fibers adhere to each other.

Sometimes only one side was smoothed to be used for writing. A pair of sheets would then be glued together with the rough sides facing each other, giving a thick, strong sheet. Al-Maqdisī says[31] that this was done in Ṣanāʾ in the Yemen, and sheets of this kind are found in Egypt. In the above-cited anonymous account of the manufacturing process, instructions are also given for antiquating the paper with the aid of saffron or fig juice. The use of such paper with an artificially aged appearance could lend itself to abuse. "Old" manuscripts might be fabricated. "Smoothing" (*ṣaql*) of the paper was done by the writer before use. If it was not first-class paper he would smear it with a white substance, then smooth it.[32]

One of the advantages of paper consisted in the fact that it could be manufactured in many different types, both of format and quality. The usual color was white, of course, but the paper might be given other colors by being dipped in or rubbed with some tinted substance; thus, blue was produced from indigo or aloe, yellow from saffron and lemon, red from the dissolved wax of a mealy bug, olive green from blue with

[31] *Aḥsan al-taqāsīm* III, 100.

[32] *Irshād* VI, 38f. The words used, *isfīdh rūy*, are not to be found in the dictionaries. They are Persian, from *safīd* (white) and *rūy* (face, surface) and may denote a tint or coloring that makes the surface white.

saffron added, green from saffron with verdigris, violet from blue and red. Great importance was attached to these different types in the chancelleries, where for each purpose there was a special type of paper. Ibn al-Nadīm gives the names of six different varieties: *al-firʿaunī*, the Pharaonic, which probably imitated Egyptian papyrus; *al-sulaymānī*, probably named after Hārūn ar-Rashīd's comptroller of finance in Khurāsān; *al-jaʿfarī*, after the above-mentioned Jaʿfar ibn Yaḥyā; *al-ṭalḥī* after Ṭalḥa ibn Ṭāhir, governor of Khurāsān 822-828; *al-ṭāhirī* after Ṭāhir ibn ʿAbdallāh, governor of the same place in 844-862; and *al-nūḥī* after Nūḥ ibn Naṣr of the house of the Sāmānids, who ruled over Transoxania in 942-954. Thus the various types, apart from the first one, are named after rulers or high officials in the province where Islamic paper was produced, and after the *wazīr*, the Barmakid Yaḥyā, who introduced the use of paper into Iraq. The varieties might also be named according to their origins or their format and quality.

Like papyrus, sheets of paper were sometimes pasted together and sold in large rolls from which the user cut suitable pieces. But most frequently the buyer received the sheets in the format in which they emerged from the frame, and this could vary widely. The sheet was folded to size, and twenty-five such standard sheets were called in Persian *dast*, "hand," translated into Arabic as *kaff*, from which subsequently the French "main de papier" was derived. Five "hands" are called a *rizma*, "bundle," which was borrowed by Italian and Spanish (*resma*) and thence taken over in different forms by other European languages—*rame* in France, *Ries* (originally *Rizz*) in German, *ris* in Danish, and of course *ream* in English. In using the paper for books, the sheets were laid inside one another to form a fascicle (*kurrāsa*), which consisted as a rule of eight folded sheets.

The ink (*ḥibr, midād*) that was employed generally looks clear and fresh even on papyrus and old paper sheets. The philosopher and theologian al-Ghazālī mentions on occasion that the ink was made of vitriol and gall-nuts,[33] the same ingredients as are still used in European manufacture. But the composition can vary widely and other ingredients may be added. A number of recipes have been handed down, usually originating from the penmen themselves. In Egypt the ashes of burnt papyri were used as carbon. Sometimes the ink has a brownish color, often with a metallic sheen, but a pure black color was the ideal. A poet of the middle ninth century speaks in one of his verses of "ink like the soaring wings of the raven, papyrus like the lustrous mirage." Other colors are used, too: blue, green, or red. Red especially was employed in Qur'āns for vowels, sūra headings, and so forth, and sometimes in other books for headings or for matter in the text that it was desired to emphasize.

It may be mentioned as a curiosity that the use of "sympathetic ink" was also known, this being ink that only became visible after special treatment. Ibn ʿAbd Rabbih (860-940) of Córdoba says in his book "The Costly Pearl,"

> As to the concealing of secrets in writings, so that none other may read them than those for whom they are written, there are methods for this that one must know. . . . The finest of these consists in your taking fresh milk and writing with it on papyrus; and he to whom it is written shall sprinkle hot ashes of papyrus upon it, whereafter that which you have written will become visible, if God will. And if you will, you may use white water of vitriol, and when he to whom you have written shall have it to hand, he shall put vitriol powder over it. And if you desire that the writing shall not be read during the day but shall be read at night, then write it with gall of the turtle.[34]

[33] *Iḥyā' ʿulūm al-dīn* IV (Cairo, 1322/1903), 177 line 36. On ink, see von Karabacek in *MSPER* 4, 77 and Grohmann, *Einführung*, p. 65.

[34] *Al-ʿiqd al-farīd* II, 178 after Abū Ḥatīm Sahl al-Sijistānī; the same in the latter's biography in Ibn Khallikān, *Wafayât* I, 318f.

In the heated political atmosphere generally prevailing in the Islamic world, there was often a use for secret written messages, but as far as books were concerned methods of this sort were naturally of little or no significance.

The writing instrument employed was exactly the same reed pen (*qalam*, from the Greek κάλαμος), used by the Mediterranean peoples before Islam. It was cut from the stems of reeds, which were especially abundant in the river Nile, as well as being found in Iraq and other places. ʿAbdallāh ibn Ṭāhir, who was governor of Khurāsān in 828-844, complained in a letter that good reeds were rare in those regions and asked that some be sent from Iraq.[35] The reed was cut with a sharp knife, and great store was set by this being done meticulously. The reed had to be hard, neither too thick nor too thin; it was best when of the brown color acquired from lying for some time in water. The reed stem must not be cut at a knot, and it must not be curved; the length must be about a hand's width. One end was sharpened so as to form a sloping plane surface, which was hollowed out a little but not too deeply. The sides of this surface were cut away to form a point, and from the point an incision was made inward along the center line of the surface. The point was cut carefully with a sharp knife (which would be spoiled by being used for anything else) in a downward direction onto a piece of bone or something similar (*miqaṭṭa*). The incision was aligned slightly differently according to the type of writing for which the pen was intended, and there were precise rules determining whether the writer should use the left or the right side of the pen, the upper or the lower part of the point, or its whole width.

[35] Al-Ṣūlī, *Adab al-kuttāb*, edited by M. Bahjat (Cairo, 1341/1922-3), pp. 68f. The letter is cited in *al-ʿIqd al-farīd* II, 182f., ʿAlī ibn al-Azhar being the author. The two works contain a number of references to the reed pen, as does al-Qalqashandī, *Ṣubḥ al-aʿshā* II (Cairo 1331/1913), 434-455. Evidence of the use of quills seems to be furnished by *Kitāb al-aghānī*, IV, 30 line 5, which deals with the age of Hārūn al-Rashīd. The word *ẓahr*, which is employed here, is otherwise applied to feathers fixed in arrow shafts.

The scribe kept his equipment in a receptacle consisting of a box with an inkwell (*dawā*) at one end. This writing set was often very beautifully decorated, either with copper with inlaid patterns or with cardbord embellished with paintings, the latter notably in Persia. It was portable, being carried in the waistband. Yāqūt mentions a penman of the twelfth century, ʿUmar ibn al-Ḥusayn, who had a particularly costly writing set that was sold for 900 dīnārs.[36] Even today these beautiful cases are still to be seen.

That writing and everything connected with it was man's business goes without saying in Islam, but even so there are individual instances of feminine participation in this pursuit. There was a female scribe in the ninth century who inspired Aḥmad ibn Ṣāliḥ, *wazīr* to the caliph al-Muʿtaḍid, to the following rapturous declaration, going down the list of writing materials: "Her script is like the beauty of her form, her ink like the back of her hair, her paper like the skin of her face, her reed pen like the point of one of her fingers, her style like the enchantment of her eye, her knife like the flash of her glance, her cutting block (*miqaṭṭa*) like the heart of her lover."[37]

Of all these writing materials, the reed pen was in a sense the most important, so that it came to symbolize the whole class of scribes, chiefly officials in the public service, who, as we have seen, were closely associated with the entire literary circle. They were called "The People of the Pen," just as the military caste were known as "The People of the Sword." In the ceremonial processions held in Egypt on New Year's Day during the Faṭimid caliphate, the canopy of the caliph was preceded by a sword and a magnificent inkwell as the symbol of "The People of the Pen," since the reed pen was considered insufficiently grand for this occasion.[38] But the reed pen did

[36] *Irshād* VI, 47.

[37] Ibn al-Ṭiqṭaqā, *Al-Fakhrī*, edited by W. Ahlwardt (Gotha, 1860), pp. 300f. In *Fihrist*, p. 7 line 18, a female slave by the name of Thanā is mentioned as a scribe.

[38] See J. Pedersen, *Islams Kultur* (Copenhagen, 1928), p. 247.

also become mystically exalted as a divine instrument with which all that happens is written down, so that it became a manifestation of God's omniscience and purpose in all things. This has its background in the Qur'ān, the 68th Sūra of which begins with an oath "by the reed pen and what they write." The reed pen becomes a symbol of all the marvelous knowledge granted to men through the Book, which filled Muḥammad with such wonder that in one of the oldest revelations it is said of God, "And your Lord is the Bountiful, who taught through the reed pen, so that Man learned that which he did not know" (Sūra 96, lines 3-5).

SIX

Arabic Script; Calligraphers

We already know something of the prehistory of the Arabic script, since we have seen that it evolved quite naturally from an Aramaic type, whereas it is not clear what the background was before Islam of the creation of a universal Arabic script of the southern Arabian type. In the Islamic literary world much attention was paid to the script and its history.[1]

The Persian-born historian al-Balādhurī (d. 892), who lived at the court of Baghdad, concludes his work on the Islamic conquests (*Futūḥ al-buldān*, "The Conquests of the Lands") with a passage about script, and from the tenth century on

[1] The following may be mentioned among the literature dealing with the Arabic script and its exponents: C. Huart, *Les calligraphes et les miniaturistes de l'orient musulman* (Paris, 1908). This book is based upon certain Persian and Turkish works of more recent times and is therefore concerned mostly with works in these languages. A. Christensen, "Boghaandvaerk og Bogkunst i Persien," *Aarbog for Bogvenner*, published by S. Dahl, 2 (Copenhagen, 1918), 22-46, deals with Persian books, especially illustrations and binding. Publications on the true Arabic script include B. Moritz, "Arabia. d. Arabic writing," *E.I*[1], *s.v.*; H. Jensen, *Die Schrift* (Glückstadt and Hamburg [1935]), pp. 221ff.; E. Kühnel, *Islamische Schriftkunst*, 2nd ed. (Graz, 1977). Script samples are to be found in these works, and also in B. Moritz, *Arabic Palaeography. A Collection of Arabic Texts from the First Century of the Hidjra till the Year 1000* (Cairo, 1905); in *Spécimens d'écritures arabes pour la lecture des manuscrits anciens et modernes par un père de la C*[ie] *de Jésus*, 19th ed. (Beirut, 1912), and in A. J. Arberry, *Specimens of Arabic and Persian Palaeography* [India Office Library] (London, 1939). Early contributions to the history of the Kufic script were made in Denmark by J.G.C. Adler in his description of Kufic manuscripts in the Royal Library, Copenhagen, 1780, and by J. D. Lindberg, *Lettre à M.P.O. Brøndsted sur quelques médailles cufiques dans le cabinet du Roi de Danemarck, récemment trouvées dans l'île de Falster et sur quelques manuscrits coufiques* (Copenhagen, 1830). He continues the work of de Sacy by giving an account of the history of the Kufic scripts, with 12 plates.

we have three authors in particular, frequently cited above, who wrote about books and so also about script, namely, the Córdoban Ibn ʿAbd Rabbih (869–940) in the work "The Costly Pearl" (*al-ʿIqd al-farīd*); and the Iraqis: al-Ṣūlī (d. 946) in the tract "The Proper Education of Scribes" (*Adab al-kuttāb*), and Ibn al-Nadīm, *warrāq* of Baghdad, whose work *al-Fihrist*, "The Index [of Books]," completed in 987, gives an exceedingly valuable survey of scripts and literature among Arabs, Jews, Syrians, Greeks, Persians, Indians, and others insofar as they fall within the compass of his knowledge. This book affords us an idea of the intellectual horizons of the literary classes of Baghdad in the tenth century.

Moving further on in time, we find that the North African Ibn Khaldūn (d. 1406) furnishes throughout his "Prolegomenon" (*al-Muqaddima*) not only an account of the culture of the period but also brief glimpses of the history of the script. At this same period the Egyptian al-Qalqashandī (d. 1418) was writing "Dawn for the Night-Blind" (*Ṣubḥ al-aʿshā*), a great work of reference in fourteen volumes for the officials of the Egyptian public service. In volume 3 there is a lengthy section on script, in which each individual letter is discussed, and detailed instructions supplied on how it is to be formed. With such jealous care was the script guarded.

The works cited have now all been printed, but it would be easy to add to them a number that are only available as manuscripts, as well as material found here and there in other literature. Interest in the script was equally keen among officials and men of letters. Yāqūt, whose biographies of literary figures have been so liberally cited here, seldom fails to include a description of the script of the person concerned. "His script was beautiful," he says frequently, and on one occasion, "His script was beautiful, with ink full-bodied [or, broad-penned], sweetly and precisely executed."[2]

[2] *Irshād* VI, 21. In W. Ahlwardt's *Verzeichnis der arabischen Handschriften der königlichen Bibliothek* (Berlin, 1887), under "Schreibkunde," are to be found the titles of 13 works, to which the editor adds in note 17 other works dealing with the art of writing.

The Islamic tradition abounds with legends identifying the originators of every possible kind of art and activity. Some of the works cited assert that the first practitioner of penmanship was Adam, who wrote on clay, which he then baked, but that after the Flood each people invented its own script. This may mean that in Islamic times clay tablets from the ruins of Iraq and Syria were known and that it was presumed, correctly, that the cuneiform characters imprinted thereon were writings from an age long past.

As to the question of which Arabic script was the oldest, Islamic tradition points both to southern Arabia and to either Ḥīra or al-Anbār in Iraq. Ibn Khaldūn joins the two streams of tradition together by declaring that the people of Ḥīra took over the script from the Himyarites of south Arabia, but wrote it badly, so that the predominant script came to diverge from the south Arabian.[3] As we have seen, it is correct that there was a link between Ḥīra in Iraq and south Arabia, but not that it was the south Arabian script that prevailed.

Most authors, curiously enough, realize this, and also realize the fact that the Arabic alphabet is derived from the Aramaic. The story goes that it was three men of the north Arabian tribe of Ṭayyi' who hit upon the idea of remodeling the "Syrian" (*suryānī*)—that is, the Aramaic—alphabet and so creating the Arabic. They taught it to the people of Anbār. Then it reached Ḥīra, where a Christian from one of the north Arabian oases learned it. He initiated some people in Mecca into the art, which thereafter became further disseminated over north Arabia and Syria. This was immediately prior to the time of the Prophet, and the authors are able to tell us who were scribes for the Prophet and later on for his successors. Thus tradition establishes a solid continuity in the development of penmanship between the era before the Prophet and the classical period of Islamic literature.

A better basis for acknowledging this continuity is furnished, however, by the written documents that have come

[3] *Muqaddima*, pp. 331ff.

down to us in the shape of stones, coins, parchments, papyrus, and paper from the earliest days of Islam, and that proliferate increasingly through the ages. If we compare the oldest Muḥammadan documents with the oldest Arabic inscriptions already mentioned, we find little difference in the script. This applies both to the oldest papyri straight from the year 22 after the *hijra*, (corresponding to A.D. 643), to the oldest inscription, from 691-692,[a] and to the oldest coins, which date from the same period.[b] We see everywhere the same heavy, somewhat clumsy shapes, which do, however, assume a more monumental character in stone inscriptions inasmuch as the letters are compact and uniform, and the lower line of the script is drawn with a strong and even stroke. The inscription in question is inside the Dome of the Rock in Jerusalem and is the work of its builder,[c] the Umayyad caliph ʿAbd al-Malik, whose name has been erased, however, and replaced by that of al-Ma'mūn, Hārūn al-Rashīd's son. The inscription reads: "This domed building was built by God's servant, the Imām al-Maʾmūn, Prince of the Faithful, in the year 72. May God receive him!" There follow a number of Qur'ānic quotations.

Arabic script, like its immediate source, Aramaic script and the latter's Canaanitic and Hebraic forerunners, as well, reads from right to left. The letters differ slightly in shape according to whether they are joined to the preceding or succeeding letter, or both, or are not joined at all. The Arabs took over an alphabet of twenty-two letters from the Nabataeans, omitting an *s* (*samekh*), whose pronunciation in Arabic coincided with another s-sound (*sīn*). Through a process of simplification, some of these twenty-two letters came to resemble one another, a situation aggravated by the fact that the twenty-two letters were insufficient to represent the Arabic consonants.

The fact is that the Arabic language has preserved many of

[a] This is the oldest architectural inscription; earlier rock inscriptions are known.

[b] The oldest coins are, in fact, several decades earlier.

[c] That is, was ordered by him.

the older Semitic speech sounds, which in Aramaic coincided with other sounds. Thus the Arabic script, but not the Aramaic, distinguishes between *d* and *dh* (*th* in the English *that*), *t* and *th* (*th* in the English *everything*), the so-called emphatic *ṭ* and the corresponding *ẓ* (Arabic *ẓill* "shadow," Aramaic *ṭᵉlālā*), the hoarse *ḥ* (in Muḥammad) and the soft-palate *kh* (like *ch* in Swiss German), the powerful guttural sound ʿ, called *ʿayn* (meaning "eye"), and the voiced soft-palate sound *gh*, called *ghayn*, and between *s* and *sh* (called *sīn* and *shīn*). Add to all this the fact that the Arabs have retained a special sound *ḍ*, of which the only remnants left in the north Semitic languages are in the recently discovered Ras Shamra dialect, and it will be seen that the Aramaic alphabet lacks distinctive characters for seven Arabic consonants. It is obvious how awkward this must have been when, in addition, there was a fortuitous confusion between the symbols for other consonants that had nothing to do with one another. This applies particularly to the consonant *t*. The latter, as will have been understood from the foregoing, was used for *th* as well, but its shape also coincided with the symbol for *b, n*, and *y* when the latter was joined to the left or to both sides. In the same way, *r* and *z*, and *f* and *q*, coincided in all positions.

An attempt was made to remedy these defects with the aid of attributive dots. Such dots seem to be present even in the oldest papyrus, from 643, and they are still plainer in one from 677. When Muslim tradition credits Abu'l-Aswad al-Du'alī with being the first man to introduce the system of dots into copies of the Qur'ān, this is due to the customary urge to prove some discoverer for everything possible, and Abu'l-Aswad is called the inventor of Arabic grammar. But papyri that have been found show that in fact these dots were already in use by his time.[d] He lived in the seventh century and was a close associate of ʿAlī, the Prophet's son-in-law. Sometimes two dots were joined to form a dash, and in certain old Qur'ānic manuscripts a system of dashes is used. The

[d] This does not, however, exclude the possibility that he invented them.

uncertainty that prevailed at first over the employment of these diacritic aids, as they are called, gradually disappeared, and a definite system emerged. There is a Leiden manuscript even as late as the ninth century (868) with a system different from the one that ultimately won the day.[4] A solitary deviant was still to be found in the Maghribi script used in the Maghrib, that is, North Africa and Spain, which indeed still predominates in North Africa today. Whereas in the normal system one dot is placed over the letter for *f* ف and two over ق, *f* is denoted in the Maghribi script as in the papyri of the early centuries by a dot under ڢ and *q* by a dot over the letter ڧ. The above-specified uniform consonants are distinguished (in the form with links on both sides) thus: *b* ـبـ, *t* ـتـ, *th* ـثـ, *n* ـنـ, *y* ـيـ.

These diacritic dots are of course a useful aid and quite satisfactory when they are positioned carefully. But in inscriptions, in letters and other writings, and in literary manuscripts, one is often faced with texts entirely devoid of dots, which of course makes reading difficult and uncertain; and in any case it has to be said that only seldom does one see a manuscript in which the positioning of diacritic dots is executed with care. The reading of an Arabic manuscript therefore almost always presents difficulties.

Another defect of the Arabic script is that, like the Canaanitic-Hebraic and the Aramaic, it is only a consonant script, though it imitated these in introducing a special symbol for the vowels. It started—it is uncertain when—by employing dots for this purpose, but probably only in Qur'āns. A dot over the letter meant that the consonant was followed by an *a*, a dot in the middle meant a *u*, and one under the letter an *i*. This brought further confusion, however, since dots were of course already in use for other functions, and so prominent a religious scholar as Mālik ibn Anas (d. 795) would not accept them in Qur'āns deposited in the mosques. In the second half of the eighth century, the system was introduced that has

[4] De Goeje, "Beschreibung," p. 781.

been used ever since, in which *u* is indicated by a small *wāw* above the consonant that it follows in speech, *a* by an oblique stroke, a horizontal *alif* ـَ, over the consonant, and *i* by a similar stroke beneath it. It seems likely that this symbol for *i* developed from an original *yā*.

For even before this—again following the example of the other north Semitic alphabet—the long vowels had been indicated with the aid of the nearest cognate consonants, *ā* by *alif* ا , *ī* by *yā* ـى, *ū* by *wāw* و. These signs cover all variations of the three vowels in the direction of *e, æ, y* and so forth. The employment of consonant signs to denote vowels was not carried through consistently, particularly in earlier times. The special vowel signs were used only to a limited extent. A manuscript in which full use is made of vowel signs is a rarity, and in Islamic books printed in the Orient virtually no vowel signs are to be seen. Quite recently some vocalizing of difficult words on European lines has been started, notably in poems and in the publication of ancient texts; this of course facilitates their study considerably.

Other reading symbols were gradually introduced too, such as a small *s* ّ, signifying *tashdīd*, "intensification"; it serves to indicate the doubling of a consonant. Other signs denote the diverse meanings taken on by the *alif* as time went on. Originally it was the symbol for a short broken sound formed in the throat and known to us through the English "glottal stop," a sound regarded in the Semitic languages as a consonant. But we have seen that it could also signify a long *ā*, and it had other uses as well, such as indicating any vowel at the beginning of the word in order to avoid commencing a syllable with two consonants, a proceeding that feels unnatural in all Semitic languages. For example, in an imperative such as *qutul*, the first *u* soon weakened, so that instead of *qtul* one said *uqtul*, unless it was preceded by a word ending in a vowel to which it could be joined, for instance, *qāla qtul*, "He said: Kill!", which is read as if it were one word. In the same way, a vowel is inserted before foreign words beginning with two consonants; for instance, Plato becomes Aflāṭūn, and the Greek word σπόγγος, "sponge" becomes *isfunj*. All these vowel affixes are indicated by an *alif*, and in order to distinguish between its various functions special signs are used, including a small ʿ*ayn* called a *hamzah* ء when it has its original consonantal function.

There is no system of punctuation, except that in the Qur'ān the ends of verses are indicated by a certain number of dots, a circle, or something of the sort. More recently some sign may occasionally be used to mark the end of a section, but there are no rules about it. Qur'ānic manuscripts often show all these signs in red ink. No word may ever be split between two lines, as is done in European languages. Much importance is attached, also, to not separating closely linked words, such as a genitive and its associated word, such as "Zayd's slave," or the brief laudations placed after God's name, or the benedictions attached to the names of the Prophet and his fellows, such as "God grant him blessings and peace" or "God have mercy upon him."

The earliest written remains show us a developing script, as may be seen from the embryonic monumental characters and the rudimentary system of dots. From these earliest forms there emerge little by little different types of Arabic script.

The most prominent type in the early centuries is the one known as Kufic. The Muslims believed it to have made its appearance in Kūfa, which became the first capital city of Iraq in 638 and long remained a seat of learning, even after the founding of Baghdad in 762. It may possibly have been used at one time by particularly skillful scribes of that town, but in fact it evolved gradually and is widely encountered over all the territories of Islam. The script is distinguished by its heavy character, its thick, firm lines and, in former times, its angular shapes. Thus, it is manifestly a development from the earliest monumental script, known to us through the building inscriptions and coins of the Umayyads. Generally speaking, it is best suited to heavier materials and is a natural product of the chisel. The words of the inscriptions often create large, harmoniously formed blocks. But its monumental character was precisely what caused it to be copiously employed in the production of Qur'āns that were to be placed in a mosque or were intended to constitute a sacred adornment in the dwelling of a potentate. Many fragments and entire copies of such Qur'āns have come down to us, and a large collection from the seventh to tenth centuries is to be found in the Dār al-Kutub in Cairo. These copies are all on parchment. Kufic script is also to be found occasionally on papyrus, and it was also employed on paper.

About the middle of the eighth century, we begin to come across new forms of Kufic script, characteristically with a substantial enlargement of many letters in the horizontal plane to counteract the impression left by the frequent upward strokes; the latter were sometimes considerably abbreviated as well, and this gave the script a strong, compact form. We encounter this type in inscriptions, on pottery, and in manuscripts. In the ninth and tenth centuries, we find a Kufic script with rounder shapes and more pronounced curves in the lines. It is as though the book script were inspired by brush produced shapes of the ceramic script; each letter with its round, broad lines is like a work of art in itself, drawn individually with a wide gap between it and the next. One is reminded of a certain scribe's response to a request for advice: "You should not write any letter without applying the whole of your energies to its writing and without considering that you are not to write anything else until you have completed it and can attend to the next one."[5]

Both the angular and the more rounded Kufic could be executed in new variations by stressing vertical rather than horizontal flow, so that the script puts one in mind of a row of stalks. Examples of it are to be found in Persia in the tenth century, in distant Samarqand, and in Egypt on pottery and textiles, where the decorative aspect naturally tended to be paramount. The latter led to the extension of the stalks into

[5] *Al-ʿiqd al-Farīd* II, 171 from bottom.

tendrils, ending in foliage and flowers, so that the whole surface became filled up. Thus evolved "florid Kufic," of which copious use was made in architecture and art handicrafts, on pottery, metalware, textiles, and woodcarvings. In the twelfth century these tendrils and flourishes could turn into an absolute wilderness, which might function as a sort of background for the script but could also entirely deprive it of power. Sometimes the letters themselves might be transformed into decorative shapes, for example, by forming the centers of the vertical shafts into interlacing patterns. This type flourished notably in Fāṭimid Egypt (969-1171).

These methods were not employed directly in the making of books, but they did exert a considerable influence on it. It was through this artistic writing that the feeling for the decorative line was developed. Whereas pictorial art never became fully accepted by Islam, Muhammadans channeled their artistic drive into the shaping of the line, and writing offered them the natural medium for doing this. Therefore in Islam the art of writing became the most respected art, and no alphabet in the world has been the object of such intense artistic labor as the Arabic. It was from ornamental writing that the arabesque evolved as an independent decorative figure,[e] in which everything depends upon the beauty of the lines themselves, upon the bold curves, refined details, and rhythmical repetition. The arabesque lacks the warmth and depth of a picture, but it expresses the elegance and abstract beauty of pure form, manifesting the genuine Muslim spirit.

The new variety of Kufic script appeared in Qur'āns in modified form, a pattern of tendrils being drawn, for instance, as a background against which to set the script. Some of the vertical elements were formed as tall, slender strokes, erect or sloping or in graceful curves. There is an eleventh-century

[e] On the contrary, ornamental Kufic—such as that of the ninth century—postdated the development of the arabesque; see E. Kühnel, *The Arabesque*, translated by R. E. Ettinghausen (Graz, 1977).

example of this originating from Persia. But by the twelfth century the heyday of the Kufic script was over.[f]

The Kufic script was artistically magnificent both as a monumental and as a book script. For day-to-day purposes a rounder, lighter, less pompous type of script was used. This was called *naskhī* (from *nasakha*, "to copy"), thus denoting it as a book script. However, it dates back to the very earliest papyri, to the texture of which it was well suited, and it is the one generally used on paper for books and letters. It won widespread acceptance in Iraq, Syria, Egypt, and the lands farther east. Its lighter shapes made it well adapted also to a more elegant script, and it is represented in a number of magnificent Qur'āns, especially in a sharp, clear form called *rayḥānī* after the penman thought to have devised it.

Naskhī was almost supreme from the twelfth century, but different variations naturally evolved, such as a chancery script known as *tawqīʿ* and later as *dīwānī*, with boldly twining lines; another was called *riqʿa*, which has a thicker stroke and a slightly more angular form. This type also came into use for monumental inscriptions. It suited this purpose best in a form with thick, rounded, boldly twining lines, called *sulus*, or more correctly *thulth*, that is, one-third, meaning one-third of the largest size of paper employed in the chancellery. This form of script is found widely disseminated, notably in Egypt in the time of the Mamlūks (1250-1517). It was also used for Qur'āns. A variety of colors were employed in order to augment the magnificence of monumental manuscripts, especially red for all diacritical marks. The use of gold was general for giving the letters luster.

That North Africa and Spain enjoyed a somewhat special position in the Islamic world, based on their peculiar political status, is attested by the fact that these countries, as noted above, created their own type of "practical script" called *al-Maghribī*, "the western," which is still supreme in North Af-

[f] This statement would be much less controversial if "thirteenth" were substituted for "twelfth."

rica, that is, the lands west of Egypt. The Maghribi script was originally called *Qayrawānī* after Qayrawān, the chief city of Tunisia, founded in 680. The script seems to have evolved in the tenth century as a variant of the Kufic script, related to the earliest types of Arabic script known. It has already been remarked that the dot below the *f* and the dot above the letter *q* have been retained, as was done occasionally in earlier times. A forerunner of this type is to be seen in the Leiden manuscript of 868 mentioned above, the script of which seems to be a cross between the Kufic script and *naskhī*. It is striking that the alphabetical order is not the same as the normal Arabic order, one of whose characteristics is that it puts letters of similar appearance together, but follows the same ancient north Semitic order as was used by the Nabataeans. The writing has the same boldness of line as does Kufic, with widely swept strokes below the line and certain characteristic letters such as *k* and *ṭ* displaying a typically Kufic form; there is often also a propensity to finish off the strokes with some kind of simple flourish. The line has a stiffer and more solid character than *naskhī*, in which the words often slant because some letters are written higher up than others. Admittedly, this happens in *Maghribī* as well, but here it is offset by the effort to maintain a rigidly horizontal principal line.

The enormously important role that the treatment of writing played for the Muslims made it natural that they should be interested in the calligrapher (*khaṭṭāṭ*, from *khaṭṭ*, "writing") as well. Calligraphers did not constitute a guild like the *warrāqs*. Although it was natural that as a rule they belonged to the latter's circle, this was not always the case, and it could be men in quite different occupations, such as public officials, who made their contribution to this art, which every cultivated person exercised to a certain degree and in which all were interested. The works cited above tell of various calligraphers who formed schools with new types of script. There are Persian and Turkish works as well, mainly of more recent date, dealing with calligraphers, and these mention not only Persians and Turks but also Arabs, for the languages of these three peoples were written with the same alphabet, and Arabic literature was common to them all. Unquestioning reliance cannot be placed upon what these more recent authors say about earlier times. In fact, it is impossible to establish who was responsible for the most important innovations in the history of writing, or what the distinctive contributions of the earlier individual calligraphers comprised.

Ibn al-Nadīm mentions as the first scribe under the Umayyads a certain Quṭba, whose work served as a foundation for the scribes of the ʿAbbāsids, and goes on to say that there was a prominent Qur'ānic scribe, Khālid ibn Abī'l-Ḥajjāj, who wrote for al-Walīd ibn ʿAbd al-Malik (705-715).[6] Ibn al-Nadīm had seen one of his Qur'ānic works, and in the Mosque of the Prophet in Medina there was a passage of the Qur'ān, from Sūra 91 to the end, executed in gold by this calligrapher. The same author enumerates various Qur'ānic scribes under the ʿAbbāsids, beginning at the time of Hārūn al-Rashīd. He also names a number of writers who formed schools and whose art was handed down from father to son. In the ninth century, according to al-Qalqashandī, Egypt in the reign of Ibn Ṭūlūn had the finest calligrapher of the age, a man named Ṭabṭab, who evoked the envy of Baghdad.[7] The leadership passed to Iraq, however, where in the course of time three men emerged as the most outstanding figures in the field of calligraphy.

The first of these, Abū ʿAlī Muḥammad ibn ʿAlī ibn Muqla, died in 940 and was an older contemporary of Ibn al-Nadīm, who puts alongside him his brother Abū ʿAbdallāh al-Ḥasan ibn ʿAlī ibn Muqla (d. 949). Ibn al-Nadīm declares them to be without equal from the earliest times to his own day, and in this posterity has agreed with him, although only the elder of the two brothers has retained his fame.[8] They had inherited the art from their father ʿAlī and grandfather Muqla, their methods having been originated by the latter; Ibn al-Nadīm had seen a Qur'ān written by Muqla. Abū ʿAlī began as a

[6] *Fihrist*, pp. 6f.

[7] *Ṣubḥ al-aʿshā* III, 17.

[8] On the contrary, posterity has reversed the verdict of Ibn al-Nadīm in that it has neglected the younger son of Ibn Muqla.

petty official but rose swiftly to high political and administrative office, first as governor of the province of Fārs, then as *wazīr* under three caliphs, al-Muqtadir, al-Qāhir, and al-Rāḍī.[8]

In this post he enjoyed both power and wealth, but like other incumbents of important positions under the ʿAbbāsids, he had a stormy life, suffering confiscations and torture several times. That great affairs were involved can be seen from the fact that on one occasion he was fined the sum of one million dīnārs, that is, about thirteen million gold francs. Eventually he had to bow before a rival, Ibn Rā'iq, who caused his right hand to be cut off. It is said that he then had his reed pen bound to his arm and showed that he could still use it, but was subjected to further torture, had his tongue cut off, and died in prison. It is characteristic of Islam that this man, who lived a violent life of political struggle and secured great riches for himself, which he distributed lavishly on all sides, and who at other times lost everything, has immortalized his name as one of Islam's greatest calligraphers. He is said to have written two magnificent copies of the Qur'ān, and pieces of writing from his hand were bought by bibliophiles in later times at high prices. Unfortunately, nothing has come down to our own day, so that we are not in a position to determine the nature of his achievement. Ibn Khallikān says that he altered the Kufic script to "the one now in use." Since it is said of several later literary figures that they wrote according to Ibn Muqla's methods, it is probable that he had some responsibility for the victory of the rounded, lighter script. His art was continued by his successors and numerous pupils.

The second great calligrapher, Ibn al-Bawwāb (d. 1022 or 1032), lived a more tranquil life, but what is known of him highlights the position of calligraphy in several ways.[9] His true name was ʿAlī ibn Hilāl, but Ibn al-Bawwāb, "the porter's son," became his nickname. He began as a decorator adorning houses with pictures—a very interesting item of

[8] See H. Bowen, *The Life and Times of ʿAlī Ibn ʿIsā* (Cambridge, 1928), index and also *Encyclopaedia of Islam*, 1st ed., II, 430f.

[9] *Irshād* V, 445ff.; Ibn Khallikān, *Wafayāt* I, 345f.

information—and went over to painting pictures in books, finally taking up calligraphy. There is no doubt that this is to be construed as meaning that he progressed to successively higher art forms. At one time he had an appointment in the mosque of Manṣūr in Baghdad as "admonisher" (*wāʿiẓ*), that is, homiletic orator, a post not to be confused with that of the official preacher at Friday religious services (*khaṭīb*).

At one time Ibn al-Bawwāb looked after Bahā' al-Daula's library in Shīrāz, and he himself tells the following little story from there, which is reported by Yāqūt: One day, in a heap of books that had been put aside, he came across a black-bound book that turned out to be part of a Qur'ān in thirty volumes written by Ibn Muqla and this aroused his greatest admiration. A search of the library brought twenty-nine volumes to light, but one was still missing. When he brought the matter before Bahā' al-Daula, the latter ordered the work to be completed, and Ibn al-Bawwāb offered to write the missing volume on condition that he received a robe of honor and one hundred dīnārs if the newly written volume could not be distinguished from the others. These terms were accepted, and Ibn al-Bawwāb hunted up in the library some old paper similar to that of the surviving volumes, wrote the missing volume in gilt, which he antiquated, then bound it, using an old cover taken from another book. When Bahā' al-Daula came to think of the matter a year later, he had the thirty volumes brought to him and scrutinized them carefully without being able to pick out the newly written one, and he then retained them all as Ibn Muqla's. Ibn al-Bawwāb did not receive the agreed remuneration, but his request for all the cut Chinese paper in the library, sufficient to last several years, was granted. There is stated to have been Samarqand paper and Chinese paper in the library.

This story indicates that Ibn al-Bawwāb's script was not far removed from Ibn Muqla's, on which it is said that he based his own. What the difference between them consisted of we do not know, but biographies of men in the twelfth and thirteenth centuries still report that they followed Ibn Muqla's or Ibn al-Bawwāb's methods. One individual is said to have used Ibn Muqla's methods for books and Ibn al-Bawwāb's for letters.[10]

Pieces of writing by both calligraphers were very much in demand by collectors and fetched high prices. Yāqūt tells of a seventy-line letter of trivial content written by Ibn al-Bawwāb's hand that was sold for seventeen dīnārs and later resold for twenty-five (over three hundred gold francs).[11] The zeal of collectors naturally encouraged forgery. We have seen that accounts of paper manufacturing also contained instructions for the artificial aging of paper, and in the episode just related Ibn al-Bawwāb himself furnishes an example of the counterfeiting of the work of an old master. Yāqūt says of one thirteenth-century calligrapher that he purchased a sheet of Ibn al-Bawwāb's script for forty dirhams. He copied it on old paper and gave the copy to a bookseller, who sold it for sixty dirhams as a script by Ibn al-Bawwāb. In the great library of Cairo some years ago a supposed autograph of Ibn Muqla was shown that, however, subsequently turned out to have been the work of a modern calligrapher.

The last of the great calligraphers was Jamāl al-Dīn Yāqūt al-Mustaʿṣimī,[12] who when a lad was purchased as a slave by al-Mustaʿṣim, the last ʿAbbāsid caliph, from whom he took his name. The caliph had him trained in literature and penmanship; he did compose a number of works, but especially displayed prodigious industry as a calligrapher in the caliph's service. His reputation for diligence was such that he was said to have written the Qur'ān 1,001 times, though this only means a very large number of times. He had numerous pupils, and his script was used as a model for a long time afterwards, being named *yāqūtī* after him. Among his methods was a

[10] *Irshād* VI, 22. Curiously enough, it is Abū ʿAbdallāh ibn Muqla, the brother of the celebrity, who is mentioned; but the two brothers employed the same methods.

[11] Ibid. V, 445f.; cf. VI, 41.

[12] On the calligrapher Yāqūt see, in addition to Huart's *Calligraphes* (cf. note 1 above), pp. 84ff., E. G. Browne, *A Literary History of Persia* II (Cambridge, 1912), 487f.; Brockelmann, *GAL Supplementband* I, 598; Ibn al-Fuwaṭī, *Ta'rīkh al-ḥawādith al-jāmiʿa* (Baghdad, 1351/1932), 500ff.

special slanting cut of the reed pen, but otherwise his script had close affinities with that of Ibn al-Bawwāb—a typical *naskhī*. He lived on for many years after the conquest of Baghdad and the murder of the caliph (1258), dying in Baghdad in 1298. Pieces of his writing are preserved in Cairo, in Istanbul, and in Paris, and include two complete Qur'āns. The script is thought to bear a certain resemblance to the later somewhat stiff Persian *naskhī,* and possibly formed the transition to it.

In subsequent centuries the art of book production enjoyed a revival, notably in the East, where Persian and Turkish calligraphers were the most accomplished. The Islamic princes, who were the patrons of literary refinement, also interested themselves in calligraphy, and many of them were considerable calligraphers themselves. The powerful ʿAḍud al-Daula of the house of the Būyids was one in the tenth century, and so especially were several of the Tīmūrids, who in the fifteenth century made cultural centers of Samarqand and other eastern towns. Calligraphy did not die out, because it at once afforded the best nourishment to the sense of delight in beauty and satisfied the urge to practice piety, for its noblest task was and remained the production of copies of the Qur'ān to an artistic standard worthy of the Holy Book. One learned man, Jamāl al-Dīn, who lived in Aleppo around 1200, was accustomed in Ramaḍān, the month of fasting, to withdraw from the world into a mosque and devote himself solely to transcribing the Qur'ān, making one or two copies according to the methods of Ibn al-Bawwāb. When he had completed his copy, he presented it to a relative, but the reed pens he had employed for his work of piety he used for writing amulets against fevers and the pains of childbirth, and it was acknowledged, says Yāqūt, that a special benison was attached to them.[13] It was the glow of holiness tingeing the activities of the calligrapher that gave him a unique importance in Islam.

[13] *Irshād* VI, 34.

SEVEN

Book Painting

THERE IS a wide and characteristic difference between the relationship of Muslims to calligraphy and their relationship to pictorial art. Calligraphy was created by Islam itself, inspired by its veneration for the Divine Book: it was an applied art that developed in harmony with literature, attaining its pinnacle, like the latter, in the ninth to thirteenth centuries; it reached out too into other art forms, being employed not only in book production but also in other handicrafts—in ceramics, metalworking, wood carving, and glassmaking, and notably in architecture. Pictorial art was not a Muslim invention; on the contrary, it was something that Islam condemned. Yet Muslim pictorial art nevertheless exists. This is accounted for by the rich tradition in this field of art that characterized each of the two mighty cultures, Byzantine and Persian, from which the culture of Islam evolved, and by Islam's inability to quell the human urge to see the impressions of the surrounding world fixed in figurative form. But unlike calligraphy, pictorial art enjoyed its heyday after the culture of Islam had passed its zenith, and it always kept its distance from the Qur'ān.

In point of fact, the Qur'ān contained no absolute ban on pictures. Sūra 5, 90 says: "O Ye who believe! wine and gaming and stone images and divining arrows are filth, a work of Satan: avoid them that you may find happiness." The reference here is only to religious images, which did not necessarily have any figurative character, and in any case scarcely had any artistic form. But in the great collections of traditions attributed to the Prophet, which are fundamental to all law and doctrine in Islam, pronouncements of an entirely different sort are to be found. Here a curse is invoked upon the "image maker" (*muṣawwir*), and we are told that the angels refuse to enter a house in which there are pictures. No one will be punished more severely on the Day of Judgment than the artist, it is said, and the argument for this is stated: he will be commanded to bring his images to life, and when he cannot do so, the punishment will fall upon him. He has presumptuously sought to imitate the Creator.[1]

It is unlikely that these pronouncements really emanate from the Prophet himself; it may even be doubted whether he ever saw a real picture. The countless dicta ascribed to the Prophet were largely shaped in the course of time as weapons in the intellectual conflicts that occupied the first few centuries after his death. There can be no doubt that it was the sacred pictures of the Christians that led to the amplification of the Qur'ānic pronouncement, and this is confirmed by the fact that in some of the dicta crucifixes are cited along with pictures as objects of denunciation. But the argument cited above goes further, inasmuch as it makes the artist's creative activity a violation of the honor of God, the only Creator. This idea is typically Islamic, and is largely responsible for the predilection for abstract art evolved through calligraphy as against the naturalism of pictorial art. However, this view is not maintained consistently. One pronouncement assumes that it applies only to representations of beings possessing souls, whereas according to another, pictures are quite in order on cushions or pillows for standing or lying on. This remains the situation: to make pictures of living beings is absolutely forbidden, but once you actually have them, a blind eye will be turned provided they are used in such a manner as to show contempt for them, as for instance by walking on them. Insofar as any distinctive

[1] References to the dicta concerning paintings to be found in the books of traditions are to be found in A. J. Wensinck, *A Handbook of Early Muhammadan Tradition* (Leiden, 1927), *s.v.* "Images." The topic is dealt with briefly by C. Snouck Hurgronje in "Ḳuṣejr ʿAmra und das Bilderverbot," in *Zeitschrift der deutschen morgenländischen Gesellschaft* 61 (1907), 186-91 (reprinted in his *Verspreide Geschriften* II [1923], 451-56).

style of pictorial art does, nevertheless, exist in Islam, this has emerged in defiance of the Law.

Muslim pictorial art is confined principally to painting, and the latter, in turn, chiefly to books.[2] All that has come down to us from ancient times in the way of painted pictures is some few fragments of papyrus and paper in Egypt. These date from the ninth and tenth centuries, and represent a wide variety of subjects: a tree with many branches, a very lifelike bird, a man and a woman reveling—this is the oldest Arabic erotic work extant—or a dog with muscles heavily emphasized. The Coptic influence is readily discernible, particularly in the representation of human figures, as for instance in a pen-and-ink drawing of a horseman with upper body leaning forward energetically, his shaggy head covered by a peaked bonnet; it bears the name of the artist, Abū Tamīm Ḥaydara.

In some cases it is possible to ascertain that the artist and the writer are one and the same person, the picture being introduced into the text as an ornament. Some of the pictures

[2] Publications on Muslim painting include the treatise by A. Christensen cited in note 1 to the previous chapter, and my *Islams Kultur*, pp. 113ff. An article by K. Madsen in *Kunstmuseets Aersskrift* 3 (1917), 1-24, discusses drawings from Indian Mughal art, to be found in the Kobberstik collection (in the print room of the Museum of Fine Arts, Copenhagen). The following are important works on the topic: E. Diez, *Die Kunst der islamischen Völker* (Berlin-Neubabelsberg, 1915), pp. 185ff.; H. Gluck and E. Diez, *Die Kunst des Islam* (Berlin, 1925); G. Migeon, *Manuel d'art musulman*, 2nd ed., I (Paris, 1927), 101-223; E. Kühnel, *Miniaturmalerei im islamischen Orient* (*Die Kunst des Ostens*, ed. W. Cohn, vol. 7) (Berlin, 1922); E. Blochet, *Les peintures des manuscrits orientaux de la Bibliothèque Nationale* (Paris, 1914-1920)—numerous publications by the same author are listed in Migeon, p. 221; F. R. Martin, *The Miniature Painting and Painters of Persia, India and Turkey from the 8th to the 18th Century*, I-II (London, 1912); F. Sarre and F. R. Martin, *Die Ausstellung von Meisterwerken muhammedanischer Kunst in München 1910*, I-III (Munich, 1912); P. W. Schulz, *Die persisch-islamische Miniaturmalerei* I-II (Leipzig, 1914); T. W. Arnold and A. Grohmann, *The Islamic Book* (Florence and Leipzig, 1929; German version *Denkmäler islamischer Buchkunst*, Munich, 1929); A. U. Pope, *An Introduction to Persian Art since the 7th Century A.D.* (London, 1930); A. U. Pope and P. Ackerman, eds., *A Survey of Persian Art from Prehistoric Times to the Present* I-VI (London and New York, 1939)—vol. III on painting by Arnold and Kühnel; vols. IV-V contain pictures.

are embodied in purely decorative ornamentation; in a picture with birds, the birds' lines and the twistings of the ornamentation intertwine, so that we see the abstract decoration growing out of the naturalistic, in the same way as we see it growing out of the letters. Abstract ornamentation was also widely employed as entirely independent decoration in manuscripts, especially on the first and last pages of a book and in the title. There are Qur'ānic manuscripts from as early as the eighth century in which sūra headings are enclosed in a frame with the Kufic script executed in gold, surrounded by tracery, twisting lines, and geometrical patterns. Sometimes the rectangular frame will be finished off on one side with a leaf-shaped pattern outside the frame. The predominant colors, apart from gold, are blue, red, green, and brown. Similar ornamentation is used in the titles of secular books.[3]

Apart from the survivals of Egyptian book painting already mentioned, no miniatures have come down to us from the period before about 1200. Diverse evidence from the very important intermediate period shows that painting had not died out. There are the magnificent fresco paintings with which the caliph al-Walīd had his desert palace east of the Dead Sea decorated shortly after 700;[a] these contain representations of human beings. The quite astonishing murals[b] discovered at the Umayyad mosque in Damascus shortly before 1930, depicting groups of trees and buildings (and thus not transgressing the ban on pictures) date from the same period. This tradition continued, inasmuch as we know that in the ninth century al-Muʿtaṣim and al-Mutawakkil embellished their palaces in Sāmarrā with paintings. It is highly remarkable that the latter caliph, who made a name as an uncompromising

[3] On this ancient art see especially the first few pages of the work by Grohmann and Arnold cited in the previous note.

[a] It is not known for certain whether it was indeed al-Walīd I who built Qusair ʿAmra. The building is a combination of a bath and a hunting box rather than a palace.

[b] These are, in fact, wall mosaics.

champion of orthodoxy, allowed himself to be portrayed on coins that are still in existence; so did al-Muqtadir (908-932).

Abundant evidence that painting flourished is furnished by ceramic art, which developed with notable brilliance in Islam and whose painted decoration, also bearing representations of living beings, we also know from the ninth century. The literature tells us that in 915 or 916, the historian al-Masʿūdī saw in Iṣṭakhr in Persia a book of Persian history containing portraits of twenty-seven Sasanian Persian kings.[4] In Egypt, where the fine arts took on a new lease of life under the Fāṭimid caliphs, we hear of painters, including one from Iraq, Ibn ʿAzīz, working under al-Mustanṣir's *wazīr*, al-Yāzūrī. There is also the information cited above about Ibn al-Bawwāb, to the effect that he first made paintings in houses and later illuminated books before becoming a calligrapher. This means that the tradition did stay alive, even if we cannot trace its path.

Sundry manuscripts with miniatures ascribed to the Baghdad or the Iraqi school have survived from the twelfth and thirteenth centuries.[c] They include astronomical and medical tracts such as translations of Dioscorides and Galen, and animal fables originating from India but translated into Arabic under the names of Kalīla and Dimna. A copy of al-Ḥarīrī's *Maqāmāt* with paintings by Yaḥyā ibn Maḥmūd dates from 1237. In the first of these there are a number of pictures of doctors and other learned men, in the second pictures of animals in the most diverse positions, but always very lifelike. In al-Ḥarīrī's book, which recounts the experiences of a vagabond, Abū Zayd, among all classes of the populace, there are a number of descriptions of the life of people in Islamic countries, and these have provided material for many book illustrators. The representations of human beings in the Iraqi works are very reminiscent of the Hellenistic-Byzantine style, insofar as the latter is known from such sources as oriental

[4] *Kitāb al-tanbīh wa'l-ishrāf*, edited by de Goeje, p. 106.

[c] The term "Iraqi school" subsumes two separate traditions: the school of Baghdad and that of Mosul.

Christian books; facial types and costumes are the same. Persons who are intended to be shown more prominently are picked out with a gold halo.[d]

However, miniature art enjoyed its real heyday in Persia and even further east. The books in which it was employed were largely Persian, but they belonged to the Muslim cultural circle, and they are included with the Islamic book as elements of the literature of the common culture. Innovations were introduced through the Mongols. These warlike people, who rampaged through Asia, crowned their career of devastation by capturing Baghdad and executing the caliph and his entire family, whereupon the former chief city of the world became relegated to the status of a provincial town of little importance. But afterwards the Mongol dynasties were responsible for a boom in the fields of architecture and handicrafts, as well as in book production.

The Manichaeans undoubtedly had a great impact on the history of Persian painting. They played an important role in Persia and Iraq in the early centuries of Islam, and for a long time during the era of violent controversy they were the heretics par excellence, for their dualism and their denial of the world conflicted with the chief dogmas of the new religion. A great persecution was launched against them, in the course of which many of them were slain while others fled to Turkestan. But in Persia the fame of their founder, "Mani the Painter," lived on, and his adherents made much use of pictorial art, especially in books. Mani's portrait and fourteen sacks of books were burned in Baghdad in 923, and in the ashes gold and silver were found.[5] This art is known to us from miniatures and frescoes of the eighth and ninth centuries found in East Turkestan. There is a certain affinity between it and the Iraqi school, which suggests that Manichaean Per-

[d] In fact, the halo is used much more indiscriminately in Iraqi painting than Pedersen suggests.

[5] A. Mez, *Die Renaissance des Islâms* (Heidelberg, 1922), p. 167, after a manuscript by Ibn al-Jauzī, the title of which he does not give.

sian painting was already an influence upon earlier Muslim book painting.

The mighty empire of the Mongols had its chief city in China, and the new efflorescence of Muslim art is due in part to inspiration from that country. The new elements from the east were absorbed without any break in the continuity of the history of Muslim painting. Alongside the traditional representations of animals we now find animals of a Chinese type, as for example in a collection accompanying Ibn Bukhtīshū's animal fables of 1295.[e] The Chinese dragon with its fantastic wings and protuberances is interpreted anew by Persian painters, as is also the bird with the long tail extending right across the heavens. Following the Chinese model, the landscape displays a stereotyped character, with serried ranks of rounded hills and no perspective of atmosphere; the Chinese sky,[f] *tai*, became a favorite theme, represented very delicately as a rippling, waving ribbon that becomes a purely conventional manifestation of a universal natural phenomenon. The people are represented as Mongol types, both on pottery and in books, with plump faces and almond eyes. Sacred individuals are no longer picked out with a round halo but with a ring of flame rising to a point in the Chinese and central Asian fashion. Silver is now used to a large extent instead of gold.

Fourteenth-century manuscripts of Rashīd al-Dīn's history of the Mongols in London and Paris contain a quantity of miniatures in the Sino-Persian style illustrating Mongol princely life.[g] One picture serviceable to Shi'ī propaganda shows the Prophet acknowledging ʿAlī as Imām. Throughout this period, the ancient Persian tradition is still to be discerned. The hunting scenes and pictures of the king sitting in a garden

[e] The latest reading of the colophon yields the date 690/1290.

[f] Pedersen is referring to cloud forms.

[g] The "London" manuscript was formerly in the possession of the Royal Asiatic Society, London; now it is in a private collection. For Paris read Edinburgh. Although there are undeniably Chinese elements in the paintings produced under the patronage of Rashīd al-Dīn, "Sino-Persian" is too simplified a description of such paintings and has no currency today.

surrounded by musicians have Sasanian forerunners that are still partly to be traced back to the Assyrians. The Sasanian King Bahrām Gūr is often represented on foot[h] shooting an arrow at an animal that is scratching itself behind the ear with its rear paw, so that he fixes the foot and the ear together. The same picture is found on Sasanian silver plates, and it was painted on a wall of the palace of al-Khawarnaq at Ḥīra.

Under Tīmūr, who acquired the power of the early Mongol rulers, Samarqand became a new cultural center, in which around 1400 numbers of artists and craftsmen were concentrated. They raised magnificent buildings and ushered in a new golden age of book production, with great libraries being established in Samarqand and Bukhārā. Tīmūr's son Shāh Rukh (1404-1447) made Harāt his capital. Under him, Chinese influence increased, and he showed a particular interest in painting. His son Baisunghur, who died before his father at the age of thirty-six, founded a library at Harāt in which he employed forty artists, calligraphers, and painters toiling at works for the library. He himself was a calligrapher and painter. One of the works produced under his aegis was the Persian national epic, the *Shāhnāma*, by Firdausī.[i] From this circle there emerged a special Persian style that was to become important to the developing Persian national sentiment.[j]

One work dating from this period is the *Miʿrājnāma*, "The Book of the Ascension," of 1436, now in Paris, which contains a picture representing the Prophet with Gabriel at the gates of Paradise.[k] Even if pictorial art was not allowed to touch the Qur'ān, it was nevertheless put at the service of

[h] This is an error; the standard iconography shows him on horseback.

[i] The *Shāhnāma* had been illustrated many times before this period. The copy in question, which is dated 1430 and is in the Gulistan Palace Library, is one of a series of luxury editions of Baisunghur's favorite texts.

[j] This was only one of several styles current in this period. Whether it had any precise relationship to Persian national sentiment remains to be demonstrated.

[k] This is, in fact, only one of many pictures in this manuscript that depict the Prophet; see M.-R. Seguy, *The Miraculous Journey of Mahomet* (London, 1977).

religious feeling in the predilection for illustrating Persian mystical poetic works that described the soul's relationship to God as a relationship between two lovers. Accordingly, we find a succession of variations on themes such as Yūsuf and Zulaykhā, Majnūn and Laylā, Khusrau and Shīrīn; and we may likewise see among the illustrations of mystical literature pictures of the ascension of the Prophet through the spheres on his steed Burāq. In addition, there were the works of Persian national history, Firdausī first and foremost, but also Rashīd al-Dīn and the Arabic writer al-Ṭabarī.

The most beautiful development of the unique Persian style was achieved by Bihzād, whose works are distinguished by their fine brushwork, by their grace of line and composition, and by their soft, delicate colors. The pictures speak clearly, but like other Persian paintings they lack perspective and modeling. Bihzād, who lived around 1500,[l] served various rulers with his art. About ten manuscripts with his miniatures are known, and a number of independent miniatures, as well, first seen as a group at the Persian exhibition in London in 1931. One of Bihzād's masterpieces is a *darwīsh* from Baghdad.[m] He enjoys particular fame for his illustrations of Tīmūr's history, in which he portrays cavalry charges and assaults on fortresses, the prince's receptions, the building of mosques, and other peaceful pursuits. He found a more realistic form for representing landscapes than the wavy Chinese lines of the previous period,[n] and he loved to paint gardens in bloom. Bihzād was buried at Tabrīz. He left behind him a school of skillful painters working under the national dynasty of the Ṣafawids.

There were thus several prominent painters working at the court of Shāh Tahmāsp (1524-1576); Sulṭān Muḥammad and Āqā Mīrak were among these. Two specially celebrated items are the splendid copy of the *Shāhnāma*, with 285 miniatures,

[l] It is generally believed that he was born about 1450; he died in 1525.

[m] This piece is no longer regarded as the work of the master.

[n] This is a somewhat puzzling and certainly inaccurate description of earlier styles of landscape painting in Persian book illustration.

in the possession of Edmund Rothschild,[o] and Nizāmī's Khamsa, in the British Library. The illustrations in the *Shāhnāma* are a glorification of the Ṣafawid court, which was also depicted through the medium of sundry portraits. Traditional hunting scenes and carousals beneath trees flourishing in the Persian landscape were painted, as well. The shāh himself was a painter, a pupil of Sulṭān Muḥammad, and sought out the company of painters.

Persian art never again reached the height to which Bihzād and his school elevated it, but a prominent painter, Riḍā-yi ʿAbbāsī, was still working under Shāh ʿAbbās (1587-1629) and enjoying the favor of the court, for a time, at any rate. He illustrated Nizāmī's "Khusrau and Shīrīn." After his time, European influence began to make itself felt, and the Persian style declined.[p] The relationship of the latter to the true Islamic book had, in fact, been gradually becoming looser and looser as Persian national sentiment became a more independent phenomenon.

The same applies to an even greater extent to India, where the descendants of the Mughal dynasty of the Tīmūrids became the creators of a new Muslim cultural type—evolved in conjunction with the Mongol-Persian one—based in Delhi as its chief city. Persian painting emerged here in a new guise. King Akbar (1556-1605),[q] particularly, took an interest in books and painting. He is said to have had a library of 24,000 volumes, and had more than a hundred painters living at his court. The king, who was intensely interested in philosophy, and who devised a hybrid religion of his own based on Islam, was himself a painter and a transcriber of books.[r] Many of the Indian miniatures consist of portraits, mostly of princes and their associates. The poses are quite stereotyped, but the

[o] Now known as the "Houghton Shāhnāma" after the owner of most of its dispersed paintings. The largest collection of these paintings in the public domain is the group of seventy-eight in the Metropolitan Museum of Art.

[p] This trend was already well marked in the lifetime of Riḍā-yi ʿAbbāsī.

[q] He is usually known as Emperor.

[r] This latter statement is inaccurate; Akbar was illiterate.

facial features are lifelife and well characterized. There are splendid depictions of animals, especially elephants and birds, and of lush landscapes with trees, flowers, and fruit. Court art also throve under Akbar's successors. Jahāngīr and Shāh Jahān, but the European influence now began to make itself felt. Under Awrangzīb (1659-1707), however, a ban on pictures was suddenly enforced, and after that there was only a brief revival of Indo-Muslim book painting. The Indian paintings have grander and more sweeping lines than does the delicate and elegant Persian art, and even if their importance to actual Islamic book production was only slight, they did nevertheless make an interesting final contribution to Muslim art, which had its origin in the Islamic book.[s]

The flair for book painting seems to diminish the farther west one travels in Islam. North Africa made no contribution, and in Egypt the art vanished when Saladin put an end to the supremacy of the Fāṭimids and strict orthodoxy was introduced.[t] Cairo under the Mamlūks enjoyed a new halcyon age in architecture and handicrafts, but painting did not revive. The Ottoman Turks, who established the last major Muslim empire, lacked the artistic feeling of their eastern kinsfolk. There was a brief period beginning in the closing years of the sixteenth century when Persian painters came to Constantinople, and these were responsible for Sultan Murād III's magnificent album of 1572, now in Vienna. Turkish painters did make their appearance, but their Persian teachers belonged to an era already on the brink of decline, and the European influence was now making itself strongly felt. Sultan Muḥammad II (1451-1481) was interested in Italian painting, and six Italian painters were in his service for a time; one of these was Gentile Bellini, who in the course of a year painted a

[s] Pedersen is not suggesting, of course, that book painting was the original inspiration of Islamic art. He means that Indian painting is relevant to Islamic painting.

[t] These statements are inaccurate and should be modified by references to the later chapters of R. Ettinghausen, *Arab Painting* (Geneva, 1962), and to J. D. Haldane, *Mamluk Painting* (Warminster, 1978).

large number of pictures and also trained a Turkish pupil. *Subḥat al-akhbār*, a work containing genealogical tables of the Ottoman princes, was furnished with a number of pictures, partly painted from the imagination. Apart from these not very significant contributions to pictorial art, which were only partially connected with books, the attitude of the Turks to book painting was negative, inasmuch as they generally maintained an orthodox position of fanatical hostility to pictures,[u] so lending an impetus to such hostility in the Muslim world at large. This has sometimes manifested itself in the rough treatment of ancient illuminated manuscripts, there being examples where human heads are pasted over with paper or even cut out.[v] There has been no revival of the ancient art in modern times.

[u] This statement is seriously inaccurate, especially since the most extensive cycle of religious paintings in Islamic art is in an Ottoman work, the seventeenth-century *Siyar al-Nabī*. For a conspectus of Ottoman painting, see the two volumes by Stchoukine listed in the bibliography.

[v] Such defacement has been practiced quite generally in the Islamic world over the centuries.

EIGHT

Bookbinding

WRITINGS ON papyrus sheets took the form of long strips, which were rolled up for storage. Parchment writings in roll form exist too, but there is no evidence in the Muslim tradition of book rolls having been used in ancient times.[1] Nevertheless, in the Heidelberg papyrus collection there is in fact an Arabic book roll, 183 cm in length, of the mid-ninth century.[2] Qur'āns in roll form appeared occasionally in very much later times. This form of book is somewhat rare in Islamic literature, however, and is something of a curiosity in subsequent ages. The general book form is the codex, which was common in Graeco-Roman literature, when Islamic literature was in its early stages. Once paper was introduced, the codex form was the only natural one.

The finished book is called by the Arabs *muṣḥaf,* a word formed from *ṣaḥīfa,* "sheet," plural *ṣuḥuf.* The word is applied especially to copies of the Qur'ān. The correct Arabic form would be *maṣḥaf,* which does sometimes occur, but the form in general use, like many other words connected with religion, was already transferred into Arabic from Abyssinian (Ethi opic) in the early days of Islam, and there is also an Arabic tradition to the effect that the Arabs learned how to use the

[1] A. Sprenger, *Das Leben und die Lehre des Mohammad* III (Berlin, 1865), pp. xl f., admittedly does mention a copy of the Qur'ān by Zayd ibn Thābit in the form of a book-roll, but the authority for this is uncertain. A tradition in al-Suyūṭī's *Itqān* (Cairo, 1343/1925) I, 59, may be so interpreted, however. It is to the effect that Zayd wrote the Qur'ān "on one sheet" during the caliphate of ʿUmar.

[2] Arnold and Grohmann, *The Islamic Book* English ed. p. 30; German ed. p. 36 and note 121.

codex form from the Abyssinians.[3] This form requires a mounting to hold the pages or sheets together, and in the early days the Qur'ān is supposed to have been held together between two wooden boards. A true book cover developed rapidly from this, the sheets being joined together and united with the wooden boards by means of a spine connecting them. During the controversy over whether material copies of the Qur'ān could be called God's eternal and uncreated word, it was said that what was between "the two covers" (*al-lawḥāni* or *al-daffatāni*) was God's word.[4]

The production of the binding was one part of the bookmaker's art that a *warrāq* had to be able to undertake. From the episode of Ibn al-Bawwāb and Bahā' al-Daula we have learned how Ibn al-Bawwāb, the celebrated calligrapher, tore off an old binding and used it to bind writings of his own. It was a black binding, and is said to have been fashioned after the style of al-Sukkarī. Just as there were types of script named after individual masters, so there were types of bookbinding, as well.

It is natural that different specialties should gradually have emerged in the book business. We hear of the trades of calligrapher (*khaṭṭāṭ*), painter (*muṣawwir*), sketcher (*ṭarrāḥ*)—that is, of ornaments, gilder (*mudhahhib*), cutter (*qāṭi'*), and bookbinder (*mujallid*). The cutter treated the sheets, and probably also helped with the processing of leather. The situation is not precisely known, however. Binding became a specialty

[3] Ibid., p. 30 (English); p. 35 (German).

[4] On Muslim bookbinding, see F. Sarre, *Islamische Bucheinbände* (Berlin, 1923), *Buchkunst des Orients*, vol. I; E. Gratzl, *Islamische Bucheinbände des 14. bis 19. Jahrhunderts* (Leipzig, 1924); M. Aga-Oglu, *Persian Bookbindings of the Fifteenth Century* (Ann Arbor, 1935). These works contain reproductions with descriptive text. Gratzl's book contains a bibliography of tracts from earlier times, including notably a series of works by P. Adam. Studies of bookbinding are to be found also in the above-cited work by Arnold and Grohmann, English ed. pp. 30-57, 98-100, German ed. pp. 35-68, 114-17, and also in Gratzl's and Sarre's works, with excellent reproductions. A brief résumé is given by C. Steinbrucker: "Islamische Bucheinbände," in *Zeitschrift der deutschen morgenländischen Gesellschaft* 84 (1930), 69-73.

at an early stage. Ibn al-Nadīm was able to cite the name of the bookbinder who worked in al-Ma'mūn's library at the beginning of the ninth century, namely, Ibn Abi 'l-Ḥarīsh, and he also gives the names of several other prominent bookbinders.[5]

Al-Maqdisī, born in Jerusalem (*Bayt al-Maqdis*), a contemporary of Ibn al-Nadīm and one of Islam's great travelers, discloses at one point in his account of the Islamic empire that he was a skillful bookbinder. He relates that during his sojourn in the Yemen he was sent a Qur'ān by the amīr for binding; he was offered two dīnārs, a very large sum, to execute the commission.[6] The Yamanīs prized handsome bindings very highly, he says. He furnishes technical information on the subject: flour paste was employed in the Yemen for gluing the sheets together and for the inside lining of the covers, whereas in Palestine he was accustomed to use asphodel glue.

Reports of interest in fine bookbindings emanate from various parts of the empire; in Persia this interest was in part a legacy from the Manichaeans. The mystic al-Ḥallāj, who—like all true mystics—declared himself to be one with God and who was executed in 922, had many disciples, and we are told that when arrested some of them had in their possession books of Chinese paper, written in gold, bound in fine leather with satin and silk on the inside of the binding.[7] And al-Maqrīzī speaks of the elegant bindings in the library of the Fāṭimids in Cairo, which were scattered to the winds before and after its conquest by Saladin; some of them lay in a great heap outside the town, and the costly bindings were used to sole the shoes of the Turkish soldiers.[8] Virtually none of these ancient bookbindings have survived, however, and

[5] *Fihrist*, p. 15 lines 2f.

[6] *Aḥsan al-taqāsīm fī ma'rifat al-aqālīm*, edited by M. J. de Goeje (Leiden, 1873), p. 100.

[7] Miskawayh, *Tajārib al-umam* I (Cairo, 1334/1918), 79; 'Arīb, *Ṣila*, edited by M. J. de Goeje (Leiden, 1897), p. 90. Cf. Mez, *Die Renaissance des Islâms*, pp. 167, 288.

[8] Al-Maqrīzī, *Khiṭaṭ* II, 254.

we lack a technical description of this ancient art, which certainly must have had close affinities with the Greek and Coptic techniques. Manuscript sources, however, do mention books on book manufacture, and especially on binding, but these date from a later age. The loose spine, universally used in Europe for the last few centuries, was not employed, of course, and because of the special methods of the Muslims, the spine of the cover is not divided by the thick transverse bands that are a feature of European bookbinding. The leather spine is glued directly on to the sheets and bears no ornamentation.[9]

The oldest surviving Muslim book cover—really only a fragment—is not of leather but of cedar wood. It dates from the Ṭulūnid period (ninth century) in Egypt, and is now in the Museum für islamische Kunst in Berlin. The wood is inlaid with a mosaic of ivory, bone, and multicolored wood. There is a trimming of zigzag lines along the edge, whereas the middle is covered with a row of arcading; the arches are filled with patterned mosaic and are separated by columnar ivory figures. This motif recurs in Ṭūlūnid architecture and in contemporary Qur'ānic ornamentation.[a] The spine of the cover is overlaid with bone mosaic in geometric patterns.[10]

This cover is unique, both in its dating, since no other book covers from the early centuries of Islamic history have come down to us, and in the material of which it is made, since it was only seldom that covers exclusively of wood were used. Normally wood covered with leather was employed in early

[9] A seventeenth-century Arabic work on bookbinding, by Abu'l-ʿAbbās al-Sufyānī, was published by P. Ricard, 2nd ed. (Paris, 1925), according to Arnold and Grohmann, *The Islamic Book*, note 131. Other Arabic books on the topic of the same period are mentioned by Maʿlūf in an article in the Arabic *Majallat al-majmaʿ al-ʿilmi al-ʿarabi, Dimashq* 3 (1923), 145. The sheets are bound together by means of transverse cords over the spine; see P. Adam, *Der Bucheinband* (Leipzig, 1890), pp. 32f. On the glued "fixed spine" see *ibid.*, p. 93.

[a] The motif of columnar figures alternating with the arches of an arcade is found neither in Ṭūlūnid architecture nor in Qur'ānic ornament. Arcading, however, is a common Ṭūlūnid feature.

[10] Sarre, Taf. I and Abb. 1; repeated in my *Islams Kultur*, p. 125.

times; subsequently the wooden board was replaced by pasteboard, which was made up by pasting together a number of sheets, first of papyrus and later of paper. Some covers have survived on Coptic books of the sixth and subsequent centuries. The leather is embellished in various ways: with ornamental leather strips sewn on and patterns rubbed or scratched in, or sometimes with tooling, inlays of leather, or braiding. A similar technique was used on books in Khocho, in eastern Turkestan, from the sixth to the ninth centuries, which suggests that the Egyptian method was carried eastward either by Christendom or by Manichaeism.[b] There are also a few ninth-century Qur'āns in the Cairo Library with wooden covers overlaid with brown leather adorned with simple ornamentation.

Not until the age of Mamlūk rule in Egypt and Syria (1250-1517), and then not really until the fourteenth century, do we have an abundance of book covers that have been sufficiently studied for particular types to be distinguished. The customary binding is not merely "whole leather" covering the spine and both sides; it is common practice in Muslim bookbinding for the leather on the back cover of the book (which corresponds to the front cover of our books) to extend over the side to form a flap covering the fore-edge of the book, and it is folded inward under the front page (the back page of our books) of the volume, where it rests. The entire book is thus protected, except for the two short edges at top and bottom.

The Egyptian covers from the Mamlūk period that have been published and described are of a type with close affinities to the Coptic ones.[11] The surface of the earlier examples is divided by lines so as to form a large rectangle filling the inner part of the board, and is surrounded by one or more borders; a border may in its turn be divided up into smaller rectangles by means of transverse lines. Within these rectangles the surface is filled with geometric patterns composed of lines and

[b] This technique could equally well be a Central Asian invention.

[11] Sarre, Taf. II-IV and Abb. 2; Gratzl, Taf. VII.

dots. A border may often contain Qur'ānic texts in ornamental script, at least in the case of Qur'āns. The pattern may be governed by twining figures instead of straight lines. The leather is brown, but part of the pattern may be gilded or colored in blue, possibly in conjunction with pinking of the leather. The pattern is produced by blind tooling, except for the gilt and blue parts; this is done with a wheel called a fillet or roll and small individual stamps. On the flap there are sometimes quite free drawings of arabesques that may turn into leaves.

Around 1500 another type of pattern emerges, in which the surface, instead of being entirely filled, is dominated by a central medallion. There may be the one type on the front and the other on the back cover of the book. The medallion may be almond-shaped, ending in points above and below filled with fine tracery in gold and blue. The remainder of the surface is without ornamentation apart from the border and small triangular segments at the corners.[12] Both the medallion and the rest of the surface may also be covered with tendrils and arabesques, whereas the borders are filled with other embellishments.[13] The medallion may be an oval formed around a circle and surrounded by small circular arcs running out into points above and below, while the corners contain fragmentary repetitions of the same pattern.[14] The medallion can also be completely circular, enclosed by rounded lines that continue above and below into arabesques extending to the border, where they meet the corner arabesques. On the binding being described here the surface of the boards is covered with a stamped latticework pattern interspersed with dots in blind tooling or gold. Between the lines of the arabesques, the leather is scored out and blue silk is pasted in to replace it.[15] This pattern may again be extended to cover most of the surface through enlargement of the medallion and the corner

[12] Sarre, Taf. V.

[13] Gratzl, Taf. X.

[14] Sarre, Taf. VI.

[15] Sarre, Taf. VII; cf. Gratzl, Taf. VIII and IX.

ornamentation so that the uncovered part of the surface comes to form a narrow figure composed of straight and curved lines. Or the medallion may fill most of the surface, which is covered both inside and outside the medallion by broad arabesques that turn into flowers and leaves.[16]

The fourteenth- and fifteenth-century Maghribi (North African) bindings that have been studied are closely allied to the Egyptian type, but use less gilding.[17] The inner rectangle of the surface of a Qur'ān binding of 1305 is covered with a geometric pattern of straight lines, in which some of the figures are filled with gilt dots. On the flap there is a fragment of the same pattern. The commonest pattern is a broad border and a circular ornament, possibly with embellishments in the middle of the rectangular or square inner surface thus formed, and further ornamentation at the corners of the rectangle.

South Arabia, where an interest in bookbinding was lauded by al-Maqdisī in the tenth century, retained this interest, as may be seen from some bindings of the fifteenth and early sixteenth centuries. They are evidence of a fine handicraft tradition, and reveal close affinities with the Egyptian and North African types discussed above.[18] Up to the present, however, only a few examples have been studied and published; the literature is Zaydī, that is, books emanating from an ʿAlid group whose present-day representatives still hold sway in the Yemen. The bindings in question are of brown leather on pasteboard. There are several borders occupying a considerable space in aggregate, so that only a relatively small inner rectangle remains. The borders are formed of small stamps, sometimes comprising lines of script containing a blessing. The medallion in the middle is usually a figure composed of circles or circular bands, and embellished with rosettes. Gilding is not used.

[16] Sarre, Taf. IX and X.
[17] Gratzl, Taf. I-VI.
[18] Gratzl, pp. 15-20 and Taf. XI-XIV.

In the types discussed so far, the insides of the bindings[19] are sometimes covered with leather, with or without ornamentation, generally in the form of arabesques, or with blue silk. In Egypt bookbindings have also been found whose inner sides—as in Coptic books—were covered by parchment with ornamentation painted on; paper was used in the same way later. The fragments so far discovered, dating from the tenth and eleventh centuries, show a vast profusion of both patterns and colors. Patterns are applied to these endpapers by painting or stamping. Woodcuts were also used, the pattern being carved on wood blocks and then impressed on the paper. Sometimes the same technique was used with paper, as we have noted in the case of leather, namely, cutting out and inlaying paper in other colors. Some of these carry bands of Kufic script.

The strides made in the art of book production, especially painting, in the eastern lands under Tīmūr and his successors benefited bookbinding, as well. The latter shows a close affinity with western techniques, and it is possible that Tīmūr did, as is reported, bring Egyptian and Syrian bookbinders to his capital. No reliably dated binding has come down to us from the fourteenth century, but we do have some from the fifteenth. The binding of a manuscript produced in 1435 for Shāh Rukh is particularly sumptuous, containing over half a million blind and gold toolings; it has been calculated that it must have taken a couple of years for one man to perform this task.[20] During the Mongol period, incidentally, a technical advance was achieved in stamping when single stamps were supplemented by the introduction of metal stamping plates capable of decorating a large surface.[21] Later on, stamps of camel hide were used for low relief, instead of metal matrices. It was now possible to have matrices for the whole binding or for the medallion or other parts alone. The tech-

[19] Arnold and Grohmann, *The Islamic Book*, English ed. pp. 50ff., German ed. pp. 58ff.

[20] Ibid., English ed. p. 99; German ed. p. 116.

[21] Aga-Oglu, *Persian Bookbinding*, p. 6.

nique of applying different tones of gold was learned, and alongside the traditional brown leather of the West, red and sometimes green leather was used. Ornamentation assumed the free, light character of Persian design.

All the innovations in fifteenth-century painting produced by the Harāt school following the initiative of Baisunghur affected the decoration of bookbindings.[c] Landscapes with trees and animals in the Chinese style—the ribbon of sky and all the other features characteristic of the painting of the age—are to be found on bindings either as blind tooling or in gilt, and the inside cover is often filled with the familiar arabesques, whose tendrils terminate in animal heads. The front cover of a book of the poems of Farīd al-Dīn ʿAṭṭār, dated 1438, to be found in Istanbul,[22] has a fairly narrow border, the entire surface being covered by a painting of a landscape. Above can be seen the snaking ribbons of cloud, and between them large birds in flight. The landscape is filled with trees, whose foliage twines about over the surface without perspective; between them monkeys and deer are visible in various postures, while below are dragonlike creatures and a deer drinking. The inside cover is reminiscent of the bindings of western Islam, with an oval medallion in the center and ornamentation at the corners of the rectangle. The ornamentation consists of vine tendrils, which in the medallion grow out of a tree in which a pheasant is sitting. On each side of the tree an animal is standing; the border, too, is filled with designs of animals. It is evident that decoration in the new Sino-Persian style has been applied to an old Muslim pattern.

The binding of the *Mathnawī* of Jalāl al-Dīn al-Rūmī,[23] of 1446, has a small landscape with a tree, monkeys, a dragon, and various animals. There is a curious scene in which a man

[c] This is too broad a generalization. Bookbinding could not well reproduce either the exquisitely precise draftsmanship of the early Harāt school or its intense purity of color, and it avoided the recondite harmonies of compositions in which the artist orchestrated large groups of figures.

[22] Aga-Oglu, *Persian Bookbinding*, pp. 5f. and pl. I-III.

[23] Ibid., pl. IV-V.

is shown fighting a bear, a revival of an ancient Near Eastern motif that appears on another binding of 1450, now in Düsseldorf, representing a man fighting a Chinese lion.[d] Above and below the picture is an Arabic inscription invoking health, happiness, and long life.[e] On the inside we again see the traditional oval medallion, this time occupied by a pair of phoenixes, their wings flapping, against a background formed by a close pattern of vines with flowers and leaves. Along with these characteristic embellishments there are also purely decorative patterns, more intricate and with more elegant details than on the older bookbindings.

The novel style created by the Harāt school spread over the East and is represented in bindings from a number of Persian towns; it was continued in Persia in the sixteenth and seventeenth centuries under the national Persian dynasty of the Ṣafawids. The pattern is freer, inasmuch as the medallion and the corners are sometimes indicated only by light strokes embodied as a design in the decoration of the whole surface.[24] The delight of the Persians in color is revealed in the copious use of gold in different variations and of inlays of orange, green, blue, and wine red. The themes of the pictures are the same: landscapes, clouds, and animals interpreted under the inspiration of Chinese art.

A new element introduced into the bookbinding art during this period was lacquered binding.[f] Here again we have a Chinese technique that was transplanted to Persia and there found employment in bookbinding. The oldest examples date from the late Tīmūrid period, shortly prior to 1500. The method consists of covering the pasteboard binding with chalk sealed by several layers of transparent lacquer. One of the

[d] The motif of a man fighting a *k'i-lin* or a dragon is a standard one in Safawid and Ottoman art, and was indeed a kind of exercise.

[e] Presumably to the owner.

[24] Sarre, Taf. XI, XIII, XVI; Gratzl, Taf. XV, XVI.

[f] For the latest comprehensive report on early lacquer in Iran, see the proceedings of the Percival David Colloquium held in London in 1981 (forthcoming).

bottom layers is painted with water colors, and the top one with gold and silver and powdered mother-of-pearl. Only the spine is of leather. One of the oldest examples, dated 1483 and to be found in Istanbul,[25] has a painted pattern of gold tendrils and leaves above the black lacquer. The medallion, corners, and inner border are stamped with another pattern of tendrils and completely covered with gold. These are the two outer covers. The inner covers are in brown leather, the top one with its inner rectangle filled with trees and animals, and with a border of tendrils and ducks in flight, all carved on a blue-painted ground, while the inner side of the back cover is filled with arabesques, with special decoration of the central medallion and corners; all this too is carved on a blue and gold background.

Lacquer bindings were particularly widespread in Persia under the Ṣafawids. One example is a binding of 1557 with a brownish-red lacquered background.[26] One of the outer covers has a small border with vine tendrils and rosettes in gold. The large area inside the border is filled by a landscape of trees, bushes, and flowers. Birds fly overhead between the fluttering ribbons of cloud. Hares and antelopes chased by a panther are running between the trees. The beasts are in gray and yellowish shades; the lines of trees and plants are touched up in gold. The ground, the rocks, and a crag are covered with powdered mother-of-pearl, while the water flowing from the crag is painted in silver, which is now black with age. The other outer cover has a similar border and also represents a landscape in which a lion is pouncing on an antelope while other beasts take to flight; underneath, a lion lies watching two herons standing at the edge of a reed-covered stretch of water. Other lacquered bindings have representations of scenes with people, sometimes court scenes with musicians as we know them from miniatures. Bookbinding with lacquered covers survived in Persia right down to the early nineteenth

[25] Aga-Oglu, *Persian Bookbinding*, p. 13, pl. X-XII.

[26] Sarre, p. 19, Taf. XXV-XXVI.

century.[g] By then the ornamentation consisted chiefly of naturalistic representations of flowers, and the bright sheen of the finish evidences the decline of the art.[27]

There was an offshoot of the Persian bookbinding art in Turkey, where from about 1500 Persian bookbinders settled in the main towns and took native apprentices who, however, lacked the artistic sense of their masters. The published examples from the eighteenth and early nineteenth centuries display the old pattern with an oval medallion at the center of a rectangle. The medallion and two accompanying small figures are filled with inscriptions in gold on a mottled red lacquered ground sprinkled with gold. The borders are filled with large naturalistic flowers or with a Qur'ānic inscription.[28] One binding is completely covered with flowers and vine tendrils on a yellowish background.[29]

Despite the innovations that have been introduced over the centuries, bookbinding has remained fundamentally the same in type. The flap folded over the fore-edge still persists, and right down to the most recent times the ornamentation retains the borders dividing the surface of the cover and the pattern with the medallion at the center of the inner rectangle. It should be remembered, however, that the bindings considered so far have been the deluxe ones. The ordinary, everyday bindings, of course, did not have the costly decoration of those described here.

In our day bookbinding has gone the way of all the other handicraft arts of Islam; mere pathetic remnants of its former glory have survived.

[g] In fact, the lacquered book cover flourished in Iran throughout the nineteenth century.

[27] See for example Gratzl, Taf. XXIII.

[28] Sarre, Taf. XXXIV and XXXV.

[29] Sarre, Taf. XXXVI.

NINE

Libraries

THE UNEXAMPLED flowering of the art of book production in Islam was due in no small degree to the ardent interest taken in books by men of wealth. Literature enjoyed such universal esteem that it was natural for those who could afford it to take some share in it and work for its advancement. We have already seen how important princes were to authors, and a number of them founded considerable libraries. Al-Qalqashandī says that there were three great libraries in Islam: the ʿAbbāsid one in Baghdad, the Fāṭimid one in Cairo, and the Spanish Umayyad one in Córdoba.[1]

The library of the ʿAbbāsids in Baghdad came into being in conjunction with the academy, *bayt al-ḥikma*, "the house of wisdom," or *dār al-ʿilm*, "the abode of learning," established by the caliph al-Maʾmūn (813-833) or possibly even earlier by his father Hārūn al-Rashīd (789-809). The first task of the academy was to procure translations of books from "the ancient sciences," namely, Hellenistic philosophy and natural science. Ibn al-Nadīm records[2] that al-Maʾmūn saw in a dream a man of pale and ruddy complexion, his forehead broad, his eyebrows meeting, bald of pate, blue of eye, dignified of bearing, seated on a throne. It was Aristotle, and the conversation that passed between them in the dream inspired al-Maʾmūn to promote the translation of Greek literature in

[1] On libraries, see F. Krenkow, and W. Heffening, "Kitābkhāna," *Encyclopedia of Islam* 1st ed., *s.v.*; Mez, *Die Renaissance des Islâms*, pp. 164ff.; O. Pinto, "The Libraries of the Arabs during the time of the Abbasids," in *Islamic Culture* 3 (1929), 211-43; J. Pedersen, "Some Aspects of the History of the Madrasa," in *Islamic Culture* 3 (1929), 525-37, and *idem*, section F5 of the article "Masdjid" in *Encyclopedia of Islam*, 1st ed.

[2] *Fihrist*, p. 243.

his academy, so that after correspondence with the Byzantine emperor he sent several men to the latter's domain, whence they returned with a number of Greek books for translation.

Al-Ma'mūn was not the first to establish a library of translations, however. A son of the Umayyad caliph Yazīd I, Khālid ibn Yazīd ibn Muʿāwiya (d. 704) is said to have preceded him,[3] and he said himself that in doing so he was seeking consolation for his disappointment at not having received the caliphate. The work of translation continued under the early ʿAbbāsids. Thus, we hear of Ptolemy's *Almagest* being translated on the initiative of the Barmakid Yaḥyā ibn Khālid, Hārūn al-Rashīd's tutor and his powerful minister for a time. We come to know through this occasion how the work of translation was carried out. First Yaḥyā had the work translated and interpreted by a number of scholars independently; but the resulting text was not satisfactory. Then he appointed two scholars—Salam, who is stated to have been director of the academy of science, was one of them—who went through the text with the translators, making corrections and improvements.[4] Other examples show that this system of using one or more translators and supervising editors was the general practice.

Al-Ma'mūn's contribution probably consisted of widening the scope of an activity already in progress. Three leading personages of the academy, namely, the above-mentioned Salam and his two colleagues Sahl ibn Hārūn and Saʿīd ibn Hārūn, are cited by name.[5] One of the many other associates was the distinguished Persian al-Khwārizmī, who numbered among his achievements the composition of various astronomical works, including astronomical tables, based upon Indian writings.[6]

[3] Ibid., pp. 242, lines 8ff., 354.

[4] Ibid., pp. 267f.

[5] Ibid., pp. 10 line 13; 120; 268 line 1; 305 lines 18f.

[6] A later version has been published by H. Suter, "Die astronomischen Tafeln des Muhammed ben Musa al-Khwārizmī," in *Kgl. Danske Videnskabernes Selskabs Skrifter*, 7 raekke, Hist. og filos. afd. III/I (Copenhagen, 1914), continuing work done by A. A. Bjørnebo and R. Besthorn.

Al-Ma'mūn was not alone in his support of this activity; it is reported, for example, that three brothers, sons of al-Munajjim, paid five hundred dīnārs a month to a group of translators.[7] Translations were much in demand at this time when Muslim literature was in process of being founded, but al-Ma'mūn's library was of course also supplied with other Arabic literature. We do not know its subsequent history; neither do we know to what extent it was accessible to others than the caliph himself and those to whom he specifically allowed admittance. It is recorded of a later caliph, al-Muʿtaḍid (892-902), that when he was planning the building of a new palace in Baghdad, he wanted an annex with residential and study accommodations for the leading personages of science and letters, so that they might be provided with board and lodging to free them for their studies.[8] The library needed for these studies may be supposed to have been the same as that with which al-Ma'mūn's name was associated, and naturally it was enlarged as time went on. When the great college (*madrasa*) known as *al-Madrasa al-Mustanṣirīya* was founded in 1234, some of the books from the caliph's library were transferred to it—some 80,000 volumes.[9]

It is upon the libraries of the Fāṭimids in Cairo that the greatest luster shines. The house of the Fāṭimids professed to be descended from the Prophet's daughter Fāṭima; thus, according to Shīʿī opinion, they had a claim to dominion over Islam. The sect whose leaders they were, a branch of the Ismāʿīlīs, became so widespread that they were able to establish an empire first in North Africa, then (967-1171), in Egypt, to which they gave a vigorous cultural impetus. They founded a completely new Cairo alongside the old, erecting there a magnificent palace and a mosque, al-Azhar, which has been a center of the Islamic world ever since. They fitted out libraries in the palace, and doubtless in the mosque as well.[10]

By the time of the second Fāṭimid ruler, al-ʿAzīz (975-996),

[7] *Fihrist*, p. 243 lines 14ff.

[8] Al-Maqrīzī, *Khiṭaṭ* IV, 192.

[9] Ibn al-Fuwaṭī, *al-Ḥawādith al-jāmiʿa*, p. 54 and the note.

[10] Al-Maqrīzī, *Khiṭaṭ* II, 253f.

the palace library had already grown enormously. On one occasion when al-Khalīl's *Kitāb al-ʿayn*, a dictionary by one of the earliest Arabian philologists, was asked for by the caliph, the librarian was able to bring him thirty-one copies, including an autographed one. He bought a copy of al-Ṭabarī's historical works for a hundred dīnārs, although there were already more than twenty, including one autograph copy. There were a hundred copies of another work of lexicography, Ibn Durayd's *Jamhara*. Altogether there were forty collections of books in the palace, that is, forty rooms filled with books; "the ancient sciences," namely, Hellenistic natural science and philosophy, were represented by 18,000 books. Al-ʿAzīz's librarian was ʿAlī ibn Muḥammad al-Shābushtī, author of a book on religious houses in Muslim lands.[11] He arranged and catalogued the books and read from them to the caliph, with whom he also conversed on literary subjects. It was by no means the case, of course, that the mighty took interest merely so that others might engage in literary pursuits; these were a part of their own interests. When there were so many copies of individual works, however, this does suggest that the library was open to a wide circle. But it has to be remembered that some works were procured because of the sumptuousness of their appointments, and also that in manuscript transmission each single copy was regarded as a separate edition of the book.

An innovation was introduced under al-Ḥākim (996-1021).[12] In an annex on the north side of the western half of the vast palace he established an academy, modeled on pre-Islamic institutions, and called, like Ma'mūn's in former times, *dār al-ʿilm* or *dār al-ḥikma*. The institution came under the jurisdiction of the government's head of propaganda (*dāʿī al-duʿāt*), which reveals the desire to use it as a means of attaching the people to the government and to the doctrines characterizing the sect it represented. But it was an institute for study with

[11] Ibn Khallikān, *Wafayāt al-aʿyān* I, 330.

[12] Al-Maqrīzī, *Khiṭaṭ* II, 334f.

a large library of its own, supplied in part from the resources of the palace library, and all branches of learning were represented there. The building was furnished with carpets on floors and walls, and as well as the books, there were paper, reed pens and ink at the disposal of the public. All and sundry might enter, and the institute was visited by different classes of the population wishing to read, to transcribe, and to be instructed. Curators, assistants, and messengers were employed at fixed wages, and scholars too were paid wages for pursuing their studies at the institute.

The budget of this institute amounted to 257 dīnārs a year, according to al-Maqrīzī. The fixed expenditures listed include: carpets from Abadān and elsewhere, 10 dīnārs; paper for transcribing, 90 dīnārs; librarian, 48 dīnārs; water, 12 dīnārs; servants, 15 dīnārs; paper, ink, and reed pens for the scholar in charge of them, 12 dīnārs; repairs of carpets, 1 dīnār; possible repairs of books and replacement of lost pages therein, 12 dīnārs; felt carpets for the winter, 5 dīnārs; other carpets for winter use, 4 dīnārs. The sums enumerated amount to a total of 209. The remainder probably went to additional expenses. Books were procured through transcription, but additions probably took the form of gifts from the caliph, as well. Bearing in mind the prices often paid for books, such as 100 dīnārs for al-Ṭabarī's history and 60 dīnārs for Ibn Durayd's *Jamhara*, the budget cited here does seem to be too modest for major book purchases. Similar libraries were established by al-Ḥākim at various other places such as al-Fusṭāṭ, Old Cairo.

The palace and academy libraries flourished during a succession of prosperous years preceding the reign of the Fāṭimid caliph al-Mustanṣir, when seven years of famine (1066-1072) resulted from the failure of the Nile to flood. During the appalling period of disintegration that now intervened, Turkish mercenary troops seized power from the feeble caliph, and they despoiled the palace of a quantity of its fantastic treasures as compensation for arrears of pay. Large numbers of books were lost during the episode, the soldiers taking them at a fraction of their worth. This happened in 1068, and affected all the books not in the inner rooms of the palace. It was a general, Nāṣir al-Daula, who was responsible for this act of plunder, but a *wazīr* was party to it. Maqrīzī's authority for the account of the affair personally saw twenty-five camels, loaded with books, brought to the residence of the *wazīr* al-Maghribī. He had taken them as settlement for 5,000 dīnārs, whereas according to expert opinion they were worth over 100,000; but they were stolen from him when Nāṣir al-Daula fled from Egypt, as also were books from the academy of science. Other quantities of books were stolen in Egyptian towns, the bindings used to sole the shoes of the soldiers, and the paper burned, while some were thrown in the water or carried off. A number of books were jettisoned in a great heap that the wind gradually filled up with sand so that it turned into a mound; it became known as "the book mound."[13]

The library was not totally destroyed, however, and in the following year it was restored and enlarged.[14] The academy became for a time an arena for religious and political contention, which seemed so dangerous to the *wazīr* al-Afḍal that he closed it in the year 1119. But after he was overthrown two years later, the academy was reestablished by his successor al-Ma'mūn in 1123, in a new building east of the palace. Thus, when Saladin came to power in Egypt in 1171 and brought the ascendancy of the Fāṭimids to an end, both the academy and the palace library were in excellent condition. But the academy, which of course was under Shīʿī influence, was closed, for now the heyday of the orthodox Sunnīs was really setting in. The wealth of the palace, including the library, was given away or sold. As usual, the figures quoted by Arabic authors vary widely, even when stating the size of the library at this time. Al-Maqrīzī gives three figures: 120,000,

[13] Ibid., II, 254.

[14] Ibid., II, 255f.; 313; 335ff.; cf. J. Pedersen, *Al-Azhar. Et Muhammedansk Universitet (Studier fra Sprog- og Oldtidsforskning, no. 124)* (Copenhagen, 1922), pp. 9f.

200,000, and 601,000 volumes; Abū Shāma says two million.[15] Both report that there were about 1,200 copies of al-Ṭabarī. All testimony agrees, at any rate, that it was one of the wonders of the world, a library without peer, embracing the entire span of Islamic learning.

Abū Shāma describes the auctioning of books. A Turkish auctioneer took the books in random lots of half a score each. One of the big purchasers was Saladin's learned *wazīr*, the bibliophile al-Qāḍī al-Fāḍil. Abū Shāma, citing several men by name as his sources, says that he went about buying by selecting all the books he wanted before the auction. Then he ripped the bindings off them and threw them into a receptacle (lit. tank) as though they were waste, so that no one paid any heed to them. Then when the auction day was over, he purchased his booty for a small sum. However that may be, the books were put to good use, for al-Qāḍī al-Fāḍil gave 100,000 volumes to the school he established, *al-madrasa al-fāḍilīya*.[16] They were subsequently lost, it is true; during a great famine in 1296 the students sold them to obtain bread. Another 100,000 volumes from the same celebrated library are said to have gone to the library of Qalā'ūn's hospital, which was built in 1284.[17] To what extent the manuscript libraries that have survived down to our own time are indirectly to the credit of the magnificent book collection of the Fāṭimids cannot, of course, be determined.

Perhaps the most important factor as far as posterity is concerned is that some members of the Fāṭimid house managed to flee to the Yemen, their descendants living there in tranquil obscurity until our own day, when a member of the family has appeared before the European public and has revealed to Orientalists that a large part of the vanished Fāṭimid literature is still preserved in the Yemen. The few items made public so far show that publication of these works will be of

[15] Al-Maqrīzī, *Khiṭaṭ* II, 253-255; Abū Shāmah, *Kitāb al-rauḍatain fī akhbār al-daulatain* I (Cairo, 1287/1870), 200 line 4.

[16] Al-Maqrīzī, *Khiṭaṭ* IV, 197f.

[17] Cf. my *Al-Azhar*.

the highest moment for our knowledge of the cultural history of Islam.

When the Fāṭimids made their entry into Egypt, there was a ruler in Córdoba, al-Ḥakam II (961-976), who occupied a prominent place among the scholars and bibliophile princes of Islam. He was a member of a dynasty that asserted its independence and laid claim to the caliphate, since it was a branch of the Umayyad family, Islam's first family of caliphs, which after the victory of the ʿAbbāsids had found in 756 an abode in the westernmost province of the empire. They founded a library, which attained its greatest growth under al-Ḥakam. He gathered scholars around him, and the chief mosque of Córdoba became a center of study. The library, which was in the palace in Córdoba, was under the management of a librarian, a eunuch named Bakīya. Copyists and bookbinders were employed, and al-Ḥakam had agents in every province who procured books for him by purchase and by transcription. Ibn Ḥazm records that Bakīya told him that the library catalogue of titles and authors' names covered forty-four quires of twenty pages each.[18] The wording of the account indicates that the library was not accessible to the general public. The splendor of the library was already dimmed under al-Ḥakam's son and successor Hishām, because the all-powerful national leader al-Manṣūr, concerned to please the orthodox religious scholars, allowed them to remove and burn those books in the library that were distasteful to them. The books involved were works of philosophy, astronomy, and so forth, namely, "the ancient sciences," the heritage of Hellenism that was always a thorn in the flesh of Sunnī orthodoxy. In 1011, when Córdoba was locked in battle with the Berbers, the minister Wāḍiḥ sold the major part of the library to obtain money for the war, and the rest was despoiled by the enemy.

Libraries continued to be established, however. They were a necessity to scholars and an adornment, at least in the eyes

[18] Identical in al-Maqqarī, *Nafḥ al-ṭīb* II, 180 and Ibn Khaldūn, *Kitab al-ʿibar* (Būlāq, 1284), IV, 146. See also R.P.A. Dozy, *Geschichte der Mauren in Spanien* II (Leipzig, 1874), 68f.; 198; 188.

of the powerful and wealthy. The petty Spanish princes who succeeded the Umayyads in 1031 also became celebrated for their libraries in Saragossa, Granada, Toledo, and elsewhere; scholars with considerable collections of books are named, as well. In Egypt the *wazīrs* had large libraries, too. Saladin's *wazīr* al-Qāḍī al-Fāḍil has already been mentioned; one of his predecessors, Yaʿqūb ibn Killīs, *wazīr* to the Fāṭimid caliph al-ʿAzīz, is said to have founded an academy for himself, on which he spent 1,000 dīnārs a month in payments to scholars, copyists, and bookbinders.[19]

Among those notables close to the ʿAbbāsid court there were several who had large libraries. Al-Mutawakkil's friend al-Fatḥ ibn Khāqān (d. 861), who is said by Ibn al-Nadīm to have been exceptionally wise and well-informed on literary matters, kept open house for men of science and letters.[20] His friend ʿAlī ibn Yaḥyā founded a library for him that was extolled for its size and splendor. This same ʿAlī, who had the nickname of al-Munajjim, "the astronomer," was himself a wealthy man, owning an estate with a palace in the vicinity of Baghdad. Here he established a large library specializing in the natural sciences, notably astronomy. He threw it open to all comers, received visits from the entire Islamic world, and entertained guests gratis when they came to study in his *khizānat al-ḥikma*, "treasure house of wisdom." It is recorded that the astronomer Abū Maʿshar came there from Khurāsān on pilgrimage to Mecca. He became so enthralled by his studies there that he abandoned his pilgrimage and even the Muslim religion.[21] This shows how difficult it was for Islam to assimilate "the ancient sciences," which played so large a role in the early libraries and still retained their importance among the Shīʿī.

During the perpetual contention that occupied the golden age of Islam, power fell into the hands of a succession of different families and parties, but we find among all of them

[19] Mez, *Die Renaissance des Islâms*, p. 169.
[20] *Fihrist*, p. 116; *Irshād* V, 459; VI, 116ff.
[21] *Irshād* V, 459, 467.

an interest in books and the founding of libraries. That ʿAbbāsid ministers who had risen through the public service were interested in libraries goes without saying. The fact that Ibn al-Furāt, who attained the rank of *wazīr* three times, left at his death in 924 a collection of books to a value of 2,000 dīnārs[22] scarcely merits being regarded as very impressive, considering that his appointment enabled him to acquire an income of many millions. The Būyids, a Persian house that exercised hegemony over Iraq and western Persia for over a hundred years (945-1055), while formally recognizing the ʿAbbāsid caliphs, themselves nourished Shīʿī sympathies. They also took into their service men capable of uniting political activity with an interest in books. From 940, the Būyid Rukn al-Daula, who ruled Rayy in western Persia, had in his service a *wazīr* named Ibn al-ʿAmīd, who was a celebrated scholar. The latter had a large library of which the historian Miskawayh was librarian.[23] Miskawayh tells of a Khurāsānī army that came to help in the struggle against the Byzantines but that, when its demands were not met by the government in Rayy, sacked the town (996). The *wazīr*'s residence was seriously ravaged, but he was concerned only for his book collection, which embraced all science and letters, and comprised altogether more than a hundred camel loads; its loss would have been irretrievable, but in the event he managed to rescue it.

Ismāʿīl ibn ʿAbbād (d. 995), Ibn al-ʿAmīd's successor as minister in Rayy, was also an author, and one of the most detailed biographies in Yāqūt's work on men of letters is devoted to him.[24] It was he who said that Sayf al-Daula's payment to al-Iṣfahānī for "The Book of Songs" had been niggardly. He remarked on that occasion that his library comprised 6,200 volumes, and that the work mentioned was the

[22] Arīb, *Ṣila*, edited by de Goeje, p. 121 lines 19f.

[23] Miskawayh, *Tajārib al-umam* II, 224f.

[24] *Irshād* II, 273-343. See also Niẓāmī-yi ʿArūḍī, *Chahār maqālah*, English translation and notes by E. G. Browne (London, 1921), pp. 19, 107.

only one that he used for nightly diversion.[25] His library meant so much to him that he refused an invitation from Nūḥ ibn Manṣūr, the Sāmānid prince in Khurāsān, to become the latter's *wazīr*, on the ground that the removal of his library would entail too much trouble. This time it was said to contain a hundred camel loads of scholarly books, the catalogue alone filling ten volumes. When Maḥmūd was advancing from Ghazna as the defender of the orthodox faith, he was told, not without justification, that this library contained much heretical literature; in 1029 Maḥmūd had some of it burnt and some sent to his capital city further east.[26]

The name of a third Būyid *wazīr*, the servant of Bahā' al-Daula, whose power encompassed Iraq and the neighboring Khūzistān, is remembered as the founder of a great library. This man was Sābūr ibn Ardashīr, who in 993 or thereabouts founded a large library in the street known as Bayn al-Sūrayn (that is, "between the two walls") in Baghdad. He made it a public institution for the use of scholars. It endured only until the conquest of Baghdad by the Seljuks in 1055, when it was burned and plundered.[27]

Among the Būyids themselves, ʿAḍud al-Daula (d. 983), Bahā' al-Daula's father, and the most important member of the family, had founded a library in Shīrāz, which, judging by al-Maqdisī's account of it, must have been on a particularly impressive scale.[28] Writing in 985, al-Maqdisī, who had himself visited the library (*khizānat al-kutub*), describes it as a complex of buildings surrounded by gardens with lakes and waterways. The buildings were topped with domes, and comprised an upper and a lower story with a total, according to the chief official, of 360 rooms. The actual stacks were located in a large vaulted room of their own, with a number of chambers adjoining. These were all equipped with cabinets of the

[25] *Irshād* V, 150.

[26] *Ibid.* II, 315.

[27] *Ibid.* VI, 359; Ibn al-Athīr, *Ta'rīkh al-Kāmil* (Cairo, 1303/1886), IX, 35 lines 6f.; X, 3 in middle.

[28] *Aḥsan al-taqāsīm*, edited by de Goeje, p, 449.

height of a man and with decorated doors. Inside the cabinets were the books, among which no book written up to that time was supposed to be missing. In each department, catalogues were placed on a shelf. All the appointments were sumptuous; the rooms were furnished with carpets, some of them also being specially designed to receive fresh, cool air through a ventilation system that functioned partly through the drawing back and forth of a number of hanging tapestries and partly through the circulation of water led around the rooms by pipes. The entire layout made such an impression on al-Maqdisī that he thought the plans for it must have been made in Paradise.

Management of the establishment was in the hands of a director (*wakīl*), a librarian (*khāzin*), and a curator (*mushrif*), but the division of functions between them is not stated. The calligrapher Ibn al-Bawwāb's description of the library, on which I have drawn above, confirms its wealth but at the same time testifies that even under Bahā' al-Daula it was already beginning to be neglected.

Libraries continued to be founded. Ibn Sawwār, a man otherwise unknown to us, established a *dār al-ʿilm*, "house of learning," in Basra, with a large library and bursaries for people who came there to study and to transcribe books; he set up another somewhat smaller library in Rāmhurmuz in the neighboring region of Persia.[29] In Mosul the scholar Jaʿfar ibn Ḥamdūn (d. 935) established a similar institute as a religious foundation (*waqf*). The library was open to all and sundry, and its founder gave money and paper to indigent students. He himself sat and labored there every day after riding.[30] There was a similar institution at Tripoli in Syria, a *dār al-ʿilm* with books on various branches of learning, notably Shīʿī literature. It developed with particular vigor under the house of ʿAmmār, but it was burned by the Crusaders in 1109 when the town was captured after a year-long siege. It was certainly

[29] *Ibid.*, p. 413 lines 15ff.

[30] *Irshād* II, 420.

a considerable library, but even so the figures given by the historian Ibn al-Furāt (d. 1404) do seem rather fantastic. He says that there were three million books, including 50,000 Qur'āns and 80,000 Qur'ānic commentaries, and that 1,800 copyists worked on the premises, thirty of them day and night![31]

The Sāmānid prince Nūḥ, who has already been mentioned and who had his residence (976-997) in Bukhārā, imitated his predecessors in gathering learned men around him, one of them being the celebrated philosopher Ibn Sīnā (Avicenna), who was summoned as a doctor to attend Nūḥ during his illness. Ibn Sīnā asked permission to use his library, and he records that there was a multitude of books arranged by rooms, with separate rooms devoted to each subject, Arabic philology and poetry, ethics, and so forth. He examined the catalogues of "the ancient sciences" and came across books whose names were known to only a few people, and which he never encountered anywhere else, either before or since.[32] Hellenistic learning still exerted its attraction, in the East as well as the West.

However, this was not to continue. The profound intellectual disputes that despite all the political turbulence gave Islams so flourishing a life in the ninth and tenth and even in the eleventh centuries, produced an intense dread of anything that might dissipate interest in, or divert it from, the vital core of Islam, the doctrine of true belief and conduct. Study of the latter had always formed the most important aspect of the learning pursued in the mosques. Hostility now became directed not only against heretical Muslim teaching but also against Hellenistic philosophy and natural science that might lead the student astray, and in any case lay outside the narrow

[31] Stated by Olga Pinto, quoting a manuscript in Vienna, in her article cited in note 1 above, pp. 235f. Whereas H. Lammens, *La Syrie* (Beirut, 1921), I, 214f., is sceptical of these huge figures, Mme Pinto appears to trust them.

[32] Ibn Abī Uṣaybiʿa, *ʿUyūn al-anbāʾ fī ṭabaqāt al-aṭibbāʾ*, II (Cairo, 1299/1882), 4 lines 4ff.

Muslim sphere of interest. This made its mark upon the libraries.

Most of the libraries discussed in the foregoing were the property of individuals, and even if the prince or wealthy magnate allowed others access to his book collection, it still retained a private character when not established as a religious foundation (*waqf*). The latter case, as we have noted, often did occur, giving the library an independent legal status, to the benefit of Muslim society. The mosques enjoyed this status from the outset, and since they were not merely devoted to worship but were also schools and seats of learning, it was natural that many people should make over their libraries to the mosques. In this way every major mosque acquired in the course of time a large library that was a public institution. Thus Ibn Jubair, a traveler of the late twelfth century, gave an account of the libraries in the two great mosques of Mecca and Medina.[33] An entire book collection might be transferred to a mosque as a self-contained library, *dār al-kutub*.[34]

The new leaning towards orthodoxy led to the establishment of a new type of school, the madrasa. It was organized as a kind of mosque with a library and with teachers who gave tuition chiefly in subjects that lay at the heart of orthodoxy, namely, Qur'ānic knowledge, instruction in the traditions of the Prophet (*ḥadīth*), and, as the basis of these subjects, jurisprudence (*fiqh*). The new institution was not a little reminiscent of the kind of foundation that used to result from a man's establishing a *dār al-ʿilm*, a house of learning with a library and bursaries for foreign students. As early as the tenth century, there was a scholar, al-Bustī (890-965), who founded such an institution with a library and living accommodation for foreign students desirous of engaging in the study of traditions and jurisprudence. The founder himself gave tuition,

[33] Ibn Jubair, *Riḥla*, 2nd ed. Edited by M. J. de Goeje (London, 1907), pp. 89 lines 5f,; 193 lines 14f.

[34] Tāj al-Mulk's library in the chief mosque of Iṣfahān may be cited as an example; see *Irshād* V, 121.

but a curator managed the establishment and lent the students books for transcribing, though only in the building itself.[35]

From this it was not a big step to the establishing by wealthy and powerful men of such madrasas and the employment in them of one or more teachers; numerous such instances are encountered in the eleventh century, mainly in the East.[36] Thus, in the first half of that century we find four institutes of this sort in Nīshāpūr, established for and named after celebrated teachers. The entire movement gathered momentum when the Seljuks rose to power in the East. These were a Turkish family who went over to Islam as strictly orthodox Sunnites. They conquered Transoxiana, Afghanistan, and Persia, and in 1055 they entered Baghdad, subsequently extending their sway over northern Syria and Asia Minor. Thus they suceeded the Būyids, and, like them, formally acknowledged the ʿAbbāsid caliph. A position of extraordinary influence was achieved by their *wazīr* Niẓām al-Mulk (1018-1092), author of the work *Siyāsat nāma*, dealing with the art of government. One of his fundamental themes was the unity of Islam through the medium of doctrinal orthodoxy fortified by the madrasa, which was to set its impress upon the official class and the world of letters. He established large madrasas bearing his name in various towns of the East. The biggest and most splendid was *al-Niẓāmīya* in Baghdad, visited by Ibn Jubair in 1185 and described by him in glowing terms. Its librarian was the prominent teacher of law al-Isfarāʾīnī.

The example of the *wazīr* was infectious, and the towns of the East filled up with madrasas that rapidly became a new type of mosque, with a pulpit and all the other simple appurtenances of the mosque. They were established with a view not only to education but to worship, as well, and in the ordinary mosques studies continued to be pursued in the cus-

[35] F. Wüstenfeld, *Der Imâm el-Schâfiʿî, seine Schüler und Anhänger bis zum J. 300 d.H.*, in *Abhandlungen der königlichen Gesellschaft der Wissenschaften zu Göttingen* 36 (1890), 163.

[36] On the *madrasa* and its history see my *Islams Kultur*, pp. 193ff., and my two articles cited in note 1.

tomary fashion. New libraries were amassed in mosques and madrasas, but the new constriction of interest determined their contents, and "the ancient sciences" were no longer represented.

Yāqūt, who stayed in Marv, in eastern Persia, around 1216-1218, records in his geographical dictionary that the town contained ten wealthy libraries, two in the chief mosque and the remainder in the madrasas. He was even permitted to take out no fewer than two hundred volumes on loan without depositing a pledge.[37] Ibn Jubair mentions thirty madrasas in Baghdad, but the most magnificent one, *al-Mustanṣirīya*, was built after his time, being founded by the caliph al-Mustanṣir in 1234. This establishment contained a large library which, as we have seen, was taken over from the caliph's library. It survived the destruction of Baghdad during the Mongol conquest of 1258, and al-Fuwatī, its librarian, has described the history of the city during these years.[38] But many other libraries were razed in the havoc wrought by the Mongols in the cities of Asia.

The madrasas spread further over Mesopotamia and Syria under the Seljuks. Zangī and Saladin were particularly active in establishing them in Damascus, and a later author, writing around 1500, enumerated about 150 madrasas in that city. When Saladin made an end of the Fāṭimids in 1171 and assumed power in Egypt and Syria, his dynasty maintained the tradition, and under the Mamlūks, who governed right down to the beginning of the nineteenth century, it still lived on. Al-Maqrīzī (d. 1442) mentions seventy-five madrasas in Cairo. The institution spread in the other Islamic countries, as well. Baisunqur established his magnificent library at Harāt during this same period, but in part it was Persian literature that

[37] *Jaqut's geographisches Wörterbuch*, edited by F. Wüstenfeld, IV (Leipzig, 1869), 509f.

[38] Ibn al-Fuwatī, *al-Ḥawādith al-jāmiʿa*; see the introduction with biography of the author. On al-Mustanṣirīyah, see Le Strange, *Baghdad during the Abbasid Caliphate*, pp. 266ff.; F. Wüstenfeld, *Die Academien der Araber und ihre Lehren. Nach Auszügen aus Ibn Schohba's Klassen der Schafeiten* (Göttingen, 1837), pp. iv and 29.

interested him and in part the artistic appointments of the books.

Amīrs and men of wealth founded madrasas for the sake of their own honor and the salvation of their souls, but little by little an imbalance appeared between this urge and the need. Orthodoxy dried up the source from which study sprang, so that around 1500 a traveler, Leo Africanus, reported that Cairo was filled with handsomely equipped institutions of study, but that no one made use of them. In this situation the funds donated for the maintenance of these establishments crumbled away, and gradually they fell into decay. When Lane lived in Cairo in the twenties and thirties of the nineteenth century there were still many large libraries in the mosques, covering in particular theology proper, Qur'ānic doctrine, traditions of the Prophet, jurisprudence, and Arabic philology; but they were all neglected, and many books disappeared to the private benefit of those charged with their superintendence.

Even in our day remnants of these libraries are to be found in the mosques; the mosque of al-Azhar in Cairo, for instance, has a fairly considerable library, and this is even more the case with the mosques of Mecca and Medina, according to the reports of recent Muslim travelers. There are many manuscripts in the Zaytūna mosque in Tunis, in Tlemcen in Algeria, and in Rabat in Morocco. In Istanbul, many manuscripts are in the possession of various mosques and a large central library; a printed catalogue of them is published, but unfortunately is not completely reliable. Most of the manuscripts in Cairene mosques have gravitated one by one into the custody of the great National (formerly Royal) Library, which was founded in 1838 and now has the character of a modern European library; in Damascus, likewise, the surviving material has been gathered in the Ẓāhirīya Library. The arrangement here and in the mosque of al-Azhar, for example, is the same as in the ancient libraries: the books are laid flat on top of one another on the shelves. The title is written on the outward-facing edge or on the case, if the book is enclosed in one. In the al-Azhar mosque fifty years ago the sheets could often be seen lying unbound inside the covers, and sometimes they would be lent out singly to the students, which of course was far from conducive to the book's preservation.

There are still many important private libraries in the Orient that contain manuscripts. Some years ago there were two private libraries in Cairo that were of particular importance: one belonged to Aḥmad Zakī Pasha and the other to Aḥmad Taymūr Pasha. The second of these, according to an article of 1923 in the Arabic *Revue de l'Académie Arabe* in Damascus, contained about 12,000 works, half of them manuscripts. Both these libraries went into public ownership on the deaths of the owners. The journal just cited has published a number of descriptions of other private libraries in the Orient.

Over the years a very substantial quantity of manuscripts has been accumulated in European libraries, which have published printed catalogues of their holdings. Much Islamic literature has thus been preserved, but large quantities have been lost. Many of the works mentioned by Ibn al-Nadīm in his *Fihrist* of the tenth century, by Yāqūt and others in their biographies, and by the Turk Ḥājjī Khalīfa in his great bibliography of the seventeenth century, therefore, are known only by name. When the thirteen-volume Leiden edition of the historical works of al-Ṭabarī was in preparation in the 1870s, it was found possible to muster a complete copy only by assembling fragments of the work from a number of libraries in Europe and the Orient; nothing approaching a complete copy existed, and even then there were isolated gaps that had to be filled from the works of other historians who had made use of al-Ṭabarī; in Mecca and Medina there was not a single fragment. This was the work of which the main libraries had held many examples in the great days, and which undoubtedly had not at that time been absent from any major library in the world of Islam. It is always possible that hitherto unknown manuscripts may still emerge from regions to which Europeans have had little access, such as Yemen, whence, as we have noted, a certain amount of Ismāʿīlī literature has appeared in recent years.

TEN

Printed Books

WHEN THE ART of book printing began to come into use in Europe in the middle of the fifteenth century, Muslim culture had passed its zenith, and no movement was to be perceived in the literary world capable of stimulating interest in novel methods of book production. It was another three or four hundred years before the Muslims took up the art that in Europe had made possible the dissemination of a new culture and the growth of a new body of literature. Even then it was only with reluctance that the Muslims adopted this European invention.[1]

Nevertheless, a number of Islamic books were printed in the meantime, although this took place in Europe, notably in Italy. Here, at Fano, Pope Julius II had a book printed in Arabic on the seven canonical times of prayer as early as 1514. An edition of the Psalms of David was printed in Hebrew, Greek, Arabic, Aramaic, and Latin in Genoa in 1516, and a book of Christian dogmatics in Rome in 1566. These books were evidently printed for Arabic-speaking Christian communities with which the Roman church had links, but the Qur'ān too was printed in Venice as early as 1530. The first

[1] On the printing of Arabic books, see M. Hartmann, *Zur literarischen Bewegung und zum Buch- und Bibliothekswesen in den islamischen Ländern*, Halle, 1905. Bibliographical details in G. Gabrieli, *Manuale di bibliografia musulmana* I, *Bibliografia generale* (Rome, 1916), pp. 274ff. The best connected account is given by L. Cheikho in a series of articles in Arabic, "Ta'rīkh fann al-ṭibāʿa fi'l-mashriq ("History of the Art of Book-Printing in the East") in the journal *al-Mashriq* ("The Orient") 3-5 (1900-1902), on which the account given here is based. A bibliography of all the works printed in Arabic until 1919 is published by Joseph Elian Sarkis (Cairo, 1930). It fills 2,024 quarto columns, and has been extended to the year 1927 by means of two supplements. It is not exhaustive, however.

Islamic book with scientific content, a geographical treatise by al-Ṣāliḥī, an Egyptian living in that period, was printed in 1584.

The beginnings of a scholarly endeavor to study the language are gradually to be noticed alongside the interest in Christian mission work. For example, in Heidelberg in 1583 Jakob Mylius printed an Arabic grammar together with a translation of the Epistle to the Galatians and a book of dogmatics.

In Italy in the sixteenth and seventeenth centuries, there were three noted Arabic printers. The Medici press, which was founded in Rome in 1584 and subsequently removed, in 1627 to Pisa and in 1684 to Florence, published many books, including the Gospels in 1591, an Arabic grammar for beginners by Joh. Raimondi in the following year, a number of Islamic scientific works, including al-Idrīsī''s description of the world, which was subsequently translated into Latin and Italian, and, most notably, the great medical treatise *al-Qānūn* by Ibn Sīnā (Avicenna), which was printed together with an extract from his metaphysical work *al-Shifā'* in 1593. There were also Greek authors in Arabic translation, such as Euclid and Porphyry, whose *Isagoge* had played a large role in the logical underpinning of Muslim science. It was printed in 1625.

The Congregation for the Propagation of the Faith (*Congregatio de propaganda fide*) founded an Arabic printing press in Rome in 1622. Here in 1627 a translation was printed of writings by Cardinal Bellarmin, the learned Jesuit theologian, who wrote a great apologia for the Roman church. Linguistic works also emerged from the press, examples being *al-ājurrūmīya* in 1633, the small popular grammar that was used by schoolboys all over the Arabic-speaking world as an introduction to the study of the language, and an Arabic-Italian dictionary in 1637. The greatest work from this press was an Arabic translation of the complete Bible, which appeared in 1671.

The third great printing press, Tipografia del Seminario,

was founded in Padua about 1680. Its most important publication was the Qur'ān, which was printed in 1698 with an Arabic text, a translation in Latin, and an introduction by Marracci. It was the third printed edition of the Qur'ān, since as well as the Venice edition of 1530 a version had been printed in Hamburg in 1694. An Italian translation was published as early as 1547; it was another century (1647) before a French translation came out, some years after a German version (1616-1623) that had been translated from the Italian. Not until 1734 was an English translation published by George Sale.

A number of Arabic books were printed in various European countries in the seventeenth century. An Arabic grammar was printed in Paris in 1613, and later on a book on "Arab Philosophers" appeared, as well as editions of the Bible and an Arabic translation of an exposition of Christian doctrine by Cardinal Richelieu himself. The New Testament was printed in Leiden in 1616 and the Pentateuch in 1622, but it was not long before actual Arabic literature began to be printed there: first Luqmān's fables in 1615, then *al-Ājurrūmīya*, the grammar mentioned above, in 1625, and al-Makīn's work of Islamic history. In London and Oxford, too, historical works such as those of Abu'l-Fiḍā' (1650) and Barhebraeus (1663) were printed. This actvity continued all through the century, and indeed has increased right up to the present day. In Russia, too, Islamic books have been printed for the benefit of the empire's Muslim subjects, the Qur'ān having been published many times since 1787.

The Turkish sultan, who was not only the nearest but also the most powerful Muslim ruler, was quick to realize what was happening in Europe, and he feared the consequences this new activity might have among his subjects. A ban on the possession of printed matter was proclaimed by Sultan Bāyazīd II as early as 1485, and was repeated and enforced in 1515 by Selīm I, who shortly thereafter became the conqueror of Egypt and Syria, the central lands of Islam, and at the same time master of the holy places in Arabia. The ban did not affect the Jews, who from 1490 printed a number of Hebrew books in Istanbul and later on also in Salonika, including the Pentateuch with the Aramaic Targum Onkelos, a free translation, and Sa'dia Gaon's commentary, the latter partly translated into Persian.

Such remained the situation until about 1700. A man named Muḥammad Efendi Chelebi and his son Saʿīd Efendi had become acquainted with the art of printing during a sojourn in Paris, and it was they who managed to convince the government that it could be of value. A firman of 1712 made permissible the printing of all books except those specially associated with religion: Qur'ānic commentaries (*tafsīr*), traditions of the Prophet (*ḥadīth*), jurisprudence (*fiqh*) and speculative theology (*kalām*), and of course the Qur'ān. Shaykh al-Islām ʿAbdallāh Efendi had delivered an opinion (*fatwā*) to the effect that such permission could be unconditional.

A printing press was now set up by Saʿīd Efendi in collaboration with Ibrāhīm Aghā, a Hungarian who understood the art of printing and had been converted to Islam. The first work printed by the partners was one of the classical Arabic dictionaries, *al-Ṣiḥāḥ*, "The Sound" or "The Entire," by al-Jauharī (d. 1002); it appeared in 1728. Some Turkish books were printed next, but then from 1745 to 1783 the press was closed. After 1800 a number of Arabic books were printed in Turkey; several presses were established in Istanbul and also in other towns beginning with Scutari and Smyrna. An edition of Euclid came out in 1801, followed by various books of religious dogma, the original restriction contained in the printing law evidently having been changed. Historical works and poetry were printed later on, as well, but attention became increasingly focused upon Turkish literature. Since the Turkish revolution, of which the break with the Arabic past was a cardinal feature, the Turks naturally have become still less interested in Arabic literature, whose characters they have stopped using for their own language. Arabic is still printed, however, and European scholars avail themselves now and then of the Istanbul printing houses for editions of Arabic texts.

In the Arabic-speaking world itself, the art of printing books was first introduced through the church. What role has been played in the lands of the Orient by Christian works printed in Italy and other European countries is a separate question, and not an easy one to answer. Among the oriental Christians themselves the first printing press to be established was at the monastery of Quzahīya, south of Tripoli, shortly after the year 1600, and in 1610 the Psalms of the Old Testament were printed there in Syriac and Arabic, but with Syriac type. No major works appeared from this press. Petermann visited the monastery in 1852, but found the monks, a hundred of them all told, quite ignorant. The library comprised about thirty books, some printed in Rome, some in the monastery.[2] After 1734 a number of religious writings in Arabic were printed at another monastery, that of Shuwayr, in the Lebanon.

Arabic type was at that time being introduced into Syria, where it was used in Aleppo in 1706 for printing the Gospels and the Psalms, and later on for other religious books on the initiative of Athanasios, the bishop of that city, who had had a number of liturgical texts in Greek and Arabic published in Bucharest some years previously. A new step was taken around 1750, when an Arabic printing press was established in the Greek Orthodox monastery of St. George in Beirut. Here the Psalms were printed in 1751, but otherwise there was not a great deal of activity in the years that followed. Printing only really became a thriving business in 1834, when American Protestant missionaries moved an Arabic printing press from Malta to Beirut. They inaugurated a new era by printing a lengthy series of books introducing European culture to the Islamic world. As well as various books of Christian dogma, they published books on geography, mathematics, physics, chemistry, zoology, and other branches of natural science, as well as a number of dictionaries that were to facilitate the learning of European languages.

The Catholic printing press, founded in 1848 and having

[2] H. Petermann, *Reisen im Orient*, 2nd ed. (Leipzig, 1865), II, 319f.

links with France, followed a parallel course. Both presses are still functioning, each now being attached to its university. The Protestant American College has made the greater impact on the populace through its long-established pedagogical activities, which have been esteemed by both Christians and Muslims. The Catholic French College, which is run by Jesuits, has made the weightier contribution to scientific research, thus becoming an important factor in European learning. Through the monthly journal *al-Mashriq*, "The Orient," which has appeared since 1898, it has functioned as an intermediary between European learning and Catholic religious culture on the one hand and the intellectual life of the Muslim Orient on the other.

Native and foreign Christians exerted a particular influence upon the genesis and subsequent development of printed literature in Syria. Of greater importance to Arabic literature, of course, has been the impact of the art of book printing within the purely Muslim milieu, especially in Egypt, which since the fall of the caliphate following the capture of Baghdad in 1258 has been the main country for Muslim education. In this, as in all other respects, the Napoleonic conquest of 1798 ushered in the modern age.

Napoleon carried with him the equipment required for setting up an Arabic printing press. It was used for issuing his army orders and his decrees for the inhabitants, and also for printing Luqmān's fables, which were printed in French at the same time. However, the French had to withdraw from the country as early as 1801, and some years later, when the British also had departed, Muḥammad ʿAlī took over the government and now embarked upon a series of reforms along European lines, bringing Europeans into his service. This ruthless, but vigorous and farsighted, politician seems to have been illiterate, but he appreciated the potential significance of the art of book printing, and in 1821 he established a government printing press in Būlāq, a suburb of Cairo. This became for many years the most important Arabic press. In 1838-1839, Muḥammad ʿAlī established a library in association with it that subsequently became the Egyptian Royal Library.[3]

Thus Egypt, unlike Turkey and Syria, got its first library by orders from above. It was received by the populace with something less than enthusiasm. Lane, after his sojourn in Cairo in the 1820s and 1830s, described the repugnance aroused by printing.[4] It was argued that God's name, which appears on every page of a Muslim book, could become defiled through this process, and it was feared that books would become cheap and fall into the wrong hands. A bookseller of Lane's acquaintance wanted to have some books printed but was held back by his doubts concerning its permissibility under holy law. He did not know, of course, that the pādishāh in Istanbul had received the word of the Shaykh al-Islām a hundred years earlier that it was permissible.

People gradually became accustomed to the new form of book production, especially, of course, after the advent of newspapers. An official weekly began publication as early as 1832, but it was not until 1876 that other papers made their appearance. The first daily newspaper, *al-Muqaṭṭam* (named after a hill outside Cairo), was launched in 1889. A number of daily newspapers were issued in the 1890s and afterwards. They were largely written by Syrians, who had received their education in one of the two institutions of learning in Beirut, which in this way attained importance beyond the frontiers of Syria. The newspaper publishers, especially the Christians, naturally tried to avoid making provocative utterances.

Even Muḥammad ʿAlī had sent young Egyptians to Europe to study, and by the last quarter of the century young Orientals were flocking to European universities, as they have done ever since. This, of course, has set its mark upon Islamic literature. European books have been translated into Arabic and printed, and Orientals themselves have written about what

[3] W. Spitta, "Neue Erscheinungen der egyptischen Presse," in *Zeitschrift der deutschen morgenländischen Gesellschaft* 30 (1876), 152.

[4] E. W. Lane, *The Manners & Customs of the Modern Egyptians* (Everyman's Library) (London, 1906), pp. 288f.

they have learned and seen. Theirs is a quest for paths that will lead to a new mode of thought, and the quest goes on still, as many of the printed works testify. The problem is far from resolved, and little of what has been written in recent generations is of lasting value. The basis of Islamic culture is still its own tradition, which was laid down in the eighth to eleventh centuries; this is the intellectual sphere in which the Islamic world continues to dwell.

The publication of early Arabic literature therefore became one of the main tasks of the printing houses, thus bringing about the curious situation in which book printing, although an important instrument in breaking the ground for a new Muslim cultural form, has simultaneously effected a renascence of the Islamic literature of the past. Some works known only in a single manuscript that lay hidden away, many of them on the point of disappearing, have been brought to the light of day and made accessible to anyone who can read Arabic. The press in Būlāq has taken a leading part in this, but since about the turn of the present century numerous other printing houses have been established in Egypt and all other Arabic-speaking countries, and early Islamic literature is now printed everywhere. Muḥammad Kurd ʿAlī, who was minister of education in Syria in the 1920s and founder of the Arab Academy in Damascus, in his work of 1926 on Syria put the number of that country's printing houses at eighty.[5]

Thus, a substantial body of Islamic literature is now in print in the Orient, while at the same time the work of publication has been going forward in Europe. All the classical collections of traditions of the Prophet (*ḥadīth*) have been printed, and the same applies to the literature on jurisprudence. Many of the most important Qur'ānic commentaries are available. The one most used was first printed in Leipzig in 1844, and since then has been published twice in Būlāq, twice in Cairo, four times in Constantinople, once in Delhi, twice in Lucknow and Bombay, once in Teheran, and three times more in the

[5] Kurd ʿAlī, *Khiṭaṭ al-shām* IV, 95.

margins of other books. About fifty works have been printed (many of them by small printing houses in Cairo) from the writings of al-Ghazālī (d. 1111), the great theologian and philosopher who fixed the pattern of orthodoxy for the future and prepared the way for its acceptance of mysticism. His principal work, "Revival of the Sciences," in four large volumes, has been published ten times. The "Book of Songs" has been printed twice in Cairo, and a third edition was in course of being printed before the war. A very considerable body of historical literature has gradually come to light, including a number of biographical works. Such a work as al-Ṭabarī's world history, on whose publication in Leiden such trouble was expended, has been reprinted in Cairo, naturally at a much lower price. In recent years, when communications with the East have become easier, European scholars have availed themselves more and more of printing houses in the Orient for publishing texts.

The former aversion to the printing of books has not totally disappeared, and is still in evidence as far as the Qur'ān is concerned. It is true that the Qur'ān has been printed, like other books, with movable type, but only a few times. The difficulties have generally been overcome by using another method, namely, lithography, in which of course it is the actual handwritten script that is transferred to the paper, even though the stone forms an intermediate stage. This method has also been used for other books, and is particularly favored in Persia. The printing of script incised on wood blocks, after the Chinese pattern, has also been employed in Islam, but only for short pieces of writing such as documents and the like.[6] The Qur'ān was printed in Calcutta in 1854, in Cairo in 1864, in Constantinople in 1872, and innumerable times since then in many formats, including a small pocket format making it suitable for carrying as an amulet.

The exterior appointments of books printed in the Orient are often very poor. The paper, commonly yellow in color,

[6] Cheikho in *al-Mashriq* 3 (1900), 79 and illustrations on p. 81.

is often very coarse and loose, and the type is frequently indistinct. As a rule, the words are set very close together, which makes reading difficult. Instead of being stitched, the sheets are usually bound by having wire passed right through them along the spine, which makes it difficult for the reader to make the book lie open. This and the carelessly glued pasteboard bindings testify to the condition of decay in which the craft still finds itself. But the books are cheap, and so attain a comparatively wide distribution. And, of course, Arabic script is so handsome that a printed page of Arabic nearly always presents an attractive appearance.

One extraordinary custom is that an independent text is commonly printed in the margin of an Arabic book. This stems from manuscripts containing a text with a commentary and possibly a super-commentary. These are usually written on the same page, next to one another. When such a work is printed, the original text, being the shorter, is placed in the margin, while the detailed commentary fills the inner area. Commentaries are often so composed as to form a connected exposition embodying the text being commented upon; the latter is then picked out by being placed within parentheses. This combined text and commentary may then be printed in the margin, while the detailed super-commentary fills the page. Alternatively, the text with the first commentary appended is placed in parentheses within the super-commentary. This custom has often led to filling the margin of a book with a work that has nothing to do with the main work; the subject is generally a cognate one, however. Al-Bayḍāwī's Qur'ānic commentaries sometimes have in the margin a second, shorter Qur'ānic commentary; Ibn al-Athīr's great history has al-Masʿūdī's history in the margin, and so on.

The procedure adopted for the publication of early literature has quite simply been the same as for the copying of a manuscript. The book would be set according to a single manuscript, the typesetter taking the copyist's place and the publisher the corrector's. When the corrector found something that seemed to him to be wrong, he corrected it. For this reason many divergencies can sometimes be found between different editions of the same work. Only in recent years have there appeared some indications of a change in this. In 1925, a commission in Cairo published an edition of the Qur'ān representing a fixed text based on painstaking study. In 1927, the great library in Cairo embarked upon a new edition of the "Book of Songs," printed on the the library's press, which has replaced the former printing press in Būlāq. This edition follows the European pattern in citing the readings that diverge from the printed text and are found in the surviving manuscripts or in other works where the same text occurs, especially in the case of poetry. A similar procedure is adopted in the library's edition of Ibn Taghrībirdī's *History of Egypt*, published in 1929. At the same time, finer varieties of paper and a distinct script have been introduced. And just as in European editions, the reader's use of the book is facilitated by supplying difficult and ambiguous words with vowels.

What the future has in store for Islamic literature is a question that cannot yet be answered, but as part of the endeavor to preserve the classical Islamic book, the developments described above represent a great advance.

BIBLIOGRAPHY

Abbott, N. "Arabic paleography." *Ars Islamica* 8 (1941), 65-104.

———. *The Rise of the North Arabic Script and Its Ḳur'ānic Development*. Chicago, 1939.

ʿAbd al-Razzāq. *Dictionary of Technical Terms*. Edited by A. Sprenger. Calcutta, 1845.

Abū Shāmah, Abu'l-Qāsim ʿAbd al-Raḥmān b. Ismāʿīl. *Kitāb al-rauḍatain fī akhbār al-daulatain* I. Cairo, 1287/1870.

Adam, P. *Der Bucheinband: seine Technik und seine Geschichte*. Leipzig, 1890.

Aga-Oglu, M. *Persian Bookbindings of the Fifteenth Century*. Ann Arbor, 1935.

Ahlwardt, W., ed. *The Divans of Six Ancient Arabic Poets*. London, 1870.

———. *Verzeichnis der arabischen Handschriften der königlichen Bibliothek I*. Berlin, 1887.

Aḥmad b. Mīr Munshī al-Ḥusainī, Qāḍī. *Calligraphers and Painters*. Translated by V. Minorsky. Washington, D.C., 1959.

Alibaux, H. "L'invention du papier." *Gutenberg-Jahrbuch*, 1939, pp. 9-30.

Amedroz, H. F., ed. *The Historical Remains of Hilâl al-Sâbî, Kitâb al-Wuzarâ*. Beirut, 1904.

Arberry, A. J. *The Koran Illuminated. A Handlist of the Korans in the Chester Beatty Library*. Dublin, 1967.

———. *Specimens of Arabic and Persian Palaeography* (India Office Library). London, 1939.

ʿArīb b. Saʿd, al-Kātib al-Qurṭubī. *Sila*. Edited by M. J. de Goeje. Leiden, 1897.

Arnold, T. W. *Painting in Islam*. London, 1928.

———, and Grohmann, A. *The Islamic Book. A Contribution*

to Its Art and History from the VII-XVIII Century. London and Florence, 1929.

Atasoy, N., and Çagman, F. *Turkish Miniature Painting*. Istanbul, 1974.

Atil, E. *Art of the Arab World*. Washington, D.C. 1975.

ʿAwwad, K. "Al-waraq aw al-kāghid." *Majallat al-Majmaʿ al-ʿIlmī al-ʿArabī* 22 (1948), 409-38.

ʿAzīza, M. *La calligraphie arabe*. Tunis, 1971.

Babinger, F. "Die Einführung des Buchdruckes in Persien." *Zeitschrift des Deutschen Vereins für Buchwesen und Schrifttum* 4 (1921), 141-42.

al-Baghdādī, ʿAbd al-Laṭīf ibn Yūsuf. *Relation de l'Égypte par Abd-Allatif, médecin arabe de Bagdad*. Edited and translated by S. de Sacy. Paris, 1810.

al-Balādhurī, Abu'l-Ḥasan Aḥmad b. Yaḥyā. *Futūh al-buldān*. Edited by M. J. de Goeje. Leiden, 1866.

Bashiruddin, S. "The Fate of Sectarian Libraries in Medieval Islam." *Libri* 17 (1967), 149-62.

Beach, M. C. *The Grand Mogul. Imperial Painting in India 1600-1660*. Williamstown, Mass., 1978.

Bergsträsser, G. "Zur ältesten Geschichte der kufischen Schrift." *Zeitschrift des Deutschen Vereins für Buchwesen und Schrifttum* 5/6 (1919), 54-66.

Bhanu, D. "Libraries and Their Management in Mughul India." *Journal of Indian History* 31 (1953), 157-73.

Binney, E. *Turkish Miniature Painting and Manuscripts*. New York and Los Angeles, 1973.

Binyon, L.; Wilkinson, J.V.S.; and Gray, B. *Persian Miniature Painting*. London, 1933.

Blieske, D. "Die Buchproduktion Irans und ihre Erfassung durch die Universitätsbibliothek Tübingen im Rahmen des Förderungs programms der Deutschen Forschungsgemeinschaft." *Der Islam* 55 (1978), 312-26.

Blochet, E. *Les peintures des manuscrits orientaux de la Bibliothèque Nationale*. Paris, 1914-1920.

Bockwitz, H. H. "Zu Karabaceks Forschungen über das Papier im islamischen Kulturkreis." *Buch und Schrift*, N.F., 1 (1938), 83-86.

Bosch, G. "The Staff of the Scribes and Implements of the Discerning: An Excerpt." *Ars Orientalis* 4 (1961), 1-13.

——— et al. *Islamic Bindings & Bookmaking*. Chicago, 1981.

Briquet, C.-M. *Le papier arabe au moyen-âge et sa fabrication*. Berne, 1888.

Brockelmann, C. *Geschichte der arabischen Literatur* I-II. Weimar, 1898-1902. With *Supplementbände* I-III. Leiden, 1937-1942.

Brown, P. *Indian Painting under the Mughals*. London, 1924.

Browne, E. G. *A Literary History of Persia* I-IV. Cambridge, 1908-1924.

Brünnow, R. E. *Brünnows Arabische Chrestomathie aus Prosaschriftstellern* 4th ed. Edited by A. Fischer. Berlin, 1928.

Bukhari, Y. K. "A Rare Manuscript on Calligraphy." *Islamic Culture* 37 (1963), 92-99.

Çagman, F., and Tanindi, Z. *Topkapi Sarayi Müzesi. Islamic Miniatures*. Istanbul, 1979.

Carter, T. F. *The Invention of Printing in China and Its Spread Westward*. New York, 1925.

———. "Islam as a Barrier to Printing." *The Muslim World* 33 (1943), 213-16.

———. "The Westward Movement of the Art of Printing. Turkestan, Persia and Egypt as Milestones in the Long Migration from China to Europe," in *Yearbook of Oriental Art and Culture* I (1924-1925), 19-28.

Cheikho, L. "Ta'rīkh fann al-ṭibāʿa fi'l-mashriq." *Al-Mashriq* 3-5 (1900-1902).

Christensen, A. "Boghaandvaerk og Bogkunst i Persien." *Abog for Bogvenner* 2 (Copenhagen, 1918), 22-46.

De Goeje, M. J. "Beschreibung einer alten Handschrift von Abû ʿObaid's Ġarîb al-ḥadîṯ'." "*Zeitschrift der deutschen morgenländischen Gesellschaft* 18 (1864), 781-807.

Demeersemann, A. "Une étape décisive de la culture et de la psychologie sociale islamiques: les données de la controverse autour du problème de l'imprimerie." *Institut des belles lettres arabes* 17 (1954), 1-48, 113-40.

Dickson, M. B., and Welch, S. C. *The Houghton Shahnameh.* Cambridge, Mass., 1981.

Diez, E. *Die Kunst der islamischen Völker.* Berlin-Neubabelsberg, 1915.

Dodge, B. *Muslim Education in Medieval Times.* Washington, D.C., 1962.

Eche, Y. *Les bibliothèques arabes publiques et semi-publiques en Mésopotamie, en Syrie et en Égypte au Moyen Age.* Damascus, 1967.

Erman, A. *Aegypten und aegyptisches Leben im Altertum.* Tübingen, 1885.

Esin, E. *Turkish Miniature Painting.* Rutland, Vt. and Tokyo, 1960.

Ettinghausen, R. *Arab Painting.* Geneva, 1962.

———. "Manuscript Illumination." In *A Survey of Persian Art from Prehistoric Times to the Present.* Edited by A. U. Pope and P. Ackerman. London and New York, 1939, pp. 1937-74.

———. *Paintings of the Sultans and Emperors of India in American Collections.* Delhi, 1961.

———. *Turkish Miniatures from the 13th to the 18th Century.* Milan, 1965.

al-Faḍā'ilī, H. *Aṭlas-i khaṭṭ, taḥqīq dar khuṭūṭ-ī islāmī.* Isfahan, 1391/1971.

Fayyad, A. *Al-ijāzāt al-ʿilmiyya ʿind al-muslimīn.* Baghdad, 1967.

Floor, W. M. "The First Printing Press in Iran." *Zeitschrift der deutschen morgenländischen Gesellschaft* 130 (1980), 369-71.

Gabrieli, G. *Manuale di bibliografia muslmana I. Bibliografia generale.* Rome, 1916.

Geiss, A. "Histoire de l'imprimerie en Egypte." *Bulletin de l'Institut Égyptien* 5th series, 1 (1907), 133-57; 2 (1908), 195-220.

al-Ghazālī, Abū Ḥamīd Muḥammad. *Iḥyāʾ ʿulūm al-dīn* IV (Cairo, 1322/1903).

Ghulam, Y. *Introduction to the Art of Arabic Calligraphy in Iran.* Shiraz, n.d.; c. 1972.

Glück, H., and Diez, E. *Die Kunst des Islam.* Berlin, 1925.

Goetz, H., and Kühnel, E. *Indian Book Painting.* London, 1926.

Goldziher, I. *Muslim Studies* II. Edited by S. M. Stern. Translated by C. M. Barber and S. M. Stern. London, 1971.

Gottschalk, W. "Die Bibliotheken der Araber im Zeitalter der Abbasiden." *Zentralblatt für Bibliothekswesen* 47 (1930), 1-6.

Gratzl, E. *Islamische Bucheinbände des 14. bis 19. Jahrhunderts.* Leipzig, 1924.

Gray, B., ed. *The Arts of the Book in Central Asia.* London, 1979.

———. *Persian Painting.* Geneva, 1961.

———, and Barrett, D. *Painting of India.* Geneva, 1963.

Grohmann, A. *Allgemeine Einführung in die arabischen Papyri nebst Grundzügen der arabischen Diplomatik.* Vienna, 1924.

———. "Arabia." In *Encyclopaedia of World Art.* Florence, 1959, *s.v.*

———. "Arabian Pre-Islamic Art." In *Encyclopedia of World Art.* Florence, 1959, *s.v.*

———. *Arabische Paläographie. I-II.* Graz, Vienna, Cologne, 1967 and 1971.

———. *Arabische Papyruskunde (Handbuch der Orientalistik i/2).* Leiden and Cologne, 1966.

———. "Bibliotheken und Bibliophilen im islamischen Orient." In *Festschrift der Nationalbibliothek in Wien, herausgegeben zur Feier des 200 jährigen Bestehens des Gebäudes.* Vienna, 1926, pp. 431-42.

———. "Djild." In *Encyclopedia of Islam.* 2nd ed. Leiden, 1960–, *s.v.*

———. *Einführung und Chrestomathie zur arabischen Papyruskunde* I. Prague, 1955.

———. *From the World of Arabic Papyri.* Cairo, 1952.

Grohmann, A. "The Problem of Dating Early Qur'āns." *Der Islam* 33 (1958), 213-31.

Grube, E. J. *Miniature islamiche*. Padua, 1976.

———. *Muslim Miniature Paintings from the XIII to XIX Century from Collections in the United States and Canada*. Venice, 1962.

Hammam, M. Y. "History of Printing in Egypt." *Gutenberg-Jahrbuch*, 1951, pp. 156-59.

Hammer-Purgstall, J. von. "Additions au mémoire de M. Quatremère sur le goût des livres chez les Orientaux." *Journal asiatique* Ser. 4/xi (1848), 187-98.

———. "Auszüge aus Saalebi's Buch der Stützen des sich Beziehenden und dessen worauf es sich bezieht." *Zeitschrift der deutschen morgenländischen Gesellschaft* 7 (1854), 499-529.

Hartmann, M. "Das Bibliothekswesen in den islamischen Ländern." *Zentralblatt für Bibliothekswesen* 16 (1899), 186ff.

———. *Zur literarischen Bewegung und zum Buch- und Bibliothekswesen in den islamischen Ländern*. Catalogue No. 4 of the Buchhandlung Rudolf Haupt. Halle, 1905.

Heffening W. "Über Buch- und Druckwesen in der alten Türkei. Ein Bericht des Preussischen Gesandten zu Konstantinopel aus dem Jahre 1819." in *Zeitschrift der deutschen morgenländischen Gesellschaft* 100 (1950), 592-99.

Herbin, A. *Essai de calligraphie orientale*. Paris, 1803.

Hitti, P. K. "The First Book Printed in Arabic." *Princeton University Library Chronicle* 4 (1942), 5-9.

Holter, K. "Der Islam." *Handbuch der Bibliothekswissenschaft* III. Wiesbaden, 1953, 188-242.

Huart, C. *Les calligraphes et les miniaturistes de l'orient musulman*. Paris, 1908.

———. "Yāḳūt al-Mustaʿṣimī." In *Encyclopedia of Islam*. 1st ed. Leiden, 1913-1934, *s.v.*

———, and Grohmann, A. "Kāg͟had." In *Encyclopedia of Islam*. 2nd ed. Leiden, 1960–, *s.v.*

———. "Kalam." In *Encyclopedia of Islam*. 2nd ed. Leiden, 1960–, *s.v.*

Ibn ʿAbd Rabbih, Abū ʿUmar Aḥmad b. Muḥammad. *Al-ʿiqd al-farīd* II. Cairo, 1322/1904.

Ibn Abī Uṣaybiʿa, Abu'l-ʿAbbās Aḥmad b. al-Qāsim. *ʿUyūn al-anbā' fī ṭabaqāt al-aṭibbā* II. Edited by A. Müller. Cairo, 1299/1882, and Königsberg, 1884.

Ibn Abī Zarʿ, Abu'l-ʿAbbās Aḥmad. *Annales regum Mauritaniae* I. Edited by C. J. Tornberg. Uppsala, 1843.

Ibn Adam, Yaḥyā. *Kitāb al-kharāj*. Edited by T. W. Juynboll. Leiden, 1896.

Ibn al-Athīr, Abu'l-Ḥasan ʿAlī b. Muḥammad. *Ta'rīkh al-Kāmil*. Cairo, 1303/1886.

Ibn Baṭṭūṭa, Abū ʿAbdallāh Muḥammad. *Riḥla*. Cairo, 1323/1905.

Ibn al-Faqīh al-Hamadhānī, Abū Bakr Aḥmad b. Muḥammad. *Kitāb al-buldān*. Edited by M. J. de Goeje. Leiden, 1885.

Ibn al-Fuwatī, Abu'l-Faḍl ʿAbd al-Razzāq. *Ta'rīkh al-ḥawādith al-jāmiʿa*. Baghdad, 1351/1932.

Ibn Iyās, Abu'l-Barakāt Muḥammad b. Aḥmad. *Die Chronik des Ibn Ijâs*. Edited by P. Kahle and M. Muṣṭafā. Leipzig, 1932.

Ibn Jubair, Abu'l-Ḥusain Muḥammad b. Aḥmad. *Riḥla*. 2nd ed. Edited by M. J. de Goeje. London, 1907.

Ibn Khaldūn, ʿAbd al-Raḥmān b. Muḥammad. *Muqaddima*. Cairo, 1322/1904.

Ibn Khallikān, Aḥmad b. Muḥammad. *Wafayāt al-aʿyān*. Cairo, 1310/1893.

Ibn Māja al-Qazwīnī, Abū ʿAbdallāh Muḥammad b. Yazīd. *Kitāb al-tijārāt, apud* his *Sunan*. Delhi, 1282/1865, and 1289/1872.

Ibn al-Nadīm, Abu'l-Faraj Muḥammad. *Al-fihrist*. Edited by G. Flügel. Leipzig, 1871.

Ibn al-Ṭiqṭaqā, Muḥammad b. ʿAlī. *Al-Fakhrī*. Edited by W. Ahlwardt. Gotha, 1860.

Imamuddin, S. M. "Hispano-Arab Libraries, Books and

Manuscripts, Muslim Libraries and Bookmen in Spain." *Journal of the Pakistan Historical Society* 7 (1959), 101–19.

Inayatullah, S. "Bibliophilism in Mediaeval Islam." *Islamic Culture* 12 (1938), 155–69.

Ipşiroğlu, M. Ş. *Das Bild im Islam*. Vienna and Munich, 1971.

al-Iṣfahānī, Abu'l-Faraj. *Kitāb al-aghānī*. 3rd ed. Cairo, 1346/1928.

al-Jāḥiẓ, Abū ʿUthmān ʿAmr b. Baḥr. *Madḥ al-kutub*. *See* Rufai, A.

James, D. "Arab Painting, 358 A.H./969 A.D.–1112 A.H./1700 A.D." *Marg* 29/3 (1976), 11–50.

———. *Qur'ans and Bindings from the Chester Beatty Library*. London, 1980.

Jensen, H. *Die Schrift*. Glückstadt and Hamburg, 1935.

Kabir, M. "Libraries and Academies during the Buwayhid Period—946 A.D. to 1055 A.D." *Islamic Culture* 33 (1959), 31–33.

Kannun, ʿAbd Allāh. "Kitāb at-Taysīr fī Sināʿat at-Tasfīr by Bakr b. Ibrāhīm al-Ishbīlī." *Revista del Instituto de Estudios Islamicos en Madrid* 7–8 (1959–1960), 1–42, 197–99.

Karabacek, J. von. "Das arabische Papier. Eine historisch-antiquarische Untersuchung." *Mitteilungen aus der Sammlung der Papyrus Erzherzog Rainer* 2–3 (1887), 87–178.

———. *Die Bedeutung der arabischen Schrift*. Nuremberg, 1877.

———. "Neue Quellen zur Papiergeschichte." *Mitteilungen aus der Sammlung der Papyrus Erzherzog Rainer* 4 (1888), 75–122.

——— et al. *Papyrus Erzherzog Rainer. Führer durch die Ausstellung*. Vienna, 1894.

al-Khaṭīb al-Baghdādī, Abū Bakr Aḥmad b. ʿAlī. *Kitāb al-kifāya fī ʿilm al-riwāya*. Hyderabad, 1357/1938.

———. *Ta'rīkh Baghdād*. Cairo 1349/1931.

Khatibi, A., and Sijelmassi, M. *The Splendour of Islamic Calligraphy*. London, 1976.

Krachkovski, I. Y. *Among Arabic Manuscripts*. Leiden, 1953.

Krenkow, F. "Kitāb." *Encyclopedia of Islam*. 1st ed. Leiden, 1913–1934, *s.v.*

———. "The Use of Writing for the Preservation of Ancient Arabic Poetry." In *A Volume of Oriental Studies Presented to Professor Edward G. Browne*. Edited by T. W. Arnold and R. A. Nicholson. Cambridge, 1922, pp. 261-68.

———, and Heffening, W. "Kitābkhāna." *Encyclopedia of Islam*. 1st ed. Leiden, 1913-1934, *s.v.*

Kühnel, E. *The Arabesque*. Translated by R. E. Ettinghausen. Graz, 1977.

———. *Islamische Schriftkunst*. 2nd ed. Graz, 1977.

———. *Miniaturmalerei im islamischen Orient*. Berlin, 1922.

Kurd ʿAlī, M. *Khiṭaṭ al-shām* IV. Damascus, 1926.

al-Kurdī, M. T. *Taʾrīkh al-khaṭṭ al-ʿarabī wa-adābuhu*. Cairo, 1358/1939.

Lammens, H. *L'Arabie occidentale avant l'hégire*. Beirut, 1928.

———. "La cité arabe de Tāif à la veille de l'hégire." *Mélanges de l'Université Saint-Joseph* 8/4 (1922), 113-327.

———. *La Syrie*. Beirut, 1921.

Lane, E. W. *The Manners & Customs of the Modern Egyptians*. Everyman's Library. London, 1906; often reprinted.

Lawrie, A. P. "Materials in Persian Miniatures." *Technical Studies in the Field of the Fine Arts* 3 (1934), 146-56.

Le Strange, G. *Baghdad during the Abbasid Caliphate*. London, 1924.

Levey, M. "Mediaeval Arabic Bookmaking and Its Relation to Early Chemistry and Pharmacology." *Transactions of the American Philosophical Society* N.S. 52/4 (1962), 3-79. Includes translation of treatise by al-Sufyānī: see below *s.v.*

Levi Della Vida, G. *Frammenti coranici in Carattere Cufico*. Vatican City, 1947.

Lindberg, J. C. *Lettre à M.P.O. Brøndsted sur quelques médailles cufiques dans le cabinet du Roi de Danemarck, récemment trouvées dans l'île de Falster et sur quelques manuscrits cufiques*. Copenhagen, 1830.

Lings, M. *The Quranic Art of Calligraphy and Illumination*. London, 1976.

———, and Safadi, Y. *The Qur'an. Catalogue of an Exhibition of Qur'an Manuscripts at the British Library, 3 April-15 August 1976*. London, 1976.

Lyall, C. J. *Commentary on Ten Ancient Arabic Poems*. Calcutta, 1894. For their text, see the edition of al-Khālidī. Vienna, 1880.

Mackensen, R. S. "Arabic Books and Libraries in the Umaiyad Period." *American Journal of Semitic Languages and Literatures* 52 (1935-1936), 245-53; 53 (1936-1937), 239-50; 54 (1937), 41-61; "Supplementary notes" 56 (1939), 149-57.

———. "Background of the History of Moslem Libraries." *American Journal of Semitic Languages and Literatures* 51 (1934-1935), 114-25; 52 (1935-1936), 22-33, 104-10.

———. "Four Great Libraries of Medieval Baghdad." *Library Quarterly* 2/iii (1932), 279-99.

———. "Moslem Libraries and Sectarian Propaganda." *American Journal of Semitic Languages and Literatures* 51 (1934-1935), 83-113.

Madsen, K. See *Kunstmuseets Aarsskrift* 3 (1917), 1-24 (*non vidi*).

al-Maʿlūf, A. See *Majallat al-majmaʿ al-ʿilmī al-ʿarabī, Dimashq* 3 (1923) (*non vidi*).

al-Maqdisī, Abū ʿAbdallāh Muḥammad b. Aḥmad. *Aḥsan al-taqāsīm fī maʿrifat al-aqālīm*. Edited by M. J. de Goeje. Leiden, 1873.

al-Maqqarī, Abu'l-ʿAbbās Aḥmad b. Muḥammad. *Nafḥ al-ṭīb*. Cairo, 1302/1885, and 1304/1887.

al-Maqrīzī, Abu'l-ʿAbbās Aḥmad b. ʿAlī. *Al-mawāʿiẓ wa'l-iʿtibār fī dhikr al-khiṭaṭ wa'l-āthār*. Cairo, 1308/1891, 1324-1326/1906-1908.

Margoliouth, D. S. *The Letters of Abū l-ʿAlā*. Oxford, 1898.

Martin, F. R. *The Miniature Painting and Painters of Persia, India and Turkey from the 8th to the 18th Century* I-II. London, 1912.

Massé, H. "L'imagerie populaire de l'Iran." *Arts asiatiques* 7 (1960), 163-78.

Massignon, L. "Études sur les ʿIsnad' ou chaînes de témoignages fondamentales dans la tradition musulmane hallagienne." In his *Opera Minora* II. Beirut, 1963, 61-92.

al-Masʿūdī, Abu'l-Ḥasan ʿAlī b. al-Ḥusain. *Kitāb al-tanbīh wa'l-ishrāf.* Edited by M. J. de Goeje. Leiden, 1894.

Meredith-Owens, G. M. *Turkish Miniatures.* London, 1963.

Meyerhof, M. "Über einige Privatbibliotheken im fatimidischen Ägypten." *Rivista degli Studi Orientali* 12 (1939-40), 286-90.

Mez, A. *Die Renaissance des Islâms.* Heidelberg, 1922. Translated into English by D. S. Margoliouth and S. Khuda Bakhsh under the title *The Renaissance of Islam.* London, 1937.

Migeon, G. *Manuel d'art musulman* I. 2nd ed. Paris, 1927.

Minorsky, V., and Wilkinson, J.V.S. *The Chester Beatty Library. A Catalogue of the Turkish Manuscripts and Miniatures.* Dublin, 1958.

Minovi, M., and Ackerman, P. "Calligraphy: An Outline History." In *A Survey of Persian Art from Prehistoric Times to the Present.* Edited by A. U. Pope and P. Ackerman. London and New York, 1939, pp. 1707-42.

Miskawayh, Abū ʿAbdallāh Aḥmad b. Muḥammad. *Tajārib al-umam* I-II. Cairo, 1333-4/1915-6.

Moritz, B. "Arabia. d. Arabic writing." *Encyclopedia of Islam.* 1st ed. Leiden, 1913-1939, *s.v.*

———. *Arabic Palaeography. A Collection of Arabic Texts from the First Century of the Hidjra till the Year 1000.* Cairo, 1905.

Mousa, A. *Zur Geschichte des islamischen Buchmalerei in Aegypten.* Cairo, 1931.

al-Munajjid, S. *Dirāsāt fī ta'rīkh al-khaṭṭ al-ʿarabī mundhu bidāyatihi ilā nihāyat al-ʿasr al-umawī.* Beirut, 1972.

———. "Ijāzāt al-samāʿ fi'l-makhṭūṭāt al-qadīma." *Revue de l'Institut des Manuscrits Arabes* 1 (1955), 232-51.

———. *Le manuscrit arabe.* Cairo, 1960.

Nakosteen, M. *History of Islamic Origins of Western Education.* Boulder, Colo., 1964.

Niẓāmī-yi ʿArūḍī al-Samarqandī, Aḥmad b. ʿUmar. *Chahār*

Maqāla. Edited by Mīrzā M. Qazwīnī. Cairo and Leiden, 1919. Revised translation by E. G. Browne. London, 1921.

Nöldeke, T. "Fünf Moʿallaqāt, übersetzt und erklärt." *Sitzungsberichte der Kaiserlichen Akademie der Wissenschaften in Wien. Philosophisch-Historische Klasse*, Bd. 140 (1899), 1-84; 142 (1900), 1-94; 144 (1901), 1-43.

——— et al. *Geschichte des Qurʾāns*. 2nd ed. Leipzig, 1938.

Palmer, E. H. *Oriental Penmanship*. London, 1886.

Pedersen, J. *Al-Azhar. Et Muhammedansk Universitet (Studier fra Sprog- og Oldtidsforskning, no. 124)*. Copenhagen, 1922.

———. *Islams Kultur*. Copenhagen, 1928.

———. "Masdjid." *Encyclopedia of Islam*. 1st ed. Leiden, 1913-1934, *s.v.*

———. Review of E. Meyer, *Ursprung und Geschichte der Mormonen. Mit Exkursen über die Anfänge des Islâms und des Christentums*. In *Der Islam* 5 (1914), 110-15.

———. "Schrift. E. Semiten." In *Reallexikon der Vorgeschichte*. Edited by Ebert, 11 (Berlin, 1927-1928), 347-57.

———. "Some Aspects of the History of the Madrasa." *Islamic Culture* 3 (1929), 525-37.

Petermann, H. *Reisen im Orient* II. 2nd ed. Leipzig, 1865.

Pihan, A. P. *Notice sur les divers genres d'ecriture . . . des Arabes. . . .* Paris, 1856.

Pinto, O. "The Libraries of the Arabs during the Time of the Abbasids." *Islamic Culture* 3 (1929), 211-43.

Pope, A. U. *An Introduction to Persian Art since the 7th Century A.D.* London, 1930.

———, and Ackerman, P., eds. *A Survey of Persian Art from Prehistoric Times to the Present* I-VI. London and New York, 1939.

al-Qalqashandī, Abu'l-ʿAbbās Aḥmad b. ʿAlī. *Ṣubḥ al-aʿshā fī ṣināʿat al-inshāʾ* II. Cairo, 1331-2/1913-4.

Qasimi, A. S. "Libraries in the Early Islamic World." *Journal of the University of Peshawar* 6 (1958), 1-15.

Quatremère, E. "Mémoire sur le goût des livres chez les Orientaux." *Journal asiatique* Ser. 3/vi (1838), 35-78.

Rao, M. R. "Libraries in Ancient and Medieval India." *Journal of the Andhra Historical Research Society* 8 (1933), 203-32.

Ribera y Tarragó, J. *Bibliófilos y Bibliotecas en la España Musulmana. Disertación leída en la Facultad de Medicina y Ciencias.* Zaragoza, 1896. Reprinted in *Disertaciones y opusculos* I (1928), 181-228.

Rice, D. S. *The Unique Ibn al-Bawwāb Manuscript in the Chester Beatty Library*. Dublin, 1955.

Robertson, E. "Muhammad ibn Abd ar-Rahman on Calligraphy." *Studia Semitica et Orientalia*. Glasgow, 1920, pp. 57-83. Translation of the *Lumʿa*.

Robinson, B. W. *A Descriptive Catalogue of the Persian Paintings in the Bodleian Library*. Oxford, 1958.

———. *Persian Miniature Paintings from Collections in the British Isles*. London, 1967.

———. "The Tehran Nizami of 1848 & Other Qajar Lithographed Books." In *Islam in the Balkans. Persian Art and Culture of the 18th and 19th Centuries.* Edited by J. M. Scarce. Edinburgh, 1979, pp. 61-74.

——— et al. *Islamic Painting and the Arts of the Book*. London, 1976.

Rosenthal, F. "Abū Ḥaiyān al-Tawḥīdī on Penmanship." *Ars Islamica* 13-14 (1948), 1-30.

———. "Significant Uses of Arabic Writing." *Ars Orientalis* 4 (1961), 15-23.

———. *The Technique and Approach of Muslim Scholarship*. Vatican City, 1947.

Rufai, A. "Über die Bibliophilie im älteren Islam nebst Edition und Übersetzung von Ǧāḥiẓ, Abhandlung *fi madḥ al-kutub*. Doctoral dissertation, Berlin, 1931, and Istanbul, 1935.

Sadan, J. "Nouveaux documents sur scribes et copistes." *Revue des Études Islamiques* 45 (1977), 41-87.

Safadi, Y. *Islamic Calligraphy*. London, 1978.

Sarkis, J. E. *Bibliography* (of book-printing in the East). Cairo, 1930 (*non vidi*).

Sarre, F. *Islamische Bucheinbände* Berlin, 1923.

Sarre, F., and Martin, F. R. *Die Ausstellung von Meisterwerken muhammedanischer Kunst in München 1910* I-III. Munich, 1912.

Schimmel, A. *Islamic Calligraphy*, Leiden, 1970.

———. "Schriftsymbolik im Islam." In *Aus der Welt der islamischen Kunst. Festschrift für Ernst Kühnel.* Edited by R. Ettinghausen. Berlin, 1959, pp. 244-54.

Schroeder, E. *Persian Miniatures in the Fogg Museum of Art.* Cambridge, Mass., 1942.

Schulthess, F. *Der Dīwān des Ḥātim Ṭej.* Leipzig, 1897.

Schulz, P. W. *Die persisch-islamische Miniaturmalerei* I-II. Leipzig, 1914.

Sellheim, R. "Ḳirṭās." *Encyclopedia of Islam.* 2nd ed. Leiden, 1960–, *s.v.*

———. "Kitāb." *Encyclopedia of Islam.* 2nd ed. Leiden, 1960–, *s.v.*

al-Shammākh. *Dīwān.* Cairo, 1327/1909.

Snouck Hurgronje, C. "Ḳuṣejr Amra und das Bilderverbot." *Zeitschrift der deutschen morgenländischen Gesellschaft* 61 (1907), 186-91.

Sourdel, D. "Le ʿLivre des sécretairesʾ de ʿAbdallāh al-Baġdādī." *Bulletin des Études Orientales de Damas* 14 (1952-1953), 115-53.

Sourdel-Thomine, J.; Alparslan, A; and Chaghatai, M. A. "Khaṭṭ." *Encyclopedia of Islam.* 2nd ed. Leiden, 1960–, *s.v.*

Sourdel-Thomine, J. "L'écriture arabe et son evolution ornementale." in *L'écriture et la psychologie des peuples. XXIIe Semaine de Synthèse.* (Paris, 1963), pp. 249-61.

———. "Les origines de l'écriture arabe à propos d'une hypothèse récente." *Revue des études islamiques* 34 (1966), 151-57.

———. "The Development of Arabic Script." In *The Cambridge History of Arabic Literature* I, chap. i. Forthcoming.

——— et al. "Kitābāt." *Encyclopedia of Islam.* 2nd ed. Leiden, 1960–, *s.v.*

Spécimens d'écritures arabes pour la lecture des manuscrits anciens et modernes par un père de la Cie de Jésus. 19th ed. Beirut, 1912.

Spitta, W. "Neue Erscheinungen der egyptischen Presse." *Zeitschrift der deutschen morgenländischen Gesellschaft* 30 (1876) 149-57.

Sprenger, A. *Das Leben Und die Lehre des Mohammad* I-II. Berlin, 1865.

Stchoukine, I. *La peinture indienne à l'époque des Grands Moghols.* Paris, 1929.

———. *La peinture iranienne sous les derniers ʿAbbâsides et les Îl-Khâns.* Brugge, 1936.

———. *La peinture turque d'après les manuscrits illustrés* I and II. Paris, 1966 and 1971.

———. *Les peintures des manuscrits de Shāh ʿAbbās Ier à la fin des Ṣafavīs.* Paris, 1964.

———. *Les peintures des manuscrits safavis de 1502 à 1587.* Paris, 1959.

———. *Les peintures des manuscrits tîmûrides.* Paris, 1954.

Steinbrucker, C. "Islamische Bucheinbände." *Zeitschrift der deutschen morgenländischen Gesellschaft* 84 (1930), 69-73.

Stern, S. M., ed. *Documents from Islamic Chanceries.* Oxford, 1965.

———, ed. *Fāṭimid Decrees: Original Documents from the Fāṭimid Chancery.* London, 1964.

———. "A Manuscript from the Library of the Ghaznawid Amīr ʿAbd al-Rashīd." In *Paintings from Islamic Lands.* Edited by R. H. Pinder-Wilson. London, 1969, pp. 7-31.

Storey, C. A. "The Beginning of Persian Printing in India." In *Oriental Studies in Honour of Cursetji Erachji Pavry.* Edited by V.D.C. Pavry. London, 1933, pp. 457-61.

al-Sufyānī, Abu'l-ʿAbbās Aḥmad b. Muḥammad. *Sināʿat tasfīr al-kutub wa-hall al-dhahab (Art de la Reliure et de la Dorure).* Edited by P. Ricard. Fez, 1919. 2nd ed. Paris, 1925.

al-Ṣūlī, Abū Bakr Muḥammad. *Adab al-kuttāb.* Edited by M. Bahjat. Cairo, 1341/1922-3.

Suter, H. "Die astronomischen Tafeln des Muhammed ben Musa al-Khwārizmī." *Kgl. Danske Videnskabernes Selskabs Skrifter* 7 raekke, Hist. og filos. afd. III/I. Copenhagen, 1914.

al-Suyūṭī, Jalāl al-Dīn. *Ḥusn al-muḥāḍara fī akhbār Miṣr wa'l-Qāhira* II. Cairo, 1321/1903.

———. *Itqān* I. Cairo, 1343/1925.

Ṭabāṭabā'ī, Sayyid M. M. "Awwal chāp-i surbī wa sipas sangī." *Rahnamā-yi Kitāb* 19/1-3 (1976), 208-16.

al-Ṭayyibī, Muḥammad b. Ḥasan. *Jāmiʿ maḥāsin kitābat wa-nuzhat ūlī al-baṣā'ir wa'l-albāb*. Edited by S. al-Munajjid. Beirut, 1962.

al-Thaʿālibī, Abū Manṣūr ʿAbd al-Malik b. Muḥammad. *Laṭā'if al-maʿārif*. Edited by P. de Jong. Leiden, 1867.

al-Tirmidhī, Abū ʿĪsā Muḥammad b. ʿĪsā. *Kitāb al-buyūʿ*. *Apud* his *Ṣaḥīḥ*. Cairo, 1292/1875.

Titley, N. M. *Miniatures from Persian Manuscripts. A Catalogue and Subject Index of Paintings from Persia, India and Turkey in the British Library and the British Museum*. London, 1977.

Tritton, A. S. *Materials on Muslim Education in the Middle Ages*. London, 1957.

Vajda. G. *Album de paléographie arabe*. Paris, 1958.

———. *Les certificats de lecture et de transmission dans les manuscrits arabes de la Bibliothèque Nationale de Paris*. Paris, 1957.

———. "Idjāza." *Encyclopedia of Islam*. 2nd ed. Leiden, 1960–, *s.v.*

———. "Un opuscule inédit d' es-Silafi." in *Bulletin de l'Institut de recherche et d'histoire des textes* 14 (1966), 85-92.

Van Regemorter, B. *Some Oriental Bindings in the Chester Beatty Library*. Dublin, 1961.

Vollers, K., ed. and tr. *Die Gedichte des Mutalammis*. Leipzig, 1903.

Weil, G. "Die ersten Drucke der Turken." *Zentralblatt für Bibliothekswesen* 24 (1907), 49-61.

———. "Mahomet savait-il lire et écrire?" In *Atti del IV Con-*

gresso Internazionale degli Orientalisti. Florence, 1880-1881, pp. 357-66.

Weisweiler, M. *Der islamische Bucheinband des Mittalalters, nach Handschriften aus deutschen, holländischen und türkischen Bibliotheken*. Wiesbaden, 1962.

Welch, A. *Artists for the Shah*. New Haven, 1976.

Welch, S. C. *A Flower from Every Meadow*. New York, 1973.

———. *Imperial Mughal Painting*. New York, 1977.

———. *Wonders of the Age. Masterpieces of Early Safavid Painting, 1501-1576*. Cambridge, Mass., 1979.

Wensinck, A. J. *A Handbook of Early Muhammadan Tradition*. Leiden, 1927.

Wiesner, J. "Die Faijûmer und Uschmûneiner Papiere. Eine naturwissenschaftliche, mit Rücksicht auf die Erkennung alter und moderner Papiere und auf die Entwicklung der Papierbereitung durchgeführte Untersuchung." In *Mitteilungen aus der Sammlung der Papyrus Erzherzog Rainer* II-III (1887), 179-260.

Wiet, G. "Recherches sur les bibliothèques égyptiennes aux Xe et XIe siècles." *Cahiers de civilisation mediévale* 6 (1963), 1-11.

———. "La valeur décorative de l'alphabet arabe." *Arts et metiers graphiques*, October 15, 1935, pp. 9-14.

Wüstenfeld, F. *Die Academien der Araber und ihre Lehren. Nach Auszügen aus Ibn Schohba's Klassen der Schafeïten*. Göttingen, 1837.

———. *Der Imâm el-Schafiʿî, seine Schüler und Anhänger bis zum J. 300 d.H. Abhandlungen der königlichen Gesellschaft der Wissenschaften zu Göttingen* 36 (1890).

Yāqūt al-Ḥamawī, Abū ʿAbdallāh Yaʿqūb b. ʿAbdallāh. *Irshād al-arīb ilā maʿrifat al-adīb*. Edited by D. S. Margoliouth. London, 1907-1926.

———. *Jacuts geographisches Wörterbuch* IV. Edited by F. Wüstenfeld. Leipzig, 1869.

Zain al-Dīn al-Maṣrif, N. *Badāʾi al-khaṭṭ al-ʿarabī*. Baghdād, 1972.

———. *Muṣawwar al-khaṭṭ al-ʿarabī*. Baghdād, 1968.

Zakī Pāshā, A. "Les bibliothèques arabes." *Muqtabas* VI/v, 385 ff. (*non vidi*).

Zayyāt, H. "Al-wirāqa wa'l-warrāqūn." *al-Mashriq* XLVII, 305-50.

Zetterstein, K. V. "Ibn ʿAbbād." *Encyclopedia of Islam*. 1st ed. Leiden, 1913-1934, *s.v.*

Ziauddin, M. *A Monograph on Moslem Calligraphy*. Visva-Bharati Studies No. 6. Calcutta, 1936.

INDEX

Sa'īd Efendi, 134
Sa'īd ibn Hārūn, 114
Saint George, 135
Saladin, 99, 103, 118-19, 121, 128
Salam, 114
Salāma ibn 'Āṣim, 45
Sale, George, 133
al-Ṣāliḥī, 132
Salīm I, 133
samā', 47
samā'an lahu, 31
Sāmānids, 67, 123, 125
Samarqand, 60-61, 64, 80, 88, 96; paper, 61-62, 64, 86
Sāmarrā, 58, 62, 92
samekh, 75
sami'a min, 22
San Felipe, 64
Ṣan'ā', 10, 63, 66
ṣaql, 66
Saragossa, 121
Sasanians, 93, 96
Sayf al-Daula, 40-41, 122
scholars, output of, 37-38; traveling, 21-22, 42, 103; wages and honoraria for, 40-42, 44, 49, 117, 121
scholarships, 40, 115, 117, 121, 124, 126
science, Islamic/Arabic, 132
scribes, as artists, 91-92
Scutari, 134
Seljuks, 123, 127
Semitic, 76; alphabet, 3; languages, 78
Seville, 41
shāh, 98
Shāh 'Abbās, 98
Shāh Jahān, 99
Shāh Rukh, 96, 108
Shāhnāma, 96-98
al-Shammākh, 8-9
Shams al-Dīn, 52
sharīf, 48
Shāsh, 61
Shāṭiba, 64
al-Sha'ūbī, 49
Shaykh al-Islām, 134, 137
al-Shifā', 132
Shuwayr, 135
Shī'ī(s), 25, 95, 115, 118, 121-22, 124
shīn, 76
Shīrāz, 86, 123
Shīrīn, 97
Sībawayh, 28, 34-35, 41-42
Sicily, 59
signed paintings, 91
al-Ṣiḥāḥ, 36, 134
Ṣila, 103, 122
silk, 54, 60, 103, 106, 108
Simeon, bishop, 9
Sīn, 75-76
Sinai, 5, 6
Sino-Persian style, 95, 109
al-Ṣiqillī, 36
Siyar al-Nabī, 100
Siyāsat nāma, 127
sketcher, 102
skin, 54-56, 62
slaves, 43, 46, 51, 87
Smyrna, 134
"Sound, the," 134
Spain, Spaniards, Spanish, 17, 21, 26, 28, 34, 37, 41, 56, 62, 64, 67, 77, 82, 113, 121
spóngos, 79
Ṣubḥ al-a'shā, 69, 73, 84
Subḥat al-akhbār, 100
ṣuḥuf, 55, 101
al-Sukkarī, *see* Abū Muḥammad 'Abdallāh ibn Yaḥyā ibn 'Abd al-Jabbār al-Sukkarī
al-Sulamī, 48
al-sulaymānī, 67
al-Ṣūlī, 69, 73
Sultan Bāyazīd II, 133
Sulṭān Muḥammad, 97-98
Sulṭān Muḥammad II, 99
Sulṭān Murād III, 99

ILLUSTRATIONS

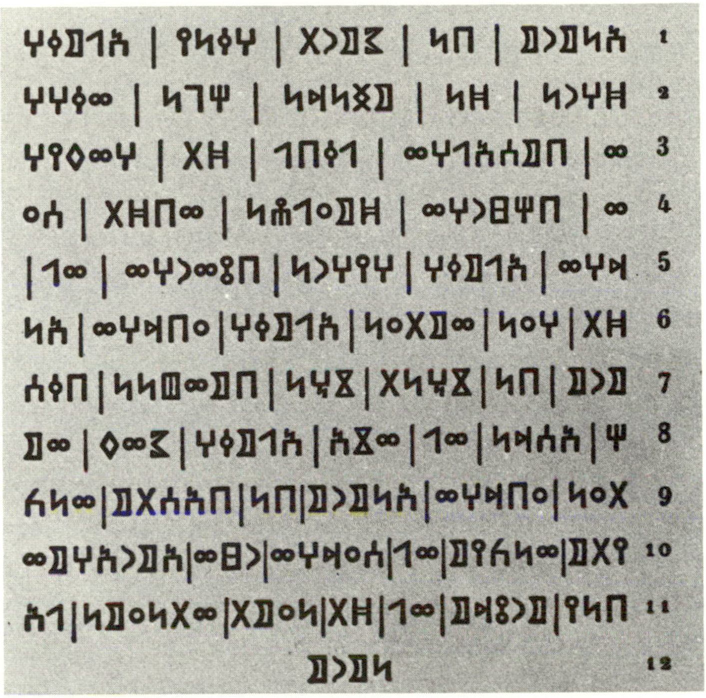

1. Sabaean Inscription Dedicated by Anmar to Ilmakkah.

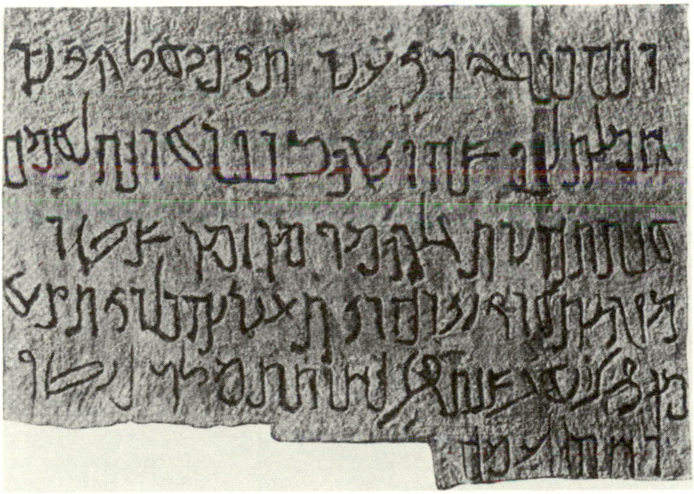

2. Nabatean Inscription.

Südsemitische Alphabete.

Transscription.	Nashi 1616.	Süd-arabisch	Lihjanisch	Tamudenisch	Safatenisch	Altes	Äthiopisch mit ä	Neueres mit ē ed. vokales	mit ā
ʾ									
b									
g									
d									
ḏ									
h									
u									
z									
ḥ									
ḫ									
ṭ									
ẓ									
i									
k									
l									
m									
n									
ʿ									
ġ									
f									
ṣ									
ḍ									
ḳ									
r									
s̀									
š									
t									
ṯ									
p̣									
p									

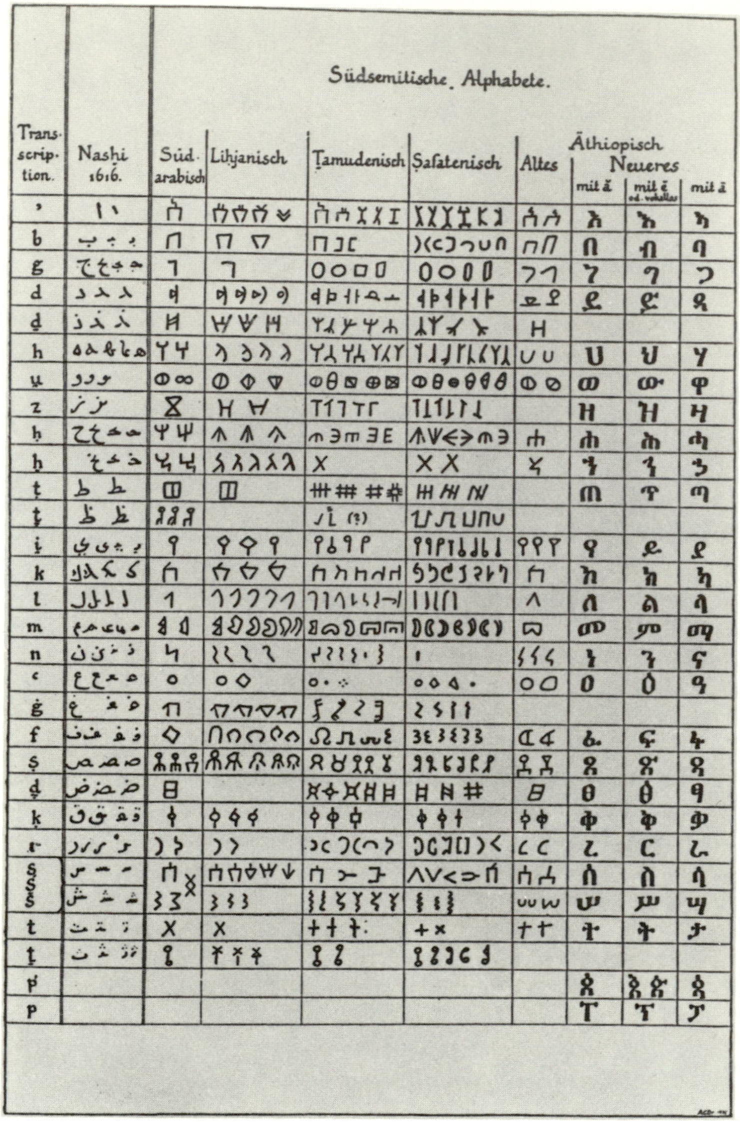

3. Comparative Table of Southern Semitic and Arabic Alphabets.

4. Chinese Papermaking.

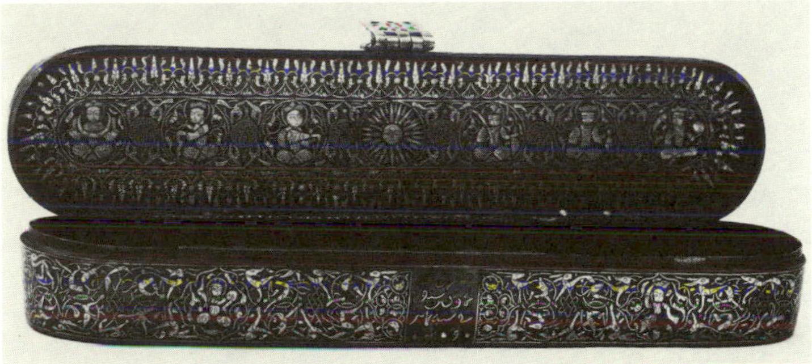

5. Penbox (*qalamdān*) signed by Maḥmūd b. Sunqur and dated 680/1281, inlaid bronze, possibly Western Iran.

6. Typical Book and Writing Utensils of Nineteenth-Century Egypt.

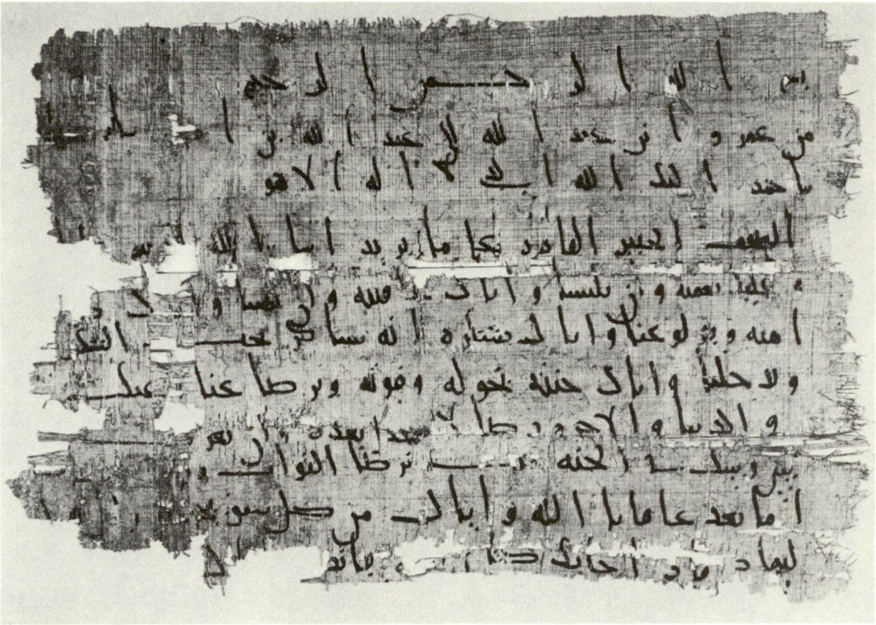

7. Papyrus, Egypt, 7th century.

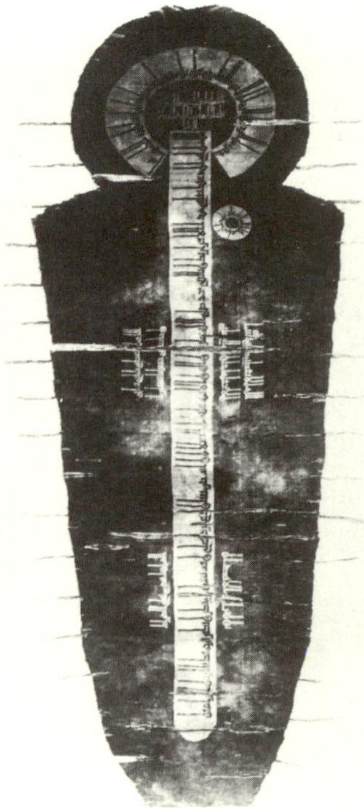

8. Pall of ʿAlī b. Muḥammad, Iran, later 4th/10th century.

9. Early Qur'ān Similar to Ma'il type, Hijaz, 2nd-3rd/8th-9th century.

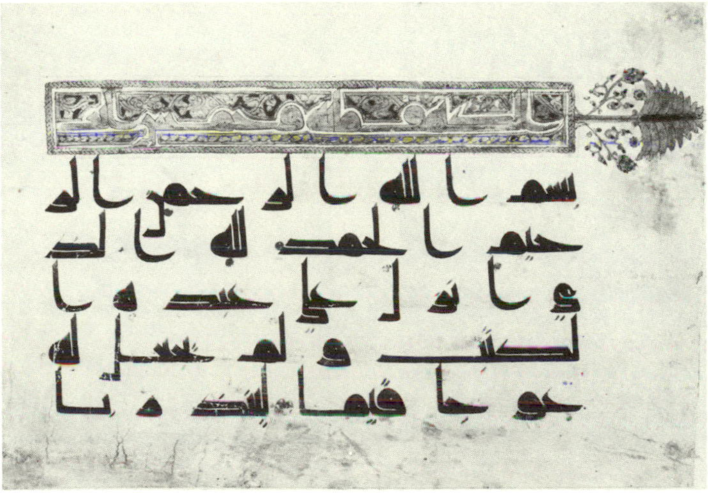

10. Fragment of Qur'ān, vellum, probably Iran. 3rd-4th/9th-10th century.

11. Fragment of Qur'ān, blue vellum, probably North Africa.

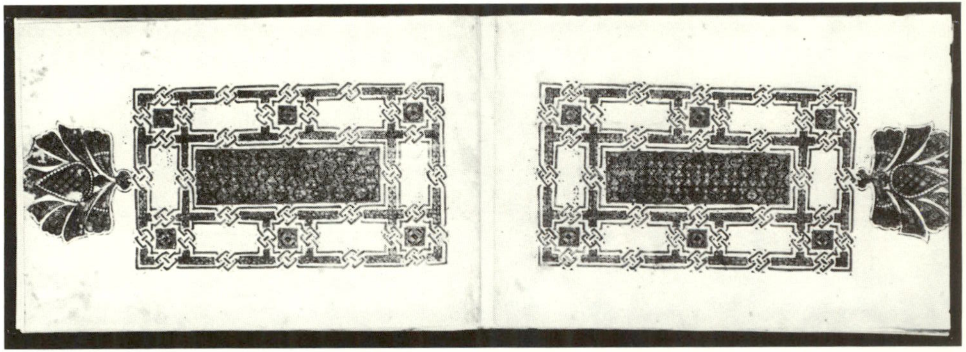

12. Illumination of Qur'ān, Near East, 3rd/9th century.

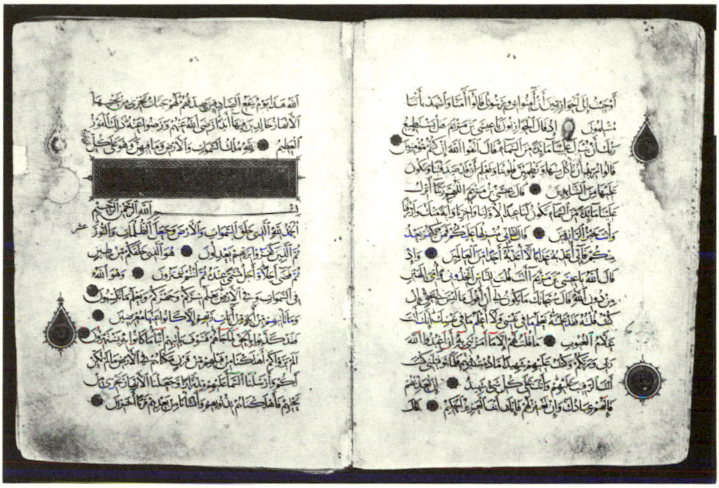

13. Leaf in Naskh, Cairo, c. 1300.

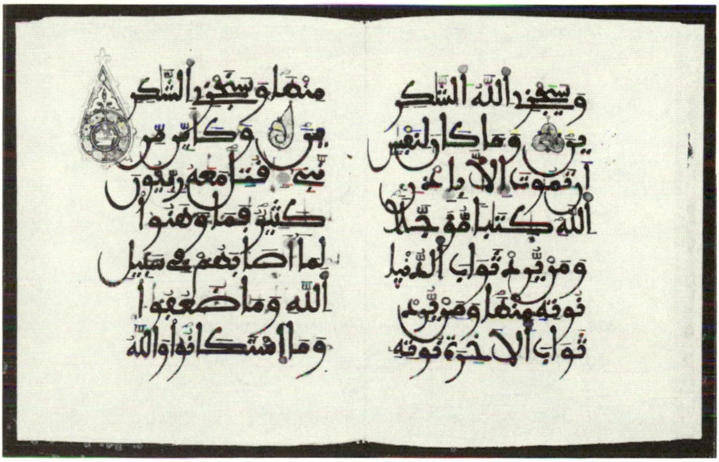

14. Leaf from Qur'ān, Morocco, late 10th/16th century.

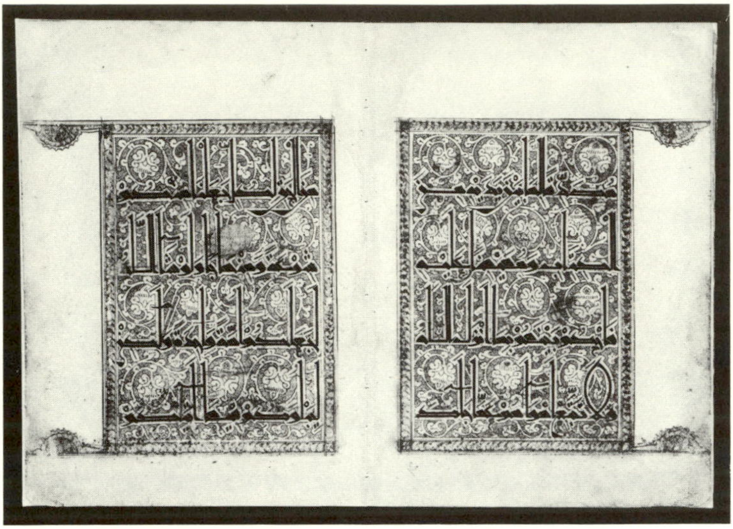

15. Leaf of Qur'ān in "Qarmatian Kufic" script, Iran, 4th-5th/10th-11th century.

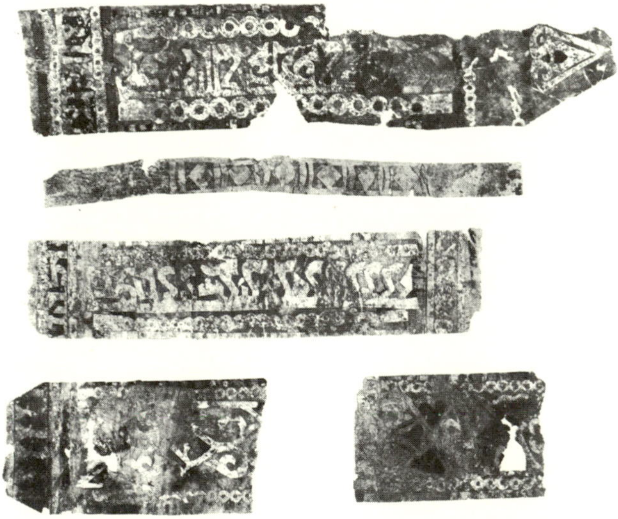

16. Fragments of Arabic end-papers in filigree work, found at al-Ushmūnain in Egypt, 4th/10th century.

17. Portrait of Riḍā-yi ʿAbbāsī by Muʿīn Muṣawwir, Iran, dated 1087/1673.

Two students.

18. Frontispiece of *De Materia Medica* of Dioscorides, Northern Iraq or Syria, 626/1229.

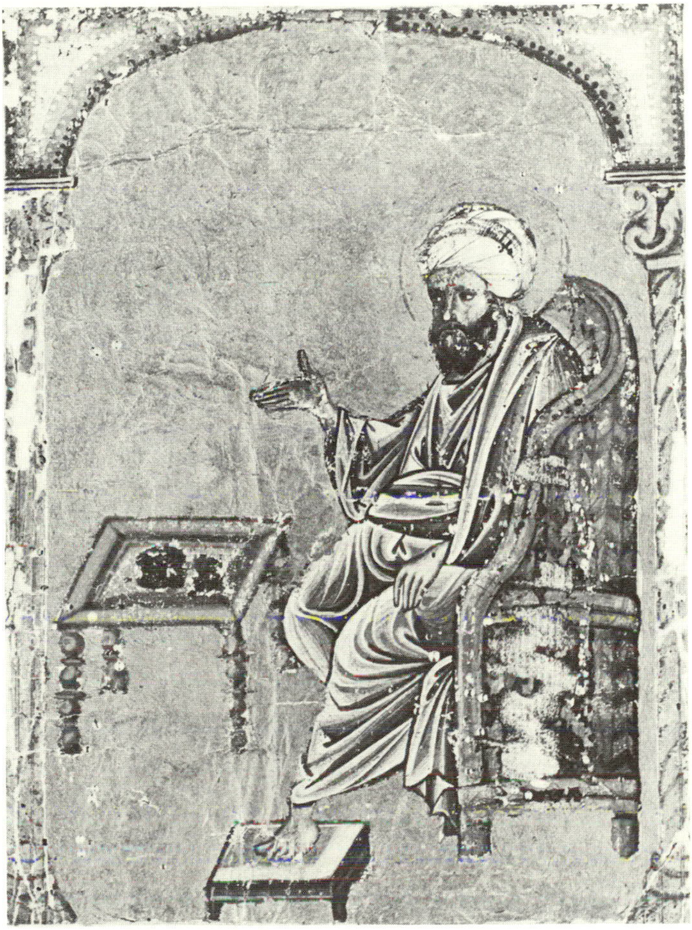

Dioscorides teaching.

19. Sultan Mahmud's Library in Medina.

20. Wooden Book Cover with Inlay Work, Egypt, 4th/10th century.

21. Detail of Fig. 20.

22. Persian Binding (possibly from Khurāsān), Early 9th/15th century.

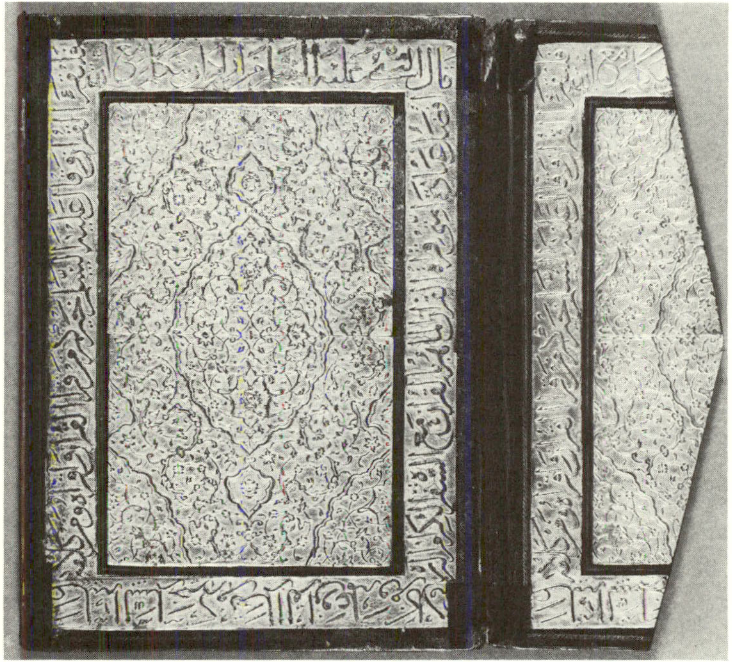

23. Persian Binding, 10th/16th century.

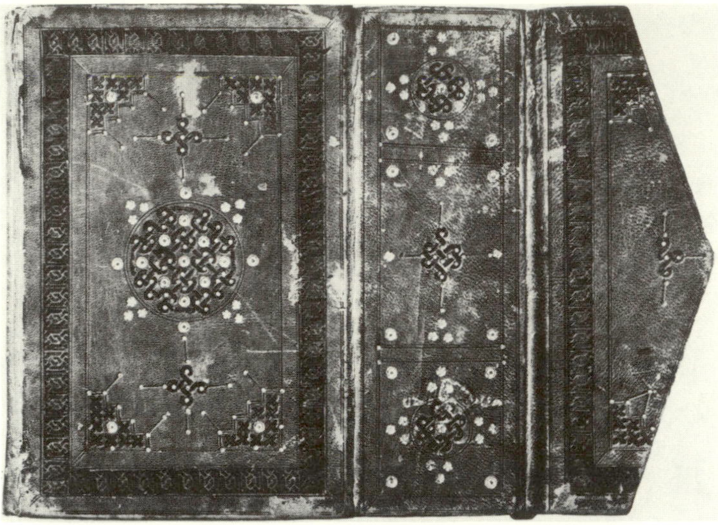

24. Maghribi binding, early 9th/15th century.

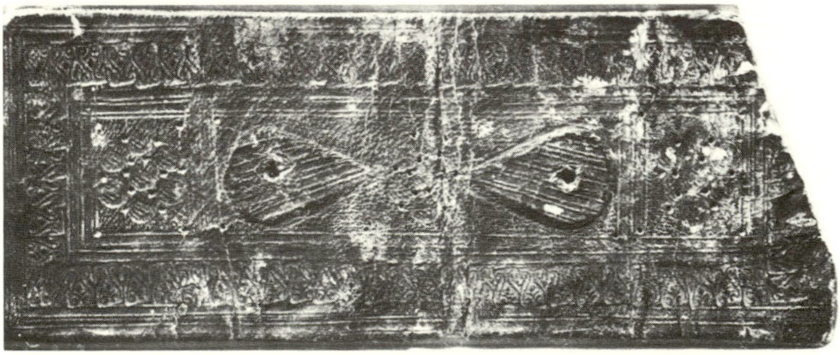

25. Fragment of Qur'ān binding in Safīna form, Egypt, 4th–5th/10th–11th century.

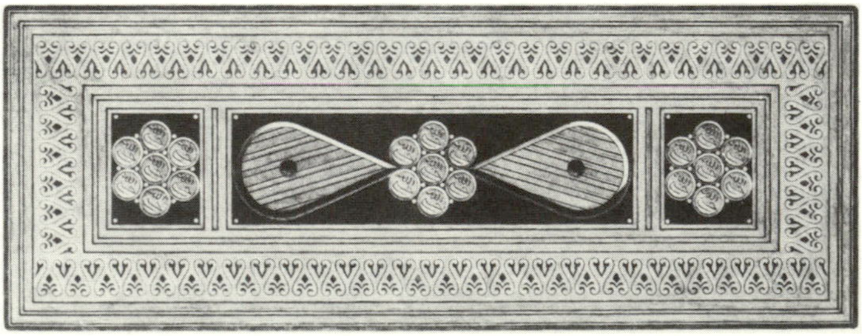

26. Conjectural reconstruction of binding illustrated in Fig. 25.

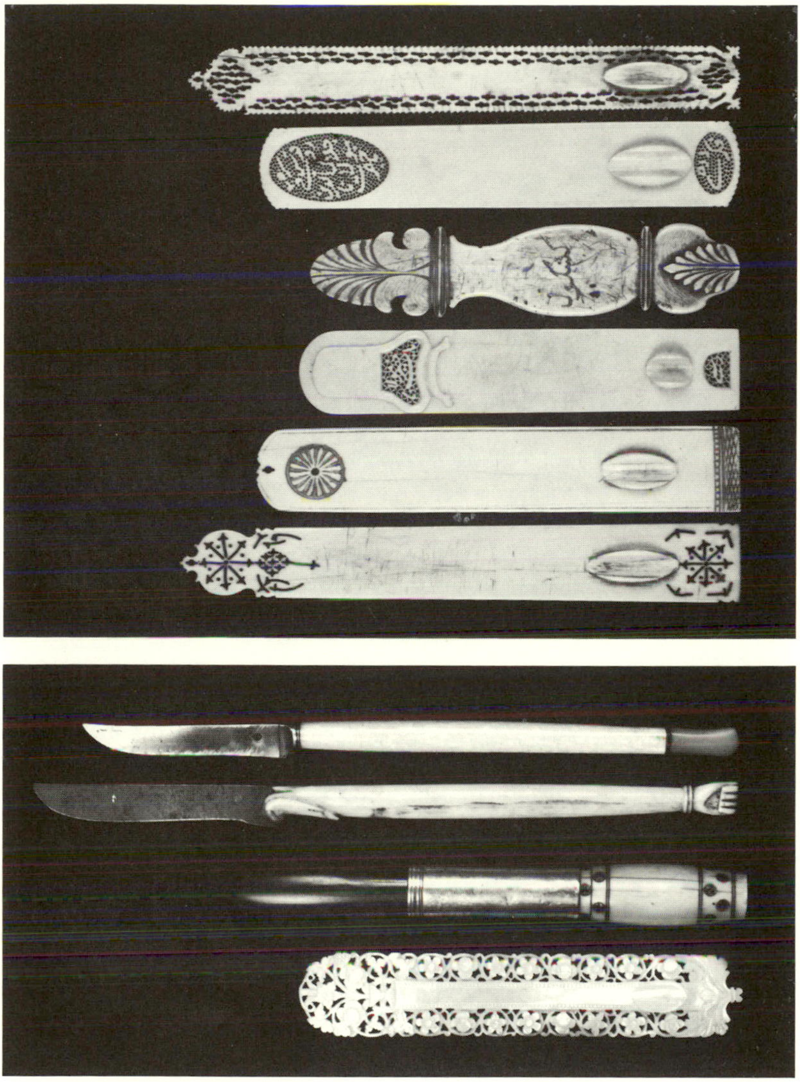

27. Implements of the Calligrapher.

28. Sample of *nastaʿlīq* Calligraphy by Mīr ʿAlī from the Jahāngīr Album, Mughal, c. 1010-1020/1600-1610.

29. A Calligrapher, detail of Fig. 28.

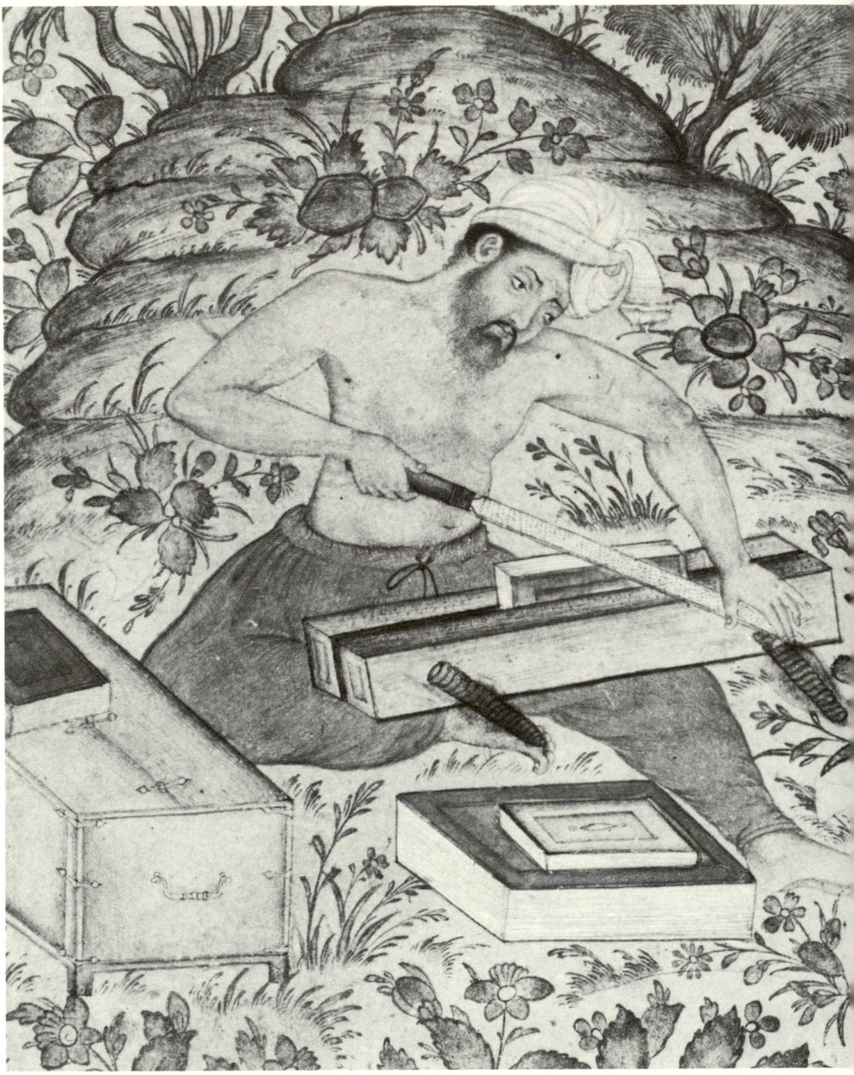

30. A Craftsman Filing the Edges of a Book, detail of Fig. 28.

31. A Craftsman Making a Wooden Bookstand, detail of Fig. 28.

32. A Craftsman Smelting Gold, detail of Fig. 28.

33. A Bookbinder Stamping the Cover of a Manuscript, detail of Fig. 28.

34. A Papermaker Polishing a Sheet, detail of Fig. 28.

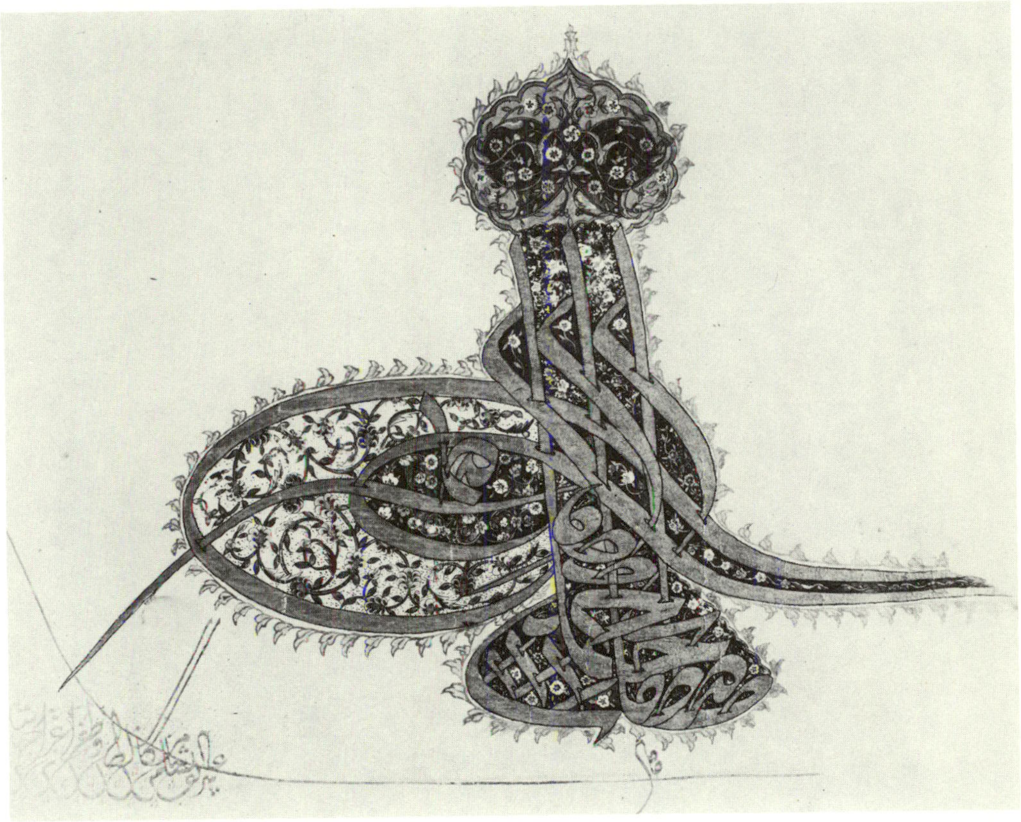

35. Ṭughrā of Sultan Muṣṭafa II (1625–1703).

36. Colophon with Signature of Ibn al-Bawwāb, Baghdad, 391/1001.

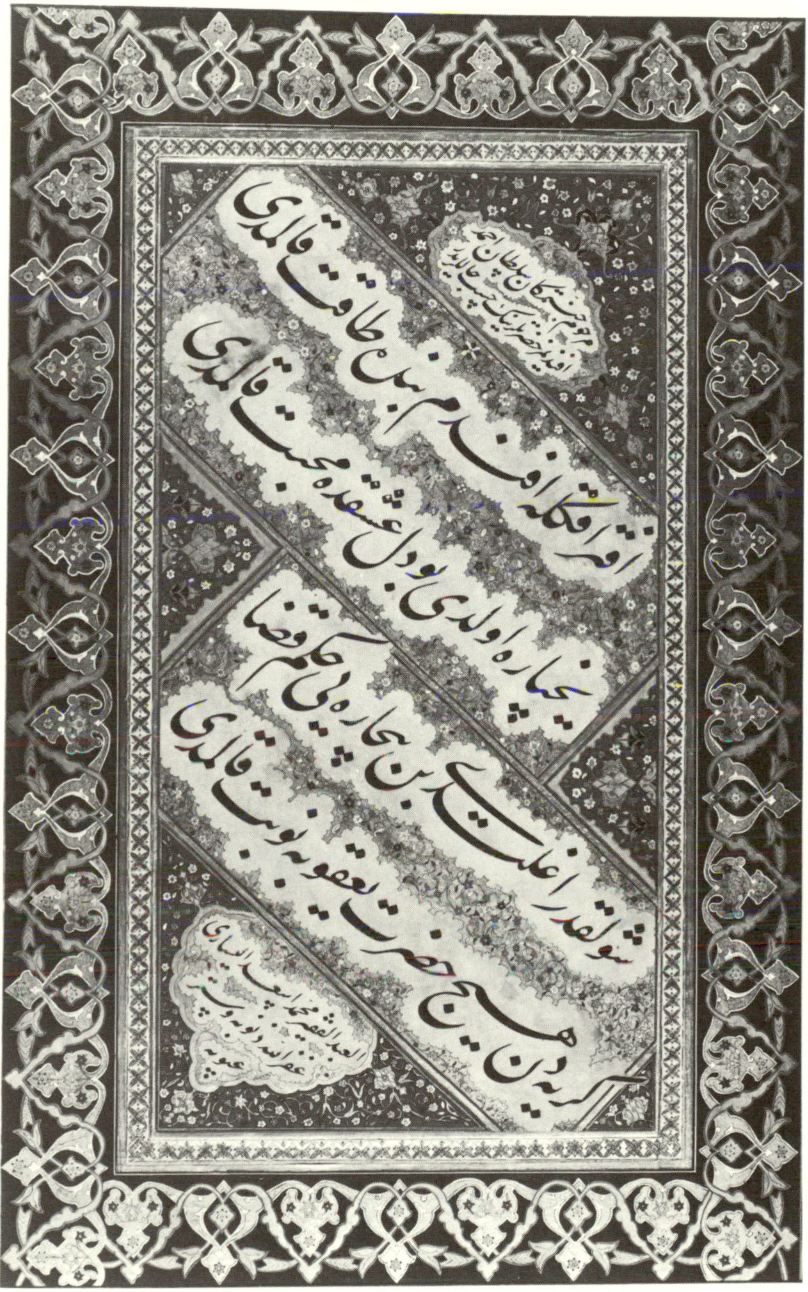

37. Calligraphic Composition, Istanbul, late 12th/18th century.

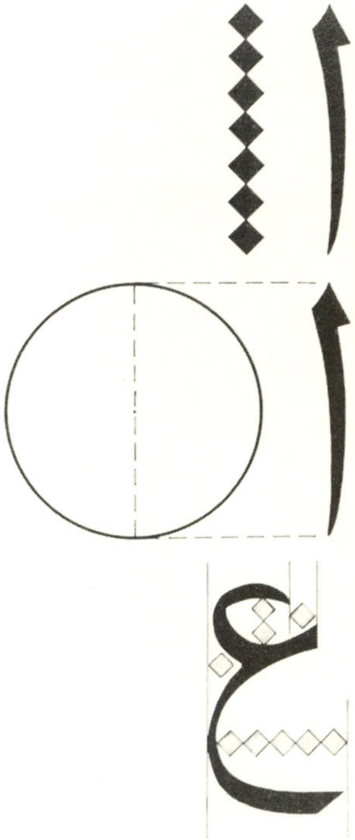

38. Conjectural Reconstruction of Ibn Muqlah's System of Proportional Writing.

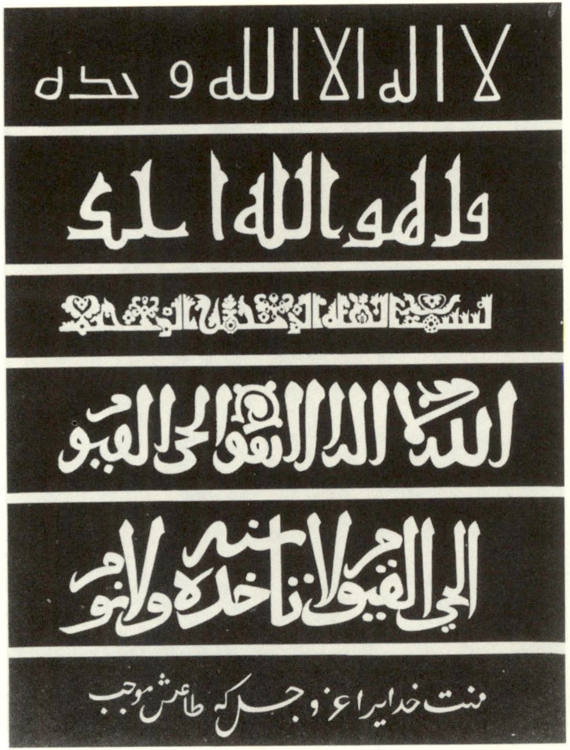

39. Major Types of Islamic Script. From top: simple Kufic, foliated Kufic, floriated Kufic, *naskhī*, *thuluth*, and *nastaʿlīq*.

40. Illumination from Manuscript Shown in Fig. 36.

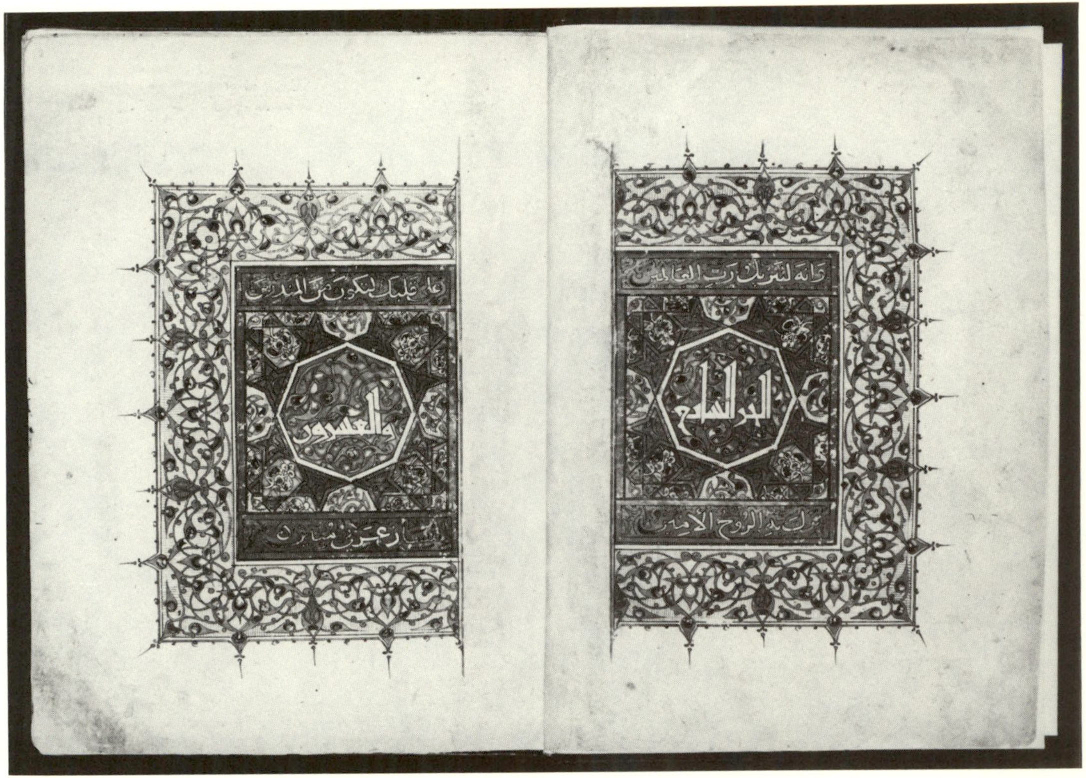

41. Mamluk Illumination, Egypt, 8th/14th century.

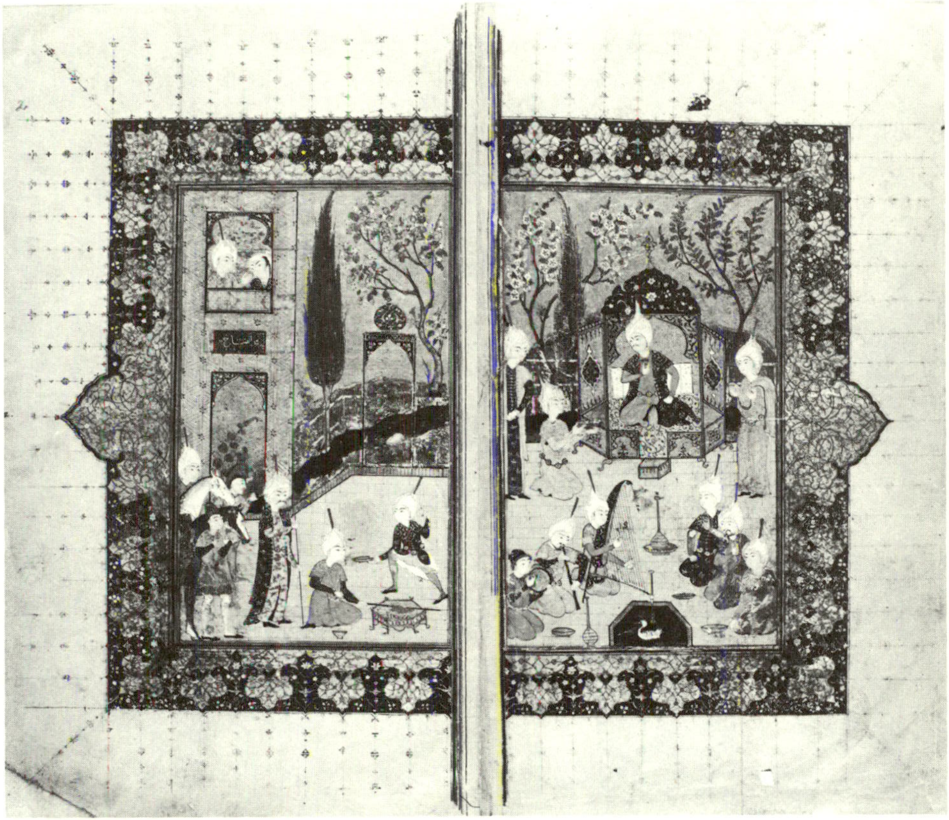

42. Enthroned Monarch with Courtiers and Musicians. Probably Tabriz. Completed 943/1536–7.

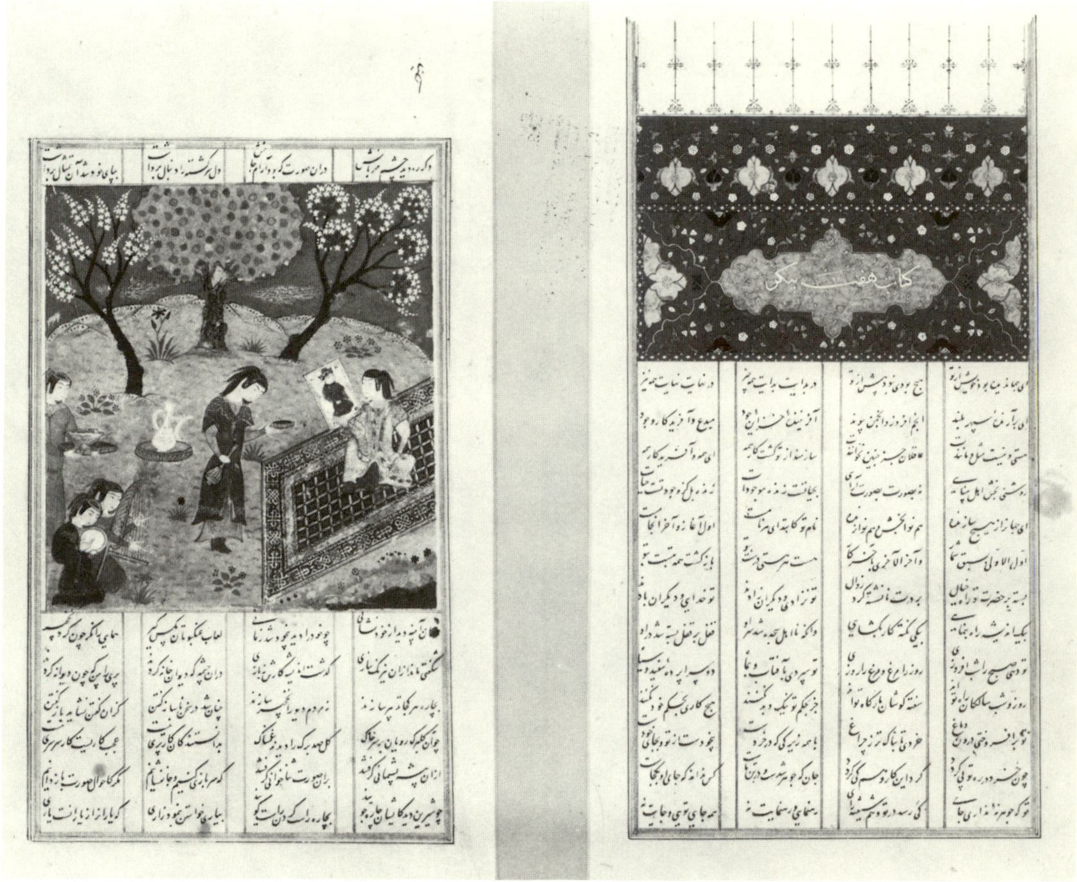

43. Shīrīn sees Khusrau's Portrait. Turkoman school, c. 1490.

44. Lacquer Penboxes. Iran. 13th/19th century.

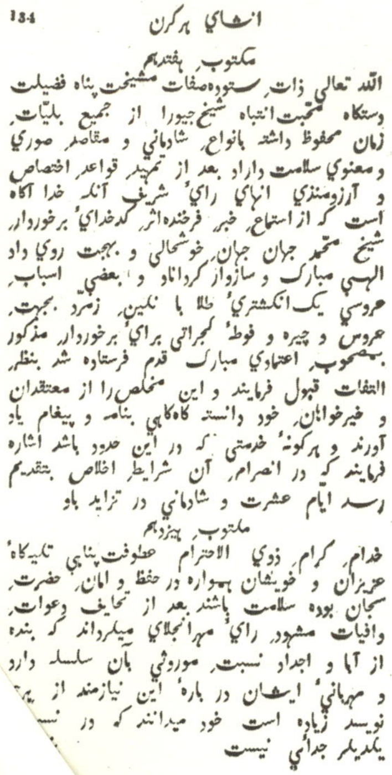

مکتوب بِقدرہم

اللّٰه تعالیٰ ذات ستودہ صفات مشیخت پناه فضیلت
و ستگاه محمّت انتباه دیده شیخ جیورا از جمیع بلیّات
زمان محفوظ داشته بانواع شادمانی و مقاصر صوری
و معنوی سلامت دارد بعد از تمهید قواعد اختصاص
و آرزومندی انبای رای شریفی آنكه خدا آگاه
است که از استماع خبر فرخنده اثر کدخدای برخوردار
شیخ محمّد جهان جهان خوشحالی و بهجت روی داد
الهی مبارک و سازوار گرداناد و بعضی اسباب
عروسی یک انکشتری ثلا با نگین زمرد بجهت
عروس و پیره و فوطه گجراتی برای برخوردار مذکور
بضمیم اعتنای مبارک قدم فرستاده شد بنظر
التفات قبول فرمایند و این منکس را از معتقدان
و خیرخواهان خود دانسته کاه‌کاهی بنامه و پیغام یاد
آورند و هرکونه خرمتی که در این حدود باشد اشاره
فرمایند که در انصرام آن شرایط اخلاص بتقدیم
رسد ایام عشرت و شادمانی در تزاید باد

ملتوب پیذدہم

خدام کرام ذوی الاحترام عطوفت پنای تایبکاه
عزیزان و خویشان همواره در حفظ و امان حضرت
سبحان بوده سلامت باشند بعد از تحایف دعوات
و افیات مشهود رای مهرانبکای میلدرانند که بنده
از آنها و اجداد نسبت موروثی بان سلسله دارد
و مهربانی ایمان در بارہ این این نیازمند از ...
نوشته زیاده است خود میدانند که در ...
یکدیگر جدایی نیست

—

...aʿlīq fount.

46. Specimen of Typical Arabic Typography
from a Multi-Author Work, Printed in Cairo in
1908, p. 218. In the margin is a work of Abū
Shujāʿ (in brackets) and the commentary of Ibn
Qāsim on it. In the main text is al-Bājūrī's
commentary on this commentary, the latter itself
in brackets.